Also by Jeffrey Rothfeder

Minds Over Matter
Heart Rhythms

PRIVACY

How Computerization Has Made

FOR

Everyone's Private Life

SALE

an Open Secret

Jeffrey

Rothfeder

Simon & Schuster

New York London Toronto Sydney Tokyo Singapore

SIMON & SCHUSTER
Simon & Schuster Building
Rockefeller Center
1230 Avenue of the Americas
New York, New York 10020

Designed by Laurence S. Horvitz
Manufactured in the United States of America

10 9 8 7 6 5 4 3 2 1

Library of Congress Cataloging-in-Publication Data
Rothfeder, Jeffrey.
    Privacy for sale : how computerization has made everyone's
private life an open secret / Jeffrey Rothfeder.
    p.   cm.
    Includes bibliographical references and index.
    1. Credit bureaus—United States—Records and correspondence—
Access control.   2. Banks and banking—United States—Records
and correspondence—Access control.   3. Confidential
communications—United States—Third parties.   4. Privacy, Right
of—United States.   5. Computer security—United States.   I. Title.
HG3751.7.R68   1992
323.44′83′0973—dc20   92-364   CIP
ISBN 0-671-73492-X

Acknowledgments

It's unlikely that this book would have been written were it not for Bob Arnold, my senior editor at *Business Week*. In mid-1989, I told Bob that I wanted to do a story on how computerization had stolen the right to privacy from Americans. Bob loved the idea immediately—and encouraged me to pursue it vigorously. Bob's excitement about the project was always obvious, and he became a willing sounding board for every outrageous anecdote about privacy intrusions and data excesses I came across. As importantly, he provided the structure for the story and gave me many more months to go after it than most editors would.

Bob also never flinched in his resolve that this story must be dramatic to be effective. Consequently, he continually encouraged me to dig deeper, be aggressive in my reporting, and stretch the craft of journalism as far as ethics and integrity would allow. Getting Dan Quayle's credit report for the article to prove how easy it is to invade the privacy of even the most powerful Americans was emblematic of Bob's and my approach to this piece. It was a delicious coup that we both reveled in. Bob's one of the best old-fashioned, straight-shooting journalists around. His support meant a lot to me.

Eventually, his faith—and mine—in the story was rewarded. In September 1989 it became a *Business Week* cover story, entitled "Is Nothing Private?" The article's impact was swift and significant. It grabbed the subject of technology's impact on privacy out of the sleepy recesses of the country's consciousness and threw it into the fore of a vibrant and ongoing public debate on Main Street and in Washington. The article also nabbed major journalism prizes: it was named a finalist in the prestigous Gerald Loeb Awards for Distinguished Business and Financial Journalism, and it won the 1990 Excellence in Technology Communications award.

When I turned the *Business Week* article into a book proposal, I was fortunate to find another capable editor who was just as enthusiastic about the story. Bob Bender at Simon & Schuster quickly realized the importance of the book and throughout the nearly two years that we worked on it, he constantly pushed me to delve further and squeeze more out of the subject. He provided much needed direction to the finished product.

There are many others, far too numerous to mention, who also contributed to the book. And there are many I'm prohibited from mentioning, because they've requested anonymity. I'm especially thankful to the publicity-shy habitués of the information underground who opened up the secrets of their hidden data networks to me, trusting that I would never reveal their true identities. For some perverse reason—probably to do with the maverick streak that imbues the information underground—they allowed a critical outsider like me inside, assuming, to their credit, that the truth has many shades and tellings.

Others, though, have nothing to hide and deserve to be publicly thanked. There are dozens of privacy and consumer advocates who tirelessly fed me information, tracked down sources, suggested people to interview, and encouraged me with their knowledge and support to keep going in the right direction. Thanks to Mary Culnan at Georgetown University, Evan Hendricks, editor of *Privacy Times,* Glen Roberts, editor of *Full Disclosure,* Vincent Brannigan at Georgetown University, Robert Ellis Smith at *Privacy Journal,* and Marc Rotenberg at the Computer Professionals for Social Responsibility.

There are also colleagues in the media who sometimes seemed just as excited about my book as I was and who passed along to me every mention of privacy and technology they came across in discussions with sources or in printed materials. Thanks to Iris Dudman at *Consumer Reports,* Jon Friedman, formerly at *Business Week,* Lisa Driscoll at *Business Week,* and Robert Ratner, a longtime writing partner.

Despite my reputation as a credit industry critic, I've developed deep respect for some key players in the business. Though we were frequently on opposite sides, the distance between us broke down often during wide-ranging discussions. My deepest regards and thanks to John Baker, senior vice president at Equifax. Baker is a decent, honest man with a kind heart, who, I'm pleased to say, is now a good friend. Thanks also to Barry Connelly at Associated Credit Bureaus and Oscar Marquis at Trans Union, my partners on "Nightline."

And then there are the victims of databanks and privacy intrusions. I met so many of them who have suffered profound scars and hardships because of computerization. Many, obviously, prefer anonymity. But there are a few whom I can mention, and they are among my favorites. Like hard-working Ernest Trent, from New Orleans, who deserved much more from life than the run-in he had with Employers

Information Service. Also Amy Freeze, James Wiggins, Tommy Robinson, and Ray Parrish. Good luck to all of you. Thanks for coming forth. Always know that I'm keenly aware how difficult that was.

Other sources I'm indebted to: Thomas Lawson, Kevin Murray, Denny Hatch, Cathleen Brueger, Jean Noonan, Heidi Beaver, David Foerster, Janet Sternberg, and Steve Mednick.

Finally, special thanks to Bob Lesnick, the best damned private investigator in the country by my thinking. I was a novice, a raw and green investigator, when we first met. But month after month he patiently taught me the upside and downside of computerization and the ins and outs of databanks. I was awed by his quick intelligence and by how capably and honestly he practices his craft. From our first meeting in a New Jersey Italian restaurant when he asked, "How much do I get out of this project," to our dozens of ensuing hour-long conversations, working with Bob was an eye-opening experience that I won't soon forget. It was worth millions to me. As is our friendship, which is extremely strong now. Working on this book was a nice way to get to know each other.

As always, the greatest appreciation is for my family: my wife, Dorie, and my children, Alexis and Ben. They are always inspiring. As a tight-knit family, we have learned from each other the value of privacy.

To my Big Three: Dorie, Alexis, and Ben

Contents

1

Glass Houses

It was a story out of a Hitchcock film: a sudden shift in fates played
out by two perfect strangers, one a defenseless, unsuspecting inge-
nue comfortably preparing for another day, the other a crazed killer
so tangled up in his own death grip that he had hopelessly misplaced
any notion of when the day begins and ends. Unfortunately for Rebecca Schaeffer, it wasn't a movie.

Early in the morning of July 18, 1989, the twenty-one-year-old costar
of the sitcom "My Sister Sam" was in her apartment on the ground
floor of an old Spanish-style building in West Hollywood, sipping
coffee and reading scripts. Relishing the quiet and tranquillity, Schaeffer didn't know that since before dawn Robert John Bardo, his emotions frazzled to the point of frenzy, had been pacing up and down the
street in front of her house. At first he was lost in an internal dialogue.
Then he started showing her picture to everybody who walked by,
asking if they knew her.

At about nine, a courier entered Schaeffer's building to deliver
script changes to her, and came out quickly. As Schaeffer began to
pore over her new lines inside, Bardo and the messenger exchanged
words outside. Bardo demanded to know whose apartment the courier had gone to and who answered the door. The messenger didn't
tell him, doing everything he could to get out of Bardo's grasp. Nothing but a crazy street person, the messenger thought as he carefully
worked his way toward his car. When the messenger drove off, Bardo
resumed his pacing.

Less than an hour later, Bardo finally screwed up enough courage to walk into the building and ring the bell to Schaeffer's apartment. Figuring that it was another messenger from the studio, Schaeffer was taken aback by the disheveled, gluey-eyed man staring at her with a dark, shadowy squint when she opened the door. He had a manila envelope in his hand. Schaeffer reached out for it, but Bardo pulled it back.

"Isn't that for me?" she asked.

Bardo nodded slowly and reached into the envelope. Never dropping his gaze from her eyes, he pulled out the picture of her.

"You sent this to me," he said as he shoved it in her face. "I'm your biggest fan. You must remember me. I've written you dozens of letters, called you many times at the studio. I just want to talk to you."

Schaeffer politely begged off: "I'm busy. Please go away. I don't have time right now." And she closed the door firmly.

Bardo left the building, but he stayed in front, talking to himself out loud now—agitated, muttering, "She's just another Hollywood whore, an immoral porn queen. She's beyond redemption." Then his body stiffened, and he stormed back into the building.

This time when Schaeffer opened the door, nobody was there, so she stepped across the threshold. Bardo burst out of the shadows, shoved a gun into her chest, and pulled the trigger. The bullet missed her heart by twelve inches. As she fell to the floor, Bardo raced out and ran toward the bus station, jettisoning into the bushes his gun and holster, as well as the manila envelope with Schaeffer's picture, a copy of *The Catcher in the Rye,* and audiotapes.

By the time Rebecca Schaeffer was pronounced dead at Cedars-Sinai Medical Center, Bardo was already on a bus en route to Tucson, Arizona, where he lived with his parents.

But he never made it home. Later that day, the twenty-one-year-old Bardo was found by police in Tucson, confused and dazed, stumbling among the cars in heavy traffic, and whispering, "I'm in trouble. I shot her."

Word went out along the police wire nationwide about Bardo and his bizarre behavior. And the Los Angeles Police Department told Tucson it wanted him. After interrogating Bardo for hours, the LAPD knew it had Schaeffer's killer. One LAPD source says, "He stalked her for a long time."

But not in the usual sense. Bardo had tailed her via computer. With the help of private investigator Anthony Zinkus, Bardo had spied on Schaeffer using computer databanks that told him where she lived, her telephone number, whom she called, what kind of car she drove, and where she shopped. Bardo, now on California's death row, stared perversely at the computer screen and voraciously drank in the data about Schaeffer as if he could see her through a window naked, with nothing to hide her most intimate secrets.

He may have been miles away from his obsession, says an LAPD source, "but the computer made him feel like he was next to her." When he saw on a credit report that Schaeffer had had dinner at a trendy Beverly Hills restaurant, he imagined a romantic night out with her. And when Schaeffer's driving record showed that the unassuming young woman drove a pickup truck, Bardo saw himself driving down the freeway in it, seated next to her.

Problem was, the moment the computer was turned off, Rebecca Schaeffer was gone also. And that was a reality too excruciating for him to endure. So to quash the pain, Bardo had to get physically close to Schaeffer or eliminate her. When she rejected him, the choice was made for Bardo.

Bardo's obsessions overwhelmed him—but it was the casual availability of personal data and the snapshot of Schaeffer emerging from this private information that fed and engorged his fantasies.

The Schaeffer case is obviously extreme in its outcome and enormity. But it's "a remarkably modern-day crime," says Stephen Mansfield, an assistant United States attorney in Los Angeles. In effect, it's a warning from the other side of sanity that we live in a world where personal data has become nothing but a commodity, bought and sold with relative ease. And, dangerously, all notions of privacy are being washed away in the backsplash.

Credit files and driving records are just the beginning. Health records, lists of the drugs we take, employment files, and the intimate details of our finances, family structures, personal tastes, buying patterns, and lifestyles are available. So are psychographic profiles (psychological portraits laced with demographic statistics), which reveal even the day-to-day fantasies and the activities of second selves that most of us would prefer to keep private.

Take Mr. Lonely, sitting at home alone late at night staring at the TV set. A long-legged, miniskirted woman appears on the screen and whispers, "Call me." Just to talk, she says, because she knows he needs a friend. Mr. Lonely is smitten and dials the 900 number on the screen.

With that step Mr. Lonely's sullen, private desires have become an open book, one that marketers are desperate to read and digest so that they can cash in on his propensities. A few days after he calls the chat line, Mr. Lonely receives a mailing from *Penthouse* urging him to subscribe to the magazine because it's clear he likes pretty girls and quality writing. A week later, he gets a call from a rack jobber who tells him that if he had a good time on the telephone the other night he could have a better time with the sex toys he'd like to sell him.

How did they find out about Mr. Lonely's potentially embarrassing and secluded moment of temptation? It wasn't difficult. Many chat lines have automatic number ID systems attached to their telephones, which display the telephone numbers of all incoming calls. Without permission, chat line managers run the phone numbers of their callers through a database to match them with their corresponding names and addresses. Then they compile lists of who's dialing in. And they sell these lists to anybody who wants them—in this case, marketers of products, like *Penthouse,* with strong sexual flavor.

They might be making money from people like Mr. Lonely, but they don't have to respect him. One list of "respondents to a variety of 900-number services including personals, lotteries, soap-operas, x-rated and multi-level marketing offers" is disdainfully named Greedy Productions 900-Number Callers.

What Mr. Lonely did—and some of what we do every moment of every day—increasingly forms the substance of what Harvard University law professor Arthur Miller calls a "computerized alter ego," a digital version of each of us to go with our public personae. Vincent Brannigan, an information specialist at Georgetown University, terms this electronic second self "the probabilistic man, whose opportunities in life are circumscribed by factors in a database."

And what makes this so dangerous is that there are few ethical rules or laws regulating the actions inspired by these computer conclusions. Citibank, for instance, says Brannigan, wouldn't dare discriminate against a black person when hiring a clerk or a vice president, "but it asks its computers to discriminate against him every day—and nobody thinks twice. When the banks wants to choose people to send credit offers to, does the computer provide a list of those living in the neighborhood where Temple Beth Shalom is located, or in the neighborhood where Mount Horizon Baptist Church is?"

Ray Parrish's computer-created "probabilistic man" almost cost him his American Express credit card in 1989. He received the card in January of that year and promptly paid bills of $331 and $204.39 in February and March. Then he got a shocking phone call from American Express. His card was cancelled, the clerk told him, because a computer belched out the fact that he didn't have enough money in his checking account to pay his April charges of $596.

American Express now admits it should never have used its technology to peek into Parrish's checkbook—especially since he was able to pay his outstanding bill easily from his savings and cash on hand. But the damage was already done, says Parrish: "I felt violated. When I gave them my bank account number, I never thought they would use it to routinely look over my shoulder."

Just think of it: there are upwards of five billion records now in the United States that describe each resident's whereabouts and other personal minutiae, and information about each of us is moved from one computer to another five times a day on average. That led the U.S. Congress's Office of Technology Assessment to say in a recent report, "It's virtually impossible for most citizens to know where files about them exist and nearly impossible for individuals to learn about, let alone seek redress for, misuse of their records."

And it doesn't stop with computer databanks. People are hired to eavesdrop regularly on cellular and portable phone conversations, using $250 radio scanners, for tidbits of personal information that could be used to someone's advantage. The practice is not illegal. What's more, at dozens of major companies, hospitals, and industrial sites inexpensive pinhole camera lenses with microphones secretly peer into employees' offices, loading docks, and locker rooms to ensure that nobody is stealing, loafing, or talking to the competition.

It's a snoop's technology boom, and "for very little cost, anybody can learn anything about anybody," says Robert Ellis Smith, editor of the *Privacy Journal,* a newsletter.

Want proof? Here's a peek at Dan Quayle's credit report, which I bought using my home computer for under $50:

As a young man, so the report says, Quayle ran up a bill of nearly $4,000 at Sears. A few years later, he had gotten this tab down to $356. At Brooks Brothers, he has been more parsimonious. The most the Vice President has ever owed the highbrow clothier is about $400, barely enough to buy a suit. The mortgage on his sprawling home in Huntington, Indiana, taken out in the early 1980s, tops $180,000. And here are some key numbers: Quayle's Social Security number ends in 4096 and the last four digits of the number of his MasterCard at First Virginia Bank are 1569. All told, he's a model citizen financially: he consistently pays his bills on time.

One would assume that getting the credit report of the man who's a heartbeat away should be a daunting task. After all, if Quayle doesn't wield the power to stop such an intrusion, who does? But it was simpler than I thought.

At the time I was an editor at *Business Week* preparing a cover story about the growing assault on privacy at the hands of ubiquitous computer databanks. Many of the privacy advocates I interviewed argued emotionally that rapid advances in technology have eliminated any control that individuals had over confidential information about themselves—and that an era of persistent prying into people's personal lives is upon us. But were these the ravings of a lunatic fringe? The only way to find out was by testing their premise. I reasoned that if a technology neophyte like me could dip into the vast pools of data coursing from one computer to another and actually view slices of confidential information undetected, the privacy advocates probably had it right.

So I contacted a so-called superbureau in the Midwest. There are dozens of companies like these around the country that buy information from credit bureaus and numerous other sources of data and then resell it to subscribers. In essence, they're a secondary marketing arm—middlemen—for the nation's primary information providers. In many cases, superbureaus are not very careful about whom they supply data to. Their customers are small accounts, and sometimes a bit on the shady side.

I told the superbureau salesman on the phone that I was an editor at McGraw-Hill (it publishes *Business Week*), and that I might be hiring an employee or two. For a background check, I needed their credit reports.

At first he was puzzled by my request. "Doesn't McGraw-Hill have accounts with the credit bureaus, to buy reports directly from them?" he asked.

"Of course," I said. "But I'm involved in a special project, outside of the normal organizational chain here. I'm hiring people discreetly for the top executives. Only a few people at McGraw-Hill know what I'm doing. So please don't mention this call to anybody."

The next day I received an application in the mail.

Where the application first asked for McGraw-Hill's federal identification number—the corporate equivalent of a Social Security number—I made one up and wrote it in. And where it asked for the federal ID number again, I filled in a different one in that space. This glaring discrepancy, which would have been discovered had the superbureau been even moderately diligent, went unnoticed by the databanker.

The application also asked for McGraw-Hill's bank account locations and credit references, as well as the company's correspondence with the federal government. I left these areas blank, explaining in an attached note that internal privacy rules prevent McGraw-Hill from releasing this type of information.

This apparently didn't arouse suspicion either. But there was one more hurdle I had to cross. "You've given me so little information for my files that before I can approve the application I have to send out somebody to do an on-site investigation," the salesman said. "It's just a formality."

Maybe to you, I thought. To me, it was the end of my experiment. How could I possibly convince an in-person investigator that I was involved in a top-secret, upper-echelon hiring project when my office was a ten-by-ten windowless box?

But my concerns were unwarranted. The investigator, an employee of Equifax, one of the nation's three big credit bureaus, wasn't terribly thorough. Without any prodding from me, he said that there was no need to see my office. It was okay, instead, to talk in the *Business Week* reception area, sitting underneath blown-up pictures of past magazine covers, six floors below McGraw-Hill's posh executive suites.

"How long has McGraw-Hill been in this building?" he asked.

"I'm not sure. Maybe twenty years."

"Does McGraw-Hill own this building?"

"I think half of it."

"Okay, sign here."

That was it. On the basis of this visit and my trumped-up application, I was given a password to tap the superbureau's electronic files at will from my Macintosh computer at home.

What's more, I was such a desirable customer that the salesman even gave me advice on how to sidestep federal credit industry guidelines and unobtrusively obtain the data I wanted. If I was using credit reports for employment purposes, I was told, the subjects would have to be notified in accordance with Fair Credit Reporting Act rules. But to bypass this regulation and keep my activities secret, the salesman on the phone said, "when you go online, just type in that you want 'pure credit reports' as opposed to 'employment-purpose credit reports.' Then no one will have to know anything."

I bought nearly a dozen credit reports from this information reseller. A bit timid initially, I first accessed the credit files of *Business Week* colleagues, with their permission, by just typing in names and addresses.

Then I asked for the credit report of liberal Congressman Richard Durbin (D-Ill.). Durbin has been an outspoken advocate of stronger privacy legislation, so I figured that if I were caught invading his privacy, he would at least be sympathetic to my clumsy attempt to shed light on a societal problem. Seconds later, Durbin's credit file appeared on my computer screen.

A bit nervously, I waited twenty-four hours for the repercussions of my deed. Perhaps a phone call from the superbureau, or even a visit from the FBI or Secret Service. Nothing happened. So the next night, I typed in the name Dan Quayle, and got what I came for.

Being privy to a person's credit files, address, Social Security number, and salary offers more than just titillation. It paves the way for finding out more about him. For example, the credit report I had on Quayle didn't have his telephone number and the only address it contained was for his home in Indiana. I wondered about his address in the Washington, D.C., area.

I called up the credit department of Sears. I told the clerk who answered that I worked for New Jersey Car Mart and that I had an application from somebody for an auto lease, but the applicant had failed to include his current address and telephone number.

"I want to give him a car," I said, "but I can't process his application until it's complete. He's hard to reach by phone—doesn't seem to be returning my calls—and I know from his credit report that he has a Sears card. So I wonder if perhaps your files have the current information I need."

"Be glad to help. What's his Sears account number?"

"54507986XXXXX," I replied.

Over the phone I heard the clerk typing it into his terminal. "That's Dan and Marilyn Quayle's account," he said slowly, suspiciously—as if to say, Hey, buster, who sent you to get me to commit an illegal act that'll cost me my job?

I knew I had to put him at ease immediately. I recalled the advice of crack New Jersey private investigator Bob Lesnick, who does so-called pretext calls like this all the time, in which he uses little white fibs to pry loose a piece of information from an unwitting source. The formula is simple, says Lesnick: tell the person you're talking to what he wants to hear, and he'll be compelled to tell you everything you need to know.

So I decided that the way to persuade this skeptical Sears clerk to cooperate was to display utter humility. I had to convince him that my station in life was below his—that I was just trying to do my job, nothing more. Surely he could relate to that. "I know that it's their account," I said, chuckling embarrassedly. "But I'm only a clerk here and I have to process this application. And nobody in the Vice President's office will help me out. For some reason, I don't know why—well, maybe I do know why, considering Quayle's reputation for not being the brightest guy in the world—he handed in an application without filling in all the blanks."

"Hold on," the clerk said, clearly still not certain that he should help me, but at the same time unsure why he shouldn't. After all, if I were calling about Jack Crack instead of Dan Quayle, the clerk would have provided Crack's address and phone number already, without hesitation. In that case, it would have come under the rubric of credit industry courtesy—one lender helping another. But Dan Quayle, the clerk was obviously thinking, deserves special attention. It's just another perk of celebrity, something that Dan Quayle commands and Jack Crack doesn't.

Because of this, I expected the clerk's supervisor, the credit manager, to come on the line next and really put my story through some horrible truth test that I could never pass. But that never happened. I was pleasantly surprised when it was only the clerk who returned. This time, though, probably under his manager's instructions, he checked my knowledge of the private Quayle even further.

"What address do you have for him?"

I read off the address on the credit report. Obviously it was the same as the one the clerk saw on his screen for Quayle's Indiana home. With that test passed, there was little more he could do but open the floodgates. "The local address we're showing," he said, "is XXXX Union Church Road, McLean, Virginia."

I gingerly took the next step. "Do you have his phone number?"
"Sure. 703-XXX-XXXX."
"Thanks a lot. You've been a big help."
But he was still unsure that he did the right thing; it was in his voice:
"Oh, by the way, this is an unpublished address and phone number, so don't pass it around to anyone."
"Of course."

Little Sister

It's clearly open season on privacy. But these attacks on personal information are not occurring in the way that they were predicted to happen when computer technology first began to be viewed as a possible threat to individual privacy, as early as four decades ago. It was popularly anticipated then that a Big Brother—with vast and powerful computers, huge centralized databases, video monitors, and communications equipment at his disposal—would use this technology to entrap individuals and force them into conformity. Every piece of pertinent information would be catalogued and then molded, enhanced, and expunged to suit the needs of Big Brother. Like medieval lords who wanted to keep the laypeople illiterate lest they understand the horrific state they were in and revolt against it, Big Brother would never give individuals access to information—even about themselves—because it might make them smart enough to topple his despotic regime.

Big Brother didn't happen here. And, ironically, because of the technology explosion, in which computers as powerful as those that once filled rooms in corporations are now the size of notebooks and available to everyone for under $2,000, he never will.

That's not to say that data collection isn't prodigious in the United States. It is. But data isn't stored and guarded jealously in a massive computer in Washington, D.C. The model is more democratic. Instead, information about every move we make—buying a car or a home, applying for a loan, taking out insurance, purchasing potato chips, requesting a government grant, getting turned down for credit, going to work, seeing a doctor—is fed into dozens and dozens of separate databases owned by the credit bureaus, the government, banks, insurance companies, direct-marketing companies, and other interested corporations. And from these databases it's broadcast to thousands and thousands of regional databanks as well as to numerous information resellers across the country. Then the data is shipped to millions of computers on corporate desktops or in people's homes throughout the country.

It's this exploding and bulging pyramid of information—"that is, the proliferation of databanks, rather than the existence of any single one of them—that poses the fundamental challenge to privacy interests," says David Flaherty, a professor of history and law at the University of Western Ontario in London, Canada, and the author of *Privacy in Colonial New England.*

And at every step of the way, much of the information contained in the pyramid is legally and instantly available from either original sources (i.e., the credit bureaus and the government) or information resellers, which purchase data from the original sources and market it broadly. And when the data is too touchy to buy from them, it can be obtained from a growing information underground in this country, the Top Guns of the business who for a price will supply anything you need to know—from bank files and telephone records to Social Security and Internal Revenue Service histories.

The result is a virtual information free-for-all. Private and public data is sorted and matched by computers of every stripe in an ever-increasing number of ways. And what has come of this unfortunately proves that Big Brother had a point: people can't be trusted with information about each other; they'll do harm with it.

Insurers use it to decide who should get life, disability, and medical coverage—and who should be denied it. Employers make hiring decisions based on it. But it's often the activities of the direct marketers that really test the bounds of probity.

Florida resident Mallory Hughes learned recently how far marketers will go to use personal data to invade an individual's privacy when he received an unsolicited mailing from evangelist Oral Roberts. Although Hughes had had no contact with Roberts previously, the letter began, "Mallory, I am your Partner and your friend, and because I am so close to you in spirit, I feel I can say something very personal to you. . . ."

Roberts continued:

> Mallory, it's time for you to get out from under a load of debt, that financial bondage that . . . makes you feel like you have nowhere

to turn. The devil tells you, "You've made your bed of debt, now you've got to lie in it. You're going to be paying on your bills for the rest of your life. . . . You're doomed with debt!"

Mallory, does the horror of those thoughts keep you awake at night? The burden, oh the burden, sometimes is too much to bear. . . . If you could just suddenly receive a big lump sum of money, all your problems would be over.

Well Mallory, I don't have a magical answer for your pile of bills and financial bondage. But I do have a miraculous answer, direct from the throne of God to your home.

As he read this letter, Hughes grew more and more shaken with each word. How did Roberts see so clearly into his private affairs and find out that he was in a bind?

It wasn't divine intervention, just databanks. Roberts had purchased Hughes's name from one of dozens of computerized files that list suspected financial deadbeats. One example is Credit Alert File, which contains the names of Americans at least sixty days past due on their credit cards. Another is the Credit Applicants Hotline, which contains the names of people whose applications for credit cards were denied in the last thirty days.

"I was sickened and scared by what Oral Roberts knew about me," says Hughes.

But if that made him queasy, Roberts's solution for Hughes's problems sent him running for the washbasin. Roberts asked Hughes to tell him "all the things you may be feeling in financial bondage to—like a car, credit cards, and other things," and write down exactly how much he owed on these items. And Roberts urged him to "plant the largest seed you've given to God toward getting your life out of financial bondage"—that is, to send a "gift of $100 to" Oral Roberts, so he could intercede with God on Hughes's behalf. That, Roberts said, would begin "the war on your debt."

"That's not all it will begin," says Denny Hatch, editor of *Who's Mailing What!*, a direct-marketing newsletter. "If Hughes tells Roberts the gory details of his crumbling financial state, Roberts will enter this data into his computer. And Hughes will likely get a follow-up appeal that says, "Mallory, I spoke to God about the $27,000 you owe on your credit cards and the $692 monthly car payment, and God told me He's working on it, but meanwhile He needs another $300.""

The government is no less intrusive—and sloppy. Thirty-seven government agencies, from the Social Security Administration to the Secret Service, regularly ask their computers to comb the databanks and create "propensity profiles" on American citizens. The purpose is to target people who, though they've committed no crimes, should be watched closely—including those who, the computers indicate, are most likely not to inform the Internal Revenue Service about changes in their income or living arrangements, and those who are most likely to try one day to shoot the President.

What's more, the government's record for protecting the personal data about U.S. residents in its computers is abysmally poor. In one of many recent incidents, Valerie Hubbard, a Social Security worker in Newark, New Jersey, was arrested for allegedly digging into the agency's computers and leaking private data on four thousand people—including where they worked, their income, and whether they were receiving disability payments—to a collection agency, Central Credit Clearing Bureau, Inc. According to federal investigators, Hubbard's take was $30 to $450 from Central Credit each time the company located a debtor from the data she allegedly supplied.

Databanking and snooping are becoming such a hot industry that, says Janlori Goldman, an attorney at the American Civil Liberties Union, "there's barely a piece of information about people that isn't used for far different purposes than it was initially gathered for, and always without approval."

This paints a disturbing picture, says Congressman Robert Wise (D-W.Va.), Chairman of the House Subcommittee on Government Information, Justice and Agriculture, who is pushing for the creation of a Data Protection Board to oversee the collection and dissemination of information in the United States: "If you buy a pregnancy test kit, you may get solicitations from diaper companies. If you go to the hospital for a checkup you may get an invitation to a diet seminar. If you take film to be developed, you might get a visit from the FBI. I'm not sure that this is a vision that makes most Americans comfortable."

It's not, according to a recent survey. In 1990, the credit bureau Equifax asked a broad cross section of Americans what they felt about threats to their privacy. A huge majority, 79 percent, said they were highly concerned about it. That's quite an increase from earlier surveys. In 1970, before Watergate and the other White House horrors, a mere 34 percent of Americans told Louis Harris and Associates researchers they felt "their privacy is being invaded." And in 1977, during the first days of the Carter administration, only 47 percent of respondents said that they were "concerned about the loss of personal privacy."

What's more, today's privacy worries cut deep. They're not just generalized, remotely felt fears. There seems to be a sense that privacy is a fundamental right that is being lost. And, like other nearly lost vestiges of old America—town meetings, quilt making, the urban stoop, among so many—its passing strips away a crucial thread in the nation's social fabric.

Indeed, if the country were being formed today, according to the Equifax survey, 79 percent of Americans would "add privacy to 'life, liberty, and the pursuit of happiness' " in the Declaration of Independence. But it's not in that document, and by a margin of 71 percent to 27 percent, respondents said that people have lost all control over how personal information about them is circulated and used.

The Founding Fathers may have committed an unfortunate oversight, but legislators and the judiciary have done little to mitigate it. Instead, they've added to the confusion by giving us nothing but a hodgepodge of ineffective legal language and legislation pertaining to privacy, most of it a vestige of the precomputer age, so dated and outmoded as to be laughable.

For instance, the commercial display of people's photographs without consent is illegal, says Robert Ellis Smith, an attorney and editor of the *Privacy Journal,* "but using a person's name or buying habits for commercial gain without consent, as the basis of direct mail and telephone solicitation campaigns, is not." Similarly, placing a wiretap on someone's phone without a warrant is prohibited, but tapping a person's medical records isn't.

Indeed, every federal privacy law—from the 1970 Fair Credit Reporting Act, to the blockbuster Privacy Act of 1974, to the Computer Matching and Privacy Protection Act of 1988—has failed to protect individuals from intrusions. Take the Right to Financial Privacy Act, passed in 1978. This bill forbids the federal government from rummaging through a person's bank account records without his consent or a judicial warrant. But nothing in the law restricts state agencies, local law enforcement officials, private employers, and even individuals from accessing bank records at will.

And because it's become an annual rite in Washington to tack on new exceptions to the legislation—in the latest round, the FBI and U.S.

attorneys were given the right to seize bank files—John Byrne, the federal legislative counsel for the American Bankers Association, says, "There's not a lot to this act anymore."

At least there's an act. There are no federal laws that offer any protection for such sensitive items as medical records, insurance files, and personnel data, to name just a few.

In fact, if you're looking for privacy, the safest place to go is the local video store. An incident involving Robert Bork, when he was a Supreme Court nominee in 1987, guaranteed that. At the time, an enterprising reporter at the *City Paper,* a Washington, D.C., weekly, went to the video outlet that Bork frequented and talked the clerk into giving him the list of titles borrowed by the judge. Obviously, he was hoping to find *Debbie Does Dallas* and *Deep Throat.* Instead, he found John Wayne movies.

The *City Paper* published the titles of the movies anyway. Lawmakers were outraged—and quickly passed the Video Privacy Protection Act of 1988. Now, retailers are not allowed to disclose video-rental records without the customer's consent or a court order. And they can't sell lists based on the records, either.

With such a dearth of privacy laws, any legislation that protects individual rights is welcome. Still, it's small comfort that people can keep to themselves the fact that they like to watch pornographic movies, but are unable to hide embarrassing and potentially damaging revelations of a far more private nature—such as whether they have tested positive for HIV, they have a drug habit they can't kick, or their finances are disintegrating and they're headed for bankruptcy.

Data Rape

There are skeptics who wonder how deep the sentiment for privacy really is. As Vincent Brannigan of Georgetown University puts it, "Generally people aren't moved by privacy as such, but only by the adverse consequences of data about them becoming known."

Taken broadly, many people want to ensure that information maintained about them is secure, but the thought of being able to uncover nearly anything about everybody else is not only of little concern, it's enticing.

The reaction I received when I published the *Business Week* cover story revealing the fact that I had obtained Dan Quayle's credit report is illustrative. Quayle predictably was offended by what I had done. He termed the invasion of privacy "disturbing," and said that "further controls should be considered." But that's not how people whose credit reports I didn't look at felt. All too typical was this letter:

> Your article in Business Week was informative. I can benefit from the information contained therein. My girlfriend is renting a room to a boarder, and I would like to do a background check on this man. I know I can get a credit report from TRW, but as my girlfriend has been assaulted before, I would very much like to obtain a lot more on this guy, starting from a police report. Can you tell me how to do this? I would also like some kind of guide to bureaus you say are so plentiful and free with information. Besides my girlfriend's current need for specific information, I am interested in accessing people's bank accounts and phone bills.

Sounds like a man to whom snooping is not a new idea—at least in his fantasies. And though he may not be aware of it, he's expressing a desire, coaxed out by high technology, that most people wouldn't be honest enough to admit. Between the lines of his letter is the notion that computers are a painless medium for prying on others, and, says Melanie Smith, a New England computer-ethics specialist, "like sex was to the Victorians, they fascinate and repel us."

Computers make the process of anonymously exploring credit records, employment files, medical histories, addresses, phone numbers, and most everything else that's personal an antiseptic one. They offer the excitement of voyeurism without its traditional taboos. When you sit in front of a keyboard in the seclusion of your home, there's little fear of getting caught, of being embarrassed publicly as a Peeping Tom. Strangely, using a computer to invade someone's private life is analogous to the way some murderers have described shooting a victim at random: you don't flinch when you pull the trigger because the weapon shields you from experiencing the hurt you're inflicting.

As the population grows more computer literate and databanks become more prevalent and sophisticated, long-distance, invisible assaults on privacy will occur more frequently. Some, unfortunately, will parallel the kind Robert Bardo had with Rebecca Schaeffer.

Even people with little computer expertise can get in on it already. The online system CompuServe is available for $10 a month to anybody who owns a personal computer and a modem. On it there's a service called PhoneFile with which you can find the address, telephone number, and household makeup of just about anyone in the United States by typing in the person's name and the state he lives in. The data in PhoneFile is collected from telephone directories, birth announcements, real estate transactions, and public agencies.

Using it, for instance, I found out that Sara Dylan—the reclusive ex-wife of rock star Bob Dylan, a woman who has shied away from any publicity, granting no interviews and even keeping private the details of their divorce—lives at XXX North Bedford Drive in Beverly Hills, California. I also got her phone number.

So much for the power to control who knows what about you.

Another readily available online service, called Nexis, is just as helpful to the would-be voyeur. In conjunction with the credit bureau TRW, Nexis supplies real estate data to anyone who presses a few buttons on his computer keyboard. It's public information—but it's never been available to millions of people sitting at computers before. And some of what you learn from this databank seems awfully private.

For instance, I found out that Arsenio Hall bought his home on Mulholland Drive in Los Angeles for $795,000 in 1988. To purchase it he took out a $499,950 mortgage from Southern California Federal Savings and Loan, and I found his account number. He has a seven-room, two-story single-family residence in average condition with a three-car garage and a pool. Arsenio Hall's phone number was also available.

Privacy is an emotionally charged issue. Nothing gets the dander of Americans up more quickly than the suspicion that someone is looking over their shoulders or peering into their private affairs. Some students of privacy call the process of how we disclose information, and to whom, "information democracy." They theorize that, in a world awash in data, we unconsciously establish trust in each other by selectively sharing information. Intimates are allowed to know a lot, but not everything. Friends are told less. Acquaintances are given mere inklings. And strangers, nothing.

Most people intuitively adopt the rules of information democracy these days without any prompting, because the thirst for privacy goes to the very core of human existence, says Washington, D.C., attorney Robert Belair, one of the theory's many proponents.

In fact, Belair says, when this thirst isn't slaked, people often describe privacy deprivation with the same words used by victims of rape: they say they feel violated, vulnerable, and ineffectual.

This powerless feeling in the face of privacy intrusions is part of a much bigger problem facing this nation. The idea of what sociologist Gunnar Myrdal called the "American Creed," which celebrates "the essential dignity of the human being," has been supplanted by pluralism. "Instead of a nation composed of individuals making their own free choices, America increasingly sees itself as composed of groups," says historian Arthur Schlesinger in his book *The Disuniting of America*.

This is a situation that, ironically, leaves the individual feeling uncomfortably alone. Increasingly, people are at the whim of not only pressure groups, but also large organizations—direct marketers, the credit bureaus, the government, and the entire information economy—that view individuals as nothing but lifeless data floating like microscopic entities in vast electronic chambers, data that exists to be captured, examined, collated, and sold, regardless of the individual's desire to choose what should be concealed and what should be made public. If his intentions are dashed in the process, no matter.

But society could pay in the end for its failure to take privacy more seriously. "When individuals are unable to control information about themselves, they become passive," says Robert Belair. "They sense that they're no longer participants in the world around them—just witnesses to it, under the thumb of decision-makers. And they stop being productive citizens."

2

The Secret Sharers

The people of New England didn't know what had hit them.

In early 1991, FCC National Bank, the nation's third-largest credit card issuer, asked a credit bureau to scour its databank quietly and examine the financial records of FCC National's customers in the New England area.

The region was stuck in a prolonged economic downturn. Bankruptcies and credit delinquencies were increasing, caused by rising unemployment and tumbling real estate values. FCC National wanted to protect itself from potential bad accounts before they actually soured.

So using high-tech forecasting tools, the credit bureau discreetly conducted a computerized analysis of every New England consumer with an FCC National credit card. Twenty-four credit characteristics were analyzed, including debt burden, number of satisfactory and past-due accounts, length of credit history, and how close card balances are to credit limits. After evaluating these characteristics, the credit bureau predicted who was on the brink of financial disaster and who was likely to survive the economic lull.

The names of the people on the bad side of the ledger were handed over to FCC National Bank. And solely on the basis of this review, FCC National canceled seventy-eight hundred cards and trimmed the credit limits of eleven hundred other cardholders—even if their credit accounts with the bank were current.

That set off a storm of protest from New England lawmakers. They accused FCC National of discrimination by burdening customers in economically depressed regions of the country with more stringent credit standards than those in untroubled areas. "When people with the same income and creditworthiness are treated differently because of where they live, then I am concerned," said Representative Joseph Kennedy II (D-Mass.), a member of the House Banking Committee.

This may have been the first time that Kennedy had heard of this practice, but more savvy credit industry watchers were aware that it was nothing new. Such unannounced inspections of credit files occur constantly. They're commonplace incursions in the $800 million credit reporting industry, which is dominated by the Big Three: TRW, Equifax, and Trans Union.

Other than the federal government, these companies are the largest repositories of information about Americans, with upwards of 450 million records on 160 million people—and most of the information they maintain is extremely confidential. Dotting their files are credit transactions and balances; Social Security numbers; birth dates; mortgage records; employment and salary histories; telephone numbers; information on legal entanglements, family makeup, bankruptcies, and tax liens; and current as well as previous addresses.

Yet despite the sensitive nature of the data they maintain, the credit bureaus, with sophisticated computer software, continually hunt through their records for subtle signs that something is awry with one individual or another—that a change in financial condition or lifestyle is in the offing. Then they immediately tell others what they have found.

When a credit bureau computer unearths the fact that a person is having trouble paying some of his bills, notification is sent to all banks and retailers subscribing to the system—even to those with which the consumer has up-to-date accounts. And it's not unusual for credit bureau computers to measure Americans by the performance of their credit records when compared with others of similar demographics and lifestyles. These scores, like marks of caste, are then appended to the credit reports, without the consumer knowing. It's all part of the daily output of the enormous credit industry databanks. And it can be dangerous.

For example, a person who is in the middle of a dispute with a key credit grantor, such as a mortgage lender, and who has stopped sending monthly payments pending resolution of the dispute could be targeted by the credit bureau databanks during a risk-assessment sweep as a likely future deadbeat. When this information is broadcast to all of his other creditors, a domino effect occurs. A black mark stains his accounts, resulting in untold harassment, and the loss of credit privileges each time he's just a day or two late paying his bills.

It wasn't always like this. For years, the credit bureaus were stingy with their data, selling it only to others who needed to review it to decide whether to do business with a consumer. It was generally accepted that the information maintained by the credit bureaus was private. As such, the attempt was made to safeguard it from unauthorized interlopers.

Indeed, TRW acknowledged this plainly in a long-standing code of ethics that it dropped just a couple of years ago: "Credit information," TRW mandated, "shall be treated by TRW credit services and its subscribers as confidential. . . . Names shall not be compiled . . . for sale."

That code of ethics is gone, and the credit bureaus now spend much of their time adding to their databanks any information they can get their hands on, hoping to discover secrets about a person that someone—perhaps a credit grantor, a private investigator, an employer, or a landlord—may want to know. And would buy a credit report or a customized list to find out.

Deteriorating financial health is not the only thing the credit bureaus watch for. Alleged fraud is another. Trans Union has a data service called Hawk that claims to weed out impostors. The credit bureau runs the names of people applying for credit against a databank of bogus addresses, Social Security numbers, and telephone numbers. The information in this databank comes from credit files, check-cashing services, mail drops, telephone-answering services, and government agencies.

When Hawk thinks it has found a phony, it attaches an "ALERT" warning on his credit report, the first and most prominent notation visible to anyone looking at the file. But Hawk makes mistakes. When a company buys information from literally dozens of sources, inaccuracies seep into even the best-maintained databanks. Trans Union admits Hawk is wrong sometimes, but, says the company's president, Allen Flitcraft, "a huge percentage [of the time] it's accurate."

That's not good enough, argues *Privacy Journal* editor Robert Ellis

Smith. Smith says he can't understand why Trans Union doesn't give the Hawk victim the opportunity to contest the credit bureau's findings before dubbing him an impostor in the databank. "Each time Hawk makes an incorrect assessment about a person—and mistakenly marks him as someone likely to defraud creditors—an innocent person receives an undeserved black eye that doesn't heal for a long time," complains Smith.

The effect that credit data can have on a person's day-to-day life—and the embarrassment that errors in these files can cause—was driven home recently when a doctor in Norwich, Vermont, tried to get a car loan. His financial condition was first-rate, so he expected to be approved without delay. But the bank held up the loan after learning from the doctor's credit report that he owed Norwich thousands in back taxes.

Town clerk Karen Porter was asked by the bank to verify the delinquency. But she couldn't. According to her records, the M.D.'s taxes were paid up. To find out why her files didn't correspond to the credit bureau's, Porter telephoned TRW—in fact, she made six calls to TRW during the next week—but, says Porter, the credit bureau never called back. In frustration, Porter told the local newspaper about the problem. When the article appeared, several Norwich residents went public with similar stories. Finally, TRW stepped in to sort out the mess.

TRW, it turned out, had made a huge blunder. Because of an inputting error, says the credit bureau, all fifteen hundred Norwich residents were erroneously listed as tax evaders on their credit reports. Further investigation uncovered the fact that the mistake didn't stop with Norwich. Tax-lien data was also tainted elsewhere in Vermont, as well as in New Hampshire, Rhode Island, and Maine. In the end, TRW had to purge its files of all tax records from these states. Before the errors were cleared up, thousands of residents suffered credit and loan rejections.

Not to mention untold embarrassment, says the Norwich physician: "I'm a small-town doctor, and I've always been a model citizen financially. Maybe I'm being overly sensitive, but I get the feeling that long after this incident is forgotten, I'll be remembered as somebody who got caught in some funny dealings when he tried to get a car loan. It's nobody's business in the first place that I was buying a new car. Now, because of TRW, I've gained notoriety by doing so."

A Company Called . . .

TRW is the number-one credit bureau. Like Kleenex and Scotch tape, its name is the industry standard. Often, getting a credit report is described by those in the credit business as "running a TRW." But being so visible is not something that TRW, a defense and electronics equipment contractor, is particularly comfortable with. Over the years, the company has made its living being cryptic and inscrutable. TRW says those days are gone. But are they?

The first time most Americans ever heard of TRW was in 1977 when Christopher Boyce and Andrew Daulton Lee were arrested. They were charged with peddling details to the Soviets of a small, highly classified CIA communications device that TRW was manufacturing. Lee made the contact with the Communists, and was the bagman. There were hints that he needed the money to support a cocaine habit. Boyce, a security clerk with top-secret clearance at TRW, supplied the information that his childhood friend sold.

Sneaking the data out was easy. The twenty-two-year-old Boyce had remarkably free rein at the company, and the databanks containing the specifications for the CIA superterrestrial communications devices, which the Soviets wanted so badly, was literally at his fingertips. After he had the specs in his hands, Boyce smuggled them out of TRW with no resistance.

It was a juicy scandal and a blow to TRW. Before the year was over, Boyce and Lee were both found guilty of being traitors to the United States. Boyce was sentenced to forty years in jail, while Lee got life imprisonment.

The trial was a sizzling one. Court testimony uncovered the fact that TRW was involved in developing highly sophisticated technology for virtually every key government operation that fed on concealment and camouflage. But TRW also had deep problems. Witness after witness offered lurid tales of liquor and drug abuse among TRW's security staffers during many a breakneck overnight at the company.

Laxness like this would be shocking at any company, but it was especially so at TRW. It was frightening to consider that this security crew, loosened up by drink and drugs, was sitting within arm's length of a powder keg of covert information, stuff that was central to the operations of not only the CIA, but also every intelligence wing of the

Justice Department, the National Security Agency, and the Pentagon. The temptation to compromise national security was as second nature to these workers as punching a time clock.

TRW had a lot of fence-mending to do with its clients after the bars locked behind Boyce and Lee. But the episode served one useful purpose: it provided the first insider's view of a puzzling company that had made impenetrability its hallmark. Now at least Americans were privy to some of the inner workings of a public riddle. And the suspicions of many were borne out: TRW was as far away from the chamber-of-commerce-clean world as you could get; it was the government's technology linchpin, way ahead of everybody else in the gleaming, strategic machine language of war and espionage.

These disconcerting recollections of TRW came rushing back to me last year as I drove up to the company's sprawling campus in Orange County, California, where its Information Services Group is housed. As a *Business Week* editor covering information companies for nearly three years, I knew TRW well.

Outwardly, TRW *has* changed a lot. For one thing, the company is pinning its future on automobile air bags, a far more benign product than advanced weaponry and surveillance devices, which used to be mainstays back when TRW was a leading defense contractor. TRW holds key long-term contracts with auto manufacturers to equip their cars with these safety devices, and the company expects to make the lion's share of its future earnings selling this equipment.

Data is a close second in projected growth for TRW. And it was TRW's decision to become a credit bureau (it got into the business in the early 1970s, and after buying numerous smaller credit agencies it became the number-one credit bureau about a decade later) that forced the company to let its protective shield slip even further and become much more accessible to the public. That happened when Washington—especially the Federal Trade Commission, based on rules written into the Fair Credit Reporting Act—started dictating to credit grantors what they had to tell consumers and how they had to tell it.

The government said that when someone is turned down for credit he must be given the chance to receive a free copy of his credit report and the opportunity to be counseled on what it says, as well as to correct any errors in it. Suddenly hundreds of thousands of people who were previously perplexed about or oblivious to what kind of company TRW was were showing up at its field offices around the country and talking over intimate financial matters with TRW representatives.

And as consumer activism ballooned during the 1980s, TRW responded with community outreach. It now advises minorities on how to get credit and how not to abuse it; it has begun a controversial service called Credentials, which, for all its faults (and there are many), at least keeps people informed of who's looking at their credit reports and what kind of information the reports contain; and its corporate leaders make numerous public appearances at grass-roots seminars. In its latest olive branch to consumers, TRW is offering to supply one free credit report per year to every American in its databank.

But old perceptions die hard and I couldn't shake the memories of the past completely as I drove up to the company's gates. I pictured an immaculate interior with high tech dripping like stalactites from the ceilings and walls, a dark cave of information technology—perhaps the nonmilitary version of the Strategic Air Command war room. I expected to find national maps with blinking lights, and computers with big tape drives spinning one-fourth counterclockwise, then stopping on a dime, then spinning again.

It wasn't like that at all. Inside, it was just like every other sanitized workplace these days. Cubicles and prefab offices, some with windows, some without. Oak-veneered paneled boardrooms overlooking vast parking lots. Computers on desktops, and big mainframes in glass-enclosed, climate-controlled rooms. But no machines moving or even humming. Nothing but quiet tech.

Then it occurred to me that TRW, despite its more visible public image, is, behind closed doors, really not much different from the way it always was. It's still, after all, dabbling in secrets, only now the silence of technology is masking its activities. Among these stolidly oblique computers; the wiring for the local-area and wide-area networks hidden and nestled in the walls, floors, and ceilings; and the transparent microwave or satellite transmissions pouring out of the building quietly travel, without detection, millions of bits of secret data per second, information of the most personal type about most Americans.

TRW knows a lot about each of us—to put it plainly, it knows many of our most intimate secrets—and it finds out more each day. Typically, information is sent electronically daily, weekly, or monthly to TRW from banks, stores, collection agencies, credit unions, and doctors, as well as from the United States Postal Service, courthouses, and numerous other government agencies—all of which keep the giant credit bureau up to date on moment-to-moment changes in our lives.

Most of the information is supplied to TRW for free. Companies that rely on TRW reports to make decisions about individuals or track their movements say it's to their advantage to help the credit bureau maintain its giant database with up-to-the-moment information. "Each new piece of information that TRW files away can potentially provide a new wrinkle about a person's background," says a credit manager at Federated Department Stores. "And it could be the difference between making a good decision about offering credit to a person or not. Or it can be the missing clue to locate somebody who's run off with $3,000 in merchandise without paying."

TRW upgrades and expands its files with information it purchases from the Census Bureau, motor vehicle agencies, magazine subscription services, telephone white pages, insurance companies, and as many as sixty other sources. "We buy all the data we can legally buy," says Dennis Benner, a TRW vice president.

For one purpose: to compile the most detailed description of the financial status, personal traits, ups and downs, and lifestyle of every American that can be assembled—and sold at a cool profit.

It's an exciting, fast-moving business. Data pours in constantly to TRW. It's collated, stored, and compared against what's already known about us. And then the computers subtly and automatically restructure our electronic profiles. Finally, the whole file, or at least pieces of it, is sent back out to TRW's customers—an amazing five hundred thousand records are sold each day.

If you miss a car payment, a pristine credit report can fade to a dubious gray in a nanosecond. If you lose your job and your salary drops to nothing from $150,000 a year, all the hard work to attain a high place in the community can be wiped out with lightning speed.

Even while we're sleeping, TRW's computers are quietly reformulating our digital dossiers with each new piece of information they get, and in seconds changing the features of our private faces. This may be invisible to us in the morning when we wake up and look in the mirror, but soon enough its impact becomes evident. "It's information like this that can make or break our lives these days, be the ticket to further success or the key that locks us out of opportunities," says Representative Andy Jacobs (D-Ind.), chairman of the House Subcommittee on Social Security. "Most of us start out talking big and say, 'Nothing in those files can hurt me; I have nothing to hide.' Well, maybe not in the criminal sense, but in the social sense, that's another story."

That's especially true with employers, landlords, credit grantors, insurers, physicians, private investigators, the police, and dozens and dozens of others able to get these credit reports, legally and illegally, with about as much resistance as Christopher Boyce met when he tiptoed out of TRW with top-secret CIA blueprints. And Jacobs is right because increasingly decisions about jobs, financial opportunities, housing, and medical care, among other things, are determined solely by what these computerized reports say.

There is a way to sanitize a bad credit report and avoid a negative decision, but you have to bump into someone like James Duke, and Duke is not an easy man to find. Duke is an eighteen-year veteran of the credit industry—most of that time counseling consumers with credit problems—and his most recent activities have forced him to keep an extremely low profile. At his request, we never met; we just communicated by fax and telephone.

Duke is emblematic of the darkest, most lethal side of the credit reporting industry. Put simply, he's a con man. Yet government officials in half a dozen states and corporate executives throughout the Southwest have paid Duke handsomely to perform the unseemly magic of his double deal, because he's figured out what few else have: "I know," he says, "everything there is to know about this stinky business."

Duke's running scared most of the time. But even on tenterhooks, he quickly proved that what he could do is remarkable. "I can take a credit report that's bad one month and make it good the next, without paying anything near what the credit grantors claim they're owed," boasts Duke.

It was hard to believe at first, but his proof was incontrovertible. On June 18, 1991, Duke's credit report looked like this:

BANK OF NY   Delinquent 60 Days   Balance: $4350
Last payment: 12/06/90
Credit Line Closed - Grantor Request

ALLIANCE MORTGAGE Last payment: 11/01/90 House in Foreclosure	Delinquent 90 Days	Balance: $75576
GE CAPITAL Last payment: 01/09/91	Delinquent 90 Days	Balance: $2776
FIRST CONSUMERS BANK Account Written Off as a Bad Debt		Balance: $3707

And that was just the beginning. There were upwards of a dozen similarly sagging accounts on Duke's credit report. Things were looking glum—especially when Duke received a letter from Alliance Mortgage in Waco, Texas. The letter began, "We have filed a Notice of Intention to Foreclose on your loan. If you wish to save your home, you must act NOW. Failure to make arrangements to pay could lead to the loss of your home."

But Duke never found out whether Alliance meant business or not. He deftly slipped out of trouble, thanks to his uncanny knack for beating the credit bureaus at their own game. In August 1991, just two months later, this is what his revised credit report looked like:

BANK OF NY Last payment: 05/31/91	Current Account	Balance: $4170
ALLIANCE MORTGAGE Last payment: 06/02/91	Current Account	Balance: $75410
GE CAPITAL Last payment: 01/09/91	Current Account	Balance: $2876
FIRST CONSUMERS BANK Paid Satisfactorily		Balance: $0

And, says Duke, armed with this credit report, he's just leased four cars and has five new credit cards. Accomplishing this feat required sleight of hand, but no actual payments. "If you know the way the databanks work, and approach it the right way, you can do anything," he explains. "It's only the poor slob that suffers in silence under the weight of the data pouring out of the credit bureaus about him."

For example, to get his mortgage listed as current on his credit report, Duke called a senior vice president at Alliance and told him a cock-and-bull story that made the VP bend over backward to accommodate Duke.

"I said, my voice trembling with fear, that his collections department has made a horrible mistake for the past six months, and I just discovered it," says Duke.

Duke explained to the bank executive that although he had religiously sent his monthly payments on time during this period, unbeknownst to him the checks were being sent back uncashed. And the worst part was, Duke told the VP, that he'd been away on assignment and hadn't opened much of his mail since late last year, so he'd been living off the cash in his checking account, blind to the fact that along with spare money he was also spending his mortgage payment, which he thought was being paid each month.

"I can't understand why we returned the checks to you," the VP said. "Did you put your account number on them?"

"I'm not sure. Maybe not. But my name was on my checks. Isn't that enough to credit my account?"

"Usually," the VP answered, puzzled. He paused a moment to think this one over. "Wait a second, you said you've been away. Have you been mailing us the checks from a location different than your home?"

"Yes, but what does that have to do with anything?"

"Well, that explains it," said the VP. And he explained to Duke that when a loan number isn't included on a check, payments are matched to an account by two items: the name on the check and the postmark that shows where it was mailed from. They both have to agree with the mortgage company's records, or the checks are sent back.

"The postmarks didn't correspond, so we must have returned your payments," the VP conceded.

Duke laughs at how easily he backed this bank VP into "admitting that his system's safeguards against mistakes had led to a massive error, though no error had even occurred. Knowing how the system worked enabled me to maneuver him into exposing a flaw in it. Next I went in for the kill."

Duke told the VP that the bank's mistake was unfortunate though forgivable. But the problem was, because of it his finances were in such disarray that "I can't pay the full amount I owe you. But I want to clear this thing up, so I'm willing to pay one fourth of what I owe you if the bank, in return, will notify the credit bureaus that the account is up to date, with an A-one rating. Your mistake is edging me closer to bankruptcy and that won't do either of us any good. I don't want that to happen and we both don't want lawsuits, so let's work a deal."

The bank executive readily agreed and, with a stroke of his pen, transformed Duke's badly blemished account—still months in arrears—into a spotless one.

The key, Duke explains, is to play to a person's ambitions. "Every corporation head is concerned only with profit and loss," says Duke. "They want money in the bank, not litigation. And every corporate vice president wants to be president. They won't get there by screwing customers and turning away payments."

There's another way to accomplish the same thing: make a lower-level contact at a creditor's collections department and convince him, by putting some money in his pocket, to slip into the databank and delete a written-off account from the company's computer system by changing it to one that's closed and paid-up satisfactorily. That's what Duke did to remove the bad First Consumers Bank debt of $3,707 from his credit report.

"Once you get somebody to do that once," Duke says, "he'll have to do it all the time. The mere threat, usually unstated, that you could report his larceny to his superiors if he gets on your wrong side is enough to keep him doing your bidding."

Duke was so skilled at fixing bad credit reports that he made a living out of it. All his business is obtained by word of mouth. And much of it comes from relationships with companies such as car dealerships and contractors that depend on credit approval to sign up customers.

When a customer wants to buy a new Mercedes but his credit report can't justify the loan, the dealership introduces him to Duke. For $2,500, Duke fixes the credit report. The car salesman is happy—he's made a sale. The customer drives away with his dream machine. Only the lender doesn't know he's been had. Odds are, though, the repo man will hear about this deal before long.

TRW officials flinch at any discussion of Duke. "He's a credit charlatan and bad for the system" is the way one TRW senior vice president put it.

The vice president is right. A credit economy can't support a lot of people like Duke. Fortunately, there are only a few. If lenders were unable to make educated credit decisions based on an accurate view of an individual's past credit performance, a dangerously large number of loans would slip into arrears, and the number of defaults would rise. That would have a trickle-down effect: the price consumers pay for merchandise would increase. Banks would offer credit only to the very wealthy. The true upside of the credit system—the chance it offers the middle class to trim the gap between it and the wealthy— would be destroyed.

Yet despite the dangers to the system that Duke represents, he's still viewed as a hero by many. Indeed, it's characteristic of the acrimony that consumers feel toward the credit bureaus—and the indifference that the credit bureaus have shown consumers—that people are not appalled when they hear about Duke's activities. Instead, the antagonistic relationship between consumers and the credit bureaus makes many people delight in what Duke does. They see him as a Robin Hood figure rather than what he really is.

Duke's business has declined significantly recently because of the emergence in his part of the country of con men, known as credit doctors, who have gone him one better. In fact, the activities of these people, who like Duke promise to clean up credit records for a fee, are often so underhanded and illegal that Duke's pale by comparison. In the process, they've managed to give all credit repair work a bad name. And now that the authorities are watching these new players closely, many customers have been scared away from dealing with anyone—Hood included—who, no matter how different, still carries the taint of being a credit doctor.

The credit M.D.s in the Southwest have made a living from compromising private databases and combining that with their ample knowledge of how to skirt credit industry regulations. The best at it, many say, were Walter "Waldo" Hilton and James Lawson, two Baptist preachers in Houston. A few years ago, the pair founded the now defunct Christian Financial Services (CFS) Inc. Unlike Duke, though, CFS apparently didn't even make a pretense of physically clearing up the credit records of clients. Instead, for about $1,500, according to authorities, Hilton and Lawson supplied deadbeat customers with new unblemished identities, at least in the eyes of the credit bureaus.

To do this, the police say, via personal computer Hilton and Lawson scoured the databanks at the Credit Bureau of Greater Houston for credit records of people with names and birthdates similar to CFS clients' but with a clean credit history. Then the two ministers took the Social Security numbers and good credit references from these files and told their customers to apply for credit by attaching this data to their real names and dates of birth. Hilton knew that this scheme would be virtually undetectable: the computers at the credit bureaus generally ignore "typos" in names and birthdates, if Social Security numbers match.

Thus, following CFS's blueprint, a Jackie Johnson, born 1952, who has a dozen delinquent accounts would apply for credit using the Social Security number of John Johnston, born 1951, who has a spotless credit file. And when he does, everything Jackie Johnson does with his new credit cards, loans and mortgages would be appended to John Johnston's file.

CFS was a big success. According to sources at the Houston police who investigated CFS, one local automobile dealer sold nearly 100 cars to buyers who had fraudulent credit reports. In another case, a down-and-out unemployed CFS client bought a $300,000 home and a Lincoln Continental with a cellular telephone. His wife, also unemployed, was outfitted with a Mercedes Benz and a $100,000 fur coat.

CFS's recipe for defrauding the credit industry was—and still is, apparently—imitated by dozens of companies in the Southwest. In fact, during the past five years about $20 million in illegal purchases were made in the Houston area as a result of phony credit data. Now, says a federal attorney who is investigating credit doctor operations nationwide, these types of incidents have spread to virtually every major city in the United States. Others agree. "Credit doctoring is an epidemic," says Joseph LaBranche, a credit-card fraud expert in Houston.

Of course, for every individual who receives thousands of dollars in new revolving credit and hundreds of thousands of dollars in mortgages the CFS way, there is someone whose credit report has been usurped to do this—and whose credit report will likely be fouled horribly when the borrower returns to his old habits and stops paying the bills. The most outrageous example is that of Jean Wright, who discovered when she received a past-due notice for a $500 electric bill belonging to someone else that the person piggybacking onto her credit file had run up $100,000 in unpaid debts using data taken from her records—and then filed for bankruptcy on her behalf.

There have been few prosecutions of these renegade credit doctors, because it's hard to get enough evidence to make a case stick. For one thing, their clients are unlikely to squeal on them, lest they end up incriminating themselves. By participating in credit doctor schemes these clients are, in effect, coconspirators to defraud individuals as well as the credit bureaus and money lenders. But CFS's misuse of credit data eventually got so obvious that Lawson and Hilton were finally cut down. In 1989, Lawson pleaded guilty to buying a car using refurbished credit data and was sentenced to five years in prison. He served about a year.

The seventy-year-old Hilton got off even better. Hilton is well known around Houston for his 1950s "Man with the Plan" radio ads, in which he promised to sell poor people refrigerators on credit. His risk was minimal. The refrigerator stopped working automatically if the buyer failed to deposit a quarter in its coin slot every day. In 1990, Hilton pleaded guilty to having unauthorized computer access codes with intent to defraud and was sentenced to a mere eight months. Hilton denies ever being a credit doctor.

That's a remarkable denial, Houston authorities say, considering how openly CFS offered its services and how many customers have come forth describing CFS's activities. Not only that, says David Hefner, the Houston police detective who nabbed him, it's likely that Hilton will return to credit doctoring soon. According to Hefner, Hilton told him when he was caught that he had a single-minded purpose: to weaken the credit industry, because it's just another example of white-domination over blacks in America. "I'm going to destroy the credit system as we know it today," Hilton reportedly told Hefner.

Everything's Permissible

The corporate chiefs I met at TRW's Information Systems Group had a strict agenda in hand. Credit "doctors" such as James Duke and credit cases like the one that pitted New Englanders against FCC National couldn't have been further from their minds. They were there to show me how carefully they guard the secrets they keep in their databanks; how important each of these digital intimacies is to them;

how seriously they regard their "sacred trust with the American people to be the central repository of personal financial information," as TRW VP Dennis Benner terms it. And they wanted to describe the diligent steps they've taken to keep credit reports out of the hands of those who would misuse the information.

William Tener is proud of what he's accomplished as TRW's director of operational and regulatory compliance. Tener is responsible for the company's security procedures. He believes in technology—and in technology's ability to fix social problems and weaknesses, even if technology itself has caused or exposed them.

To Tener, the answer lies solely in the right technocountermeasure. He says: "Desktop computers may have made it easier to get at someone's credit report from your own home, even if you don't have a legitimate right to do so, but that doesn't mean that I can't shut down the abusers with better technology than they have at their disposal. It's a war, and the winner is the person that has the more creative technology on his side."

The centerpiece of Tener's arsenal is Discovery, the first truly advanced security system in the credit industry, one based on a model developed by the rocket scientists at TRW's Space Park. Discovery has artificial intelligence. It reasons like a human in attempting to identify and outwit people trying to steal data from the company's files by impersonating TRW subscribers.

"Think of it like this," Tener says. "Suppose a stranger called you up and said, 'Hi, son. It's mom.' Even if she mimicked your mother's voice perfectly, you'd pick up certain clues in what she says—either the content, the context, or the colloquialisms she uses—that would unmask her as a fraud. That's what Discovery does. When a person claims to be a subscriber and dials in for a credit report, it looks for characteristics that are uncharacteristic of that subscriber. It looks for the subtle signs that someone other than the subscriber is accessing the TRW system."

To outfox frauds, Discovery knows how each TRW customer typically requests a credit report. Does he input the subject's name and address or just his name and Social Security number? At what hours does he call, and from what region of the country? What type of equipment does he use to access the system—a personal computer, telephone, mainframe, workstation, or TRW terminal? How many credit reports does he commonly buy at a time? And dozens of other items.

Then, each time a subscriber asks for a TRW report, Discovery compares his current MO against its customer profile database, and "when something doesn't look right, the security staff is alerted," says Tener.

A Discovery "hit" is followed by a call from TRW security to the subscriber, telling him there's reason to believe a credit report was purchased using his password by somebody who doesn't have a legitimate right to see this report. On occasion, says Tener, one of a customer's employees has illegally accessed the system. Then the credit bureau warns the company that if it happens again, TRW will close the account and possibly sue or bring charges.

"But mostly," says Tener, "it's a false alarm, and nothing untoward has gone on." We've got statistics, Tener says—and he starts to rattle them off—which prove that because of Discovery the number of people illegally accessing the TRW system is down to virtually none.

I had to stop Tener there. The fact is, in a matter of minutes I can gain access to anybody's credit report—yours, the Vice President's, my best friend's, or that of somebody I've never even met. And I can do it undetected by any multimillion-dollar security system. If I were dangerous I could use this information, as a growing number of malicious people do, for crimes against property and privacy—financial scams, blackmail, larceny, and voyeurism that results in threats on people's lives or worse.

To prove this, I showed Tener a copy of the falsified application I completed to gain access to the databank that sells TRW credit reports via personal computer to anyone who pays the $495 sign-up fee. Then I showed him Dan Quayle's credit report, which I had bought from this information reseller. And I reminded Tener that I could still be buying credit reports—anybody's—from this databanker today without even an eyebrow being raised had I not published the details of my journalistic exercise in *Business Week* and alerted my credit-report supplier to my shady activities.

Then I described to Tener the time I called up a Long Island credit bureau, a TRW affiliate, and told it the same little fib about how McGraw-Hill needed credit reports to check on potential employees. The credit bureau's manager asked me which reports I needed. I gave him the name and address of my senior editor and identified him as the first job applicant I wanted to investigate.

A couple of hours later, the manager telephoned me and revealed something about his personality that shouldn't have surprised me, considering everybody's propensity for snooping and gossip. Nevertheless, I was shocked because it ran totally counter to the rules of the credit industry of which he is a part.

It turns out the manager was just as nosy as I was. He told me that he had examined the editor's credit report and wasn't sure if he was a good hiree, especially if the job required handling large sums of money. "This guy's mortgage is ominously large," the credit bureau manager warned. "Unless his salary is quite high, he's going to be tempted to make off with some of McGraw-Hill's money just to pay for his home."

Then the manager did something else that proved credit reports are not, in his mind, very private: though I didn't ask him to, he faxed the editor's credit report to me, sending it to a facsimile machine used by every editorial staffer at *Business Week*. As the fax machine spewed it out—and, indeed, as it sat in the paper catcher of the machine for hours before it was delivered to me—the report was an open book. The senior editor's personal financial data and other confidential information about him, including his Social Security number, were available to be read by hundreds of people—among them colleagues who know him well.

Tener was nonplussed by my anecdotes, and he didn't want to talk about this issue anymore. But the credit bureaus couldn't maintain a low profile on it for long. Soon after my visit to TRW, the House Subcommittee on Consumer Affairs and Coinage held a series of hearings on amendments to the Fair Credit Reporting Act.

In the first stage of these sessions, Representatives were upset about my *Business Week* story and the apparent ease with which I obtained so many credit reports without detection. They demanded to know how such private documents—even the Vice President's personal files—could be accessed so freely and what the credit industry felt could be done about this problem.

In response, Al Flitcraft, president of Trans Union, suggested that the solution is "to strengthen the law in . . . terms of the penalty [for illegally accessing a credit report]. Maybe $5,000 isn't enough. Maybe one year in jail isn't enough. Maybe if it was twenty years in jail and a million dollars those people wouldn't do it."

That led to the following exchange between Flitcraft and Representative Nancy Pelosi (D-Calif.):

Pelosi: So what you're saying is that the mechanics of the operation are such that you really cannot guarantee the privacy and safety of the consumer?

Flitcraft: Not without tearing the system apart and having no system. Because what your question implies would be an ability to have a safeguard—

Pelosi: A guarantee. . . . Maybe I'm not understanding it. In other words, somebody could call up and say I'm thinking about hiring somebody or renting an apartment or selling a house or making a loan and I want to know about the creditworthiness of John Doe—

Flitcraft: Not . . . anybody can do that, only a legitimate credit grantor or somebody who testifies in a document that they sign that they're going to do a preemployment check. . . .

Pelosi: So anybody can do that, though? This is frightening to me. . . . Somebody's privacy has been invaded and . . . we can't even calculate or convey what that might do to that person's personal life. So I would hope that the industry, recognizing that there is a need for what you do, could contribute some ideas about how to protect and guarantee the rights of consumers.

Flitcraft: I don't see how that's possible, ma'am.

Pelosi: Well I'm glad to hear that on the record.

That admission of impotence against intruders—especially those like me who barely cover their tracks—worried me. It reminded me of the stories I'd heard of people whose lives have been suddenly turned upside down by somebody illegally accessing their credit reports. I've met dozens of these people during the last few years, but one story stands out because it was sadder than the rest.

Chandler Corcoran was seventy-two years old when I met her, and lived in a chichi apartment on New York's East Side, in the same building where Greta Garbo for decades before her death wrapped herself in a veil of privacy.

Corcoran's apartment was awash in crystal and elegant charm. High-backed wing chairs with antique doilies over flaring armrests. Lipstick plants in full bloom, their bloodred flowers shooting out of nature's perfect imitation of plastic tubes. Over the mantel a portrait of her dead husband, Ernest, posed in pinstripes, his corporate demeanor dictatorial yet unexplainably warm.

As Corcoran spoke, her voice quivered—at times it was soft, at other times tense, but it hardly ever rose above a cracking whisper. "I have cancer. I've gone through months of painful chemotherapy. And now this," she said. With shaking hands she passed a sheaf of papers to me: her credit records, letters she'd recently written to the authorities, and notes she'd received from them.

It was compelling reading, a step-by-step introduction to an intricate and perfidious credit card scam that had left Chandler Corcoran in a huge fix. And she'd only learned about it because four months after it began an eagle-eyed Visa security staffer noticed a jarring discrepancy in a request for a supplemental card on one of her credit card accounts. The application asked that the new credit card, and all future bills for this account, be sent to an address in Harlem, New York City's black ghetto—an address that seemed inconsistent with Corcoran's financial profile.

"He called me and told me that in reviewing the application something seemed awry," Corcoran said. "He wanted to know if there was some mistake, perhaps a typo, or if I really wanted this person, who was obviously from a different ethnic and economic background, to share my card."

Corcoran was bewildered. So the Visa clerk suggested she immediately telephone all her creditors and find out if any other supplemental cards for her accounts had been applied for and issued recently. It was likely, he told her, that this wasn't the first such request. And the others were probably approved.

So Corcoran, just home from a four-month stay at New York Hospital, weakened by chemotherapy, began the round of telephone calls.

What she found out amounted to a pattern of shameless activity. "Look at my credit report, it's all there in black and white," Corcoran said, her voice suddenly firm, drenched with indignation.

I glanced at the report quickly and was stunned by what I saw. Credit card piled on top of credit card, many with the same account numbers, and all of them spent to the limit. An inordinate number had gone unpaid for so long that they were closed due to delinquency.

"I get goose bumps every time I see that credit report," Corcoran said. "It's like looking at your paralyzed body lying on the white sand being pecked at by vultures."

"I don't get it. Is this report accurate or not?"

"It's accurate, all right," Corcoran explained. "It seems that a group of people led by somebody named Denise Davis has obtained nearly a dozen supplemental credit cards on my accounts. There were three extra American Express cards alone, and two extra Citibank Visas.

And they were running up thousands of dollars in bills on these cards."

The call from Visa was fortunate. Without it, Corcoran would have remained in the dark about what was going on. All her monthly bills were being sent to the Harlem address. And in her diseased condition, with so much of her energy focused on sheer survival, she never even noticed that she wasn't receiving bills in the mail anymore. Denise Davis obviously had no intention of paying these bills, so the accounts were badly in arrears.

Experts familiar with similar credit card scams explain how this one probably worked: It's likely that Denise Davis, or one of her cohorts, was employed at New York Hospital in some capacity. Tapping the computerized records system for patients living in well-heeled zip codes, Davis and her cohorts found Chandler Corcoran and downloaded her address and Social Security number. Then, using this information as a passport to obtain additional data, they ran Corcoran's credit report and got the account numbers of open credit cards in her name that had a lot of cash available on them. Finally, they applied for additional cards on these accounts—and received them without a snag. Most financial institutions, where scrutiny of credit applications is notoriously lax, respond to requests like these with *pro forma* approval.

Chandler Corcoran's creditors empathize with her plight, and don't hold her responsible for any of the purchases charged to her account that she didn't make. But it could take a year to clear up the mess her accounts are in, and to set right her badly besmirched credit record. And it might be months before she'll be able to use her credit cards again—at least without getting the third degree from every retailer she hands the plastic to.

One thing Corcoran's creditors won't do, though, is ask Denise Davis to pay for her crime. Typical is the response of the desk manager Corcoran spoke to at American Express's fraud department: "He told me," she said, "that he's inundated with thousands of cases just like mine. They're piling up on his desk, and he doesn't have the manpower to do anything about any of them."

What Corcoran went through has left an eerie, haunting, helpless feeling. At a time when she's battling simply to stay alive, Corcoran said, she doesn't deserve to be the victim of somebody's wretched practical joke, of somebody's unsavory gain at her expense.

"I have to tell you something I did that was so uncharacteristic of me," she said, looking down at her hands, a sheepish, embarrassed expression on her face. "You have to understand, when you have cancer there's nobody to lash out at for giving you the disease, though you want to desperately. You have no choice but to be passive. This Denise Davis thing was too much—on top of getting cancer. I couldn't stand back and let that happen to me, too, without confronting it, because if I did nothing, I'd have to admit that my fate forever was to be only a victim. That's the way I would go to my death. It was unacceptable, I thought."

So one day, in utter frustration, Corcoran called Directory Assistance for Denise Davis's phone number. Then Corcoran telephoned Davis. "But when she answered the phone, I froze," Corcoran said, now staring at me, obviously wanting me to say something comforting, to tell her that anybody in that situation would have done the same thing. I regret that I didn't.

"I couldn't say a word to her," she continued. "I got so scared, face-to-face, as it were, with somebody that's doing me so much harm when she doesn't even know me. I was afraid of how else she might hurt me, if she found out that I knew who she was and where she lived. So I hung up without speaking."

The worst part is that Denise Davis and her cohorts probably committed dozens of crimes like the one they visited on Chandler Corcoran. Estimates of the amounts that credit grantors write off because of illegal credit transactions range from $1 billion to $4 billion annually.

What started out as isolated incidents is rapidly becoming an epidemic of mayhem spread mostly by mobs of young foreign nationals—chiefly Africans, Japanese, Chinese, and Arabs, according to the Secret Service, the FBI, and other federal law enforcement agencies. These youths have set up little-known, tight-knit intelligence networks in the United States that secretly carry private data about Americans nonstop.

"Ethnic gangs using confidential data as a weapon," says David Leroy, chief of domestic intelligence for the Drug Enforcement Administration, "appear to be the new trend in crime."

According to a statement issued in September 1986 by a Senate subcommittee after it held hearings on the ethnic underworld, these groups have "become especially adept at credit card fraud, bank fraud, insurance fraud and entitlement [government benefits] fraud."

They are, in short, information rapists who violate people by turning their own intimacies against them.

Typical of the victims of entitlement fraud is Doris Manuel. What happened to her is puzzling and Kafkaesque—and, unlike Chandler Corcoran, she'll be paying for it for quite some time.

Manuel's nightmare began with a letter she received from the Internal Revenue Service. The IRS told her a routine audit had disclosed that she hadn't paid income tax for more than five years on the wages from her job at a garment factory in New York. Manuel, a medical secretary, was shocked by this news. She says she never worked in the garment industry in her life.

It turned out that Manuel was a victim of a complex information scam. An Ecuadoran immigrant named Maria Cortez, who *is* a garment factory worker, has been using Manuel's Social Security number as her own, under the name Doris Cuevas, Manuel's maiden name. And Maria Cortez has not paid a cent in income tax.

Which means, says the IRS, that about $60,000 in salary—earned by Maria Cortez, but reported to Doris Cuevas's tax account—has gone untaxed. As far as the IRS is concerned, somebody's going to have to pony up, namely Doris Manuel. After all, explains the IRS, it's Manuel's Social Security number that is assigned to the job. And the IRS means business. The agency is already dunning three fourths of Manuel's weekly paycheck.

"It's a horrible feeling," says Manuel. "You feel totally invaded."

As for Maria Cortez, she's inscrutable. She won't say where she got Manuel's Social Security number from, except to admit that "a friend gave it to me." She has refused to provide his name, however. And she adds enigmatically and without remorse, "My name is Maria Cortez, and my Social Security number is Doris Cuevas."

The authorities claim that the most notorious of the ethnic gangs committing databank crimes are Nigerian. Reportedly, members of this group conceal their true background by claiming to be from the Virgin Islands. After signing up for federal scholarships available to citizens of American protectorates, they enroll in universities across the nation, and use these conveniently insulated locales as meeting places.

Meanwhile, others, says New York postal inspector Martin Biegelman, "obtain security guard positions, which are generally low-paying and hard to fill. Then, when they're assigned to a building at night, these individuals are given free rein to patrol the offices and the computers located there. They go through personnel files and even employees' desks to obtain names, job titles, Social Security numbers, home addresses, and whatever other personal information is available."

This data, along with additional items obtained from credit reports and other computerized information sources, is placed on the Nigerians' national network. Then, gang members freely sort the data, says Dale Boll, assistant director in charge of fraud at the Secret Service, to get credit cards "with fraudulent applications. These cards are used to buy thousands of dollars in merchandise and to rent expensive automobiles, all of which are brought down to the port and shipped back home where they're sold"—before anybody knows about it.

Ensuing profits are shared by whichever gang is masterminding the scheme. An individual's take, according to the Secret Service, can top $10,000 per day. As many as one hundred thousand fraudulent credit transactions like these occur annually, an unreleased internal TRW memo admits.

It's crime that pays. On the few occasions that a gang member is tracked down and actually caught, he's often out of jail even before the victim has undone the damage to his personal affairs.

Typical is the prosecution of thirty-four-year-old Nigerian Bola Allen. A few years ago, with information obtained from financial databanks, Allen took on the identity of Houston native Keith Closius. He obtained numerous fraudulent credit cards and opened up a bogus checking account in Closius's name.

Closius was unrelenting in his resolve to nab Allen. That's a far cry from what usually occurs, says Wallace Zeringue, a county prosecutor in Texas. "Keith Closius is an exceptional case because he didn't give up," notes Zeringue. Generally, most victims, finding no support from creditors, banks, or the police, simply tire of trying to apprehend the criminal who's turned their lives upside down. But Closius, after nearly a year of seeking out Allen, mostly on his own time and with his own money, finally cornered him. Soon after, Allen was sentenced to fifteen years in prison. But Allen cut a deal, agreeing to give authorities a worm's-eye view of what goes on in the Nigerian network—though he refused to rat on any of his colleagues. And Allen was paroled after serving fewer than twenty-four months in a Texas prison.

Although individuals are feeling the pinch of these scams, the crimes go unchecked mainly because creditors do little to stop them. "The industry has some cleaning up to do," says Secret Service agent Boll. "Marketing departments set the tone for how the business is run at most financial institutions. Their goal is simply to get more credit cards out there and nothing else. Losses from fraud are not their problem or concern."

Apparently, neither is unauthorized credit report access, which allows people such as Denise Davis and Bola Allen to victimize unsuspecting people quietly. For that, the credit bureaus have only themselves to blame. They single-handedly shoehorned language into the 1970 Fair Credit Reporting Act (FCRA), the law that oversees credit bureau activities, allowing anyone "with a permissible business purpose" to purchase credit reports. This remarkably broad exception in the law doesn't require that a credit report buyer produce proof of permissible purpose. The mere claim that a credit report is needed to do business with an individual, whether that claim is legitimate or not, will do.

It's a sloppy and vague loophole that is all the worse because nobody has ever bothered to police it, especially with the emergence of desktop computers a decade or so after the FCRA was passed. Via computer, requests for data are made anonymously, screen-to-screen. Under cover of electronics, it's virtually impossible to ascertain the validity of these requests.

That the permissible-purpose rule would make credit reports an uncontrollable commodity and thus have serious consequences for individual privacy clearly wasn't on the credit bureaus' mind when they forced its insertion into the FCRA. They were only concerned with commercial considerations, with imposing the fewest restrictions on credit report sales.

It wasn't difficult for the credit bureaus to have their way with the FCRA when the law was first being considered more than two decades ago. Nobody was watching very closely then. When the FCRA was adopted, few outside of Congress and a handful of consumer advocates were paying much attention to the credit bureaus, which were little known and understood. It would have been difficult at the time to predict that twenty years later credit data would be such a critical determinant of one's quality of life, or even the catalyst for crimes. Simply put, when the FCRA was passed, we were a nation of babes in terms of our understanding of how a credit transaction works or how retailers, gasoline companies, or banks make credit-granting decisions.

The credit economy was nascent then. And most consumers were delighted by the new financial potential credit cards offered. It meant that they didn't have to save up years to pay in full, in cash, for that expensive couch anymore. It could be paid out in small monthly installments. People who previously never could consider a vacation in Europe were given the opportunity to travel like the Rockefellers—for less than $100 per month, payable after they returned.

As it turned out, it was easier to go on a safari in Kenya using plastic as currency than to get a copy of your credit report. In the early days of the credit economy, the credit bureaus never let individuals see the data they maintained on them. The way the credit bureaus structured their rapidly growing industry was to keep consumers out of the "need to know" loop.

Some Congressmen had other ideas, though. Especially when they started hearing horror tales from irate constituents who were brusquely and unaccountably denied credit, or were turned down by six banks for a mortgage, or couldn't get a loan to buy a car to go to work so they lost their job, or couldn't even rent an apartment for their family of ten after their previous one burned down—all because of some inexplicable and erroneous bad-debt entry in a new and confounding thing called a credit report.

Led by Senator William Proxmire (D-Wisc.), a small number of Washington legislators drafted the FCRA to give consumers the right to review their credit records and to change or delete incorrect items on them. Proxmire envisioned much more for the FCRA. Unfortunately, the rest never saw the light of day.

Proxmire, who retired in 1988 after a stellar thirty-one-year career in the Senate, was a tough, prominent, anti-big-government, pro-individual-rights legislator. During the writing of the FCRA, Proxmire's eyes were opened to the vast amount of personal information credit reports contained.

This data was so sensitive, Proxmire thought, that to protect the privacy of the individual, the FCRA had to do much more than just give everybody easy access to their own credit reports. The law also had to ensure that credit reports were understood to be private and confidential, and that they would be viewed by only a select few outsiders who had to see them in order to make credit-granting decisions.

This was important because it was becoming increasingly clear that though consumers were woefully ignorant about what their credit reports contained, credit bureaus were already selling them to virtually anybody willing to pay. CBS News, for instance, obtained a handful in the late 1960s by creating a fictitious company and sending letters to the credit bureaus asking for reports on people selected at random from telephone directories.

But Proxmire didn't count on how violently the credit bureaus would react to his proposal to limit access to credit reports. Even at that early stage in their development, the credit bureaus foresaw the huge revenue potential in selling credit reports to as many different types of customers as possible. If they could peddle reports only to credit grantors such as banks and retailers, they feared their sales potential would be sliced too narrowly. There were other customers—employers, landlords, private investigators, marketers, and attorneys among them—who were already buying a lot of credit reports, and who represented a big long-term market. And, as the credit bureaus saw it, cutting out any group of possible customers would shred future profit margins drastically.

They passed this message along in no uncertain terms to their Congressmen, whom "they tend to know very well," says Kenneth McLean, a former aide to Proxmire. And before the brouhaha over the FCRA had ended, the open-ended permissible-purpose rule had been inserted as a sop to the credit bureaus.

The credit bureaus had won a significant victory—and they crowed about it. The FCRA, as John Spafford, president of the Associated Credit Bureaus, put it succinctly and, inexplicably, without embarrassment, "is an industry bill."

Proxmire and his supporters were dismayed by this turn of events. Typical were the disappointed comments of Arthur Miller, a Harvard University law professor who worked closely with the Senator on the FCRA: "The original Proxmire bill has been butchered; it was drawn and quartered and its vitals were left on the committee's chopping block. How that came to pass is no mystery. Industry lobbyists and bank-oriented Senators engaged in the dissection, while advocates of consumer protection quietly relied on the legislative process to produce a bill that would respond to the needs of the public."

Proxmire attempted to repair the FCRA's inadequacies three times after the law was passed. In 1973, 1975, and 1979 he tried to push amendments through that would have put strict limitations on access to credit reports. He failed each time. And with only one minor exception—in 1978 the time period for reporting bankruptcies on credit reports was reduced from fourteen to ten years—the FCRA has never been amended.

Loose Change

Today the credit bureaus are in the midst of their most radical overhaul since the passage of the Fair Credit Reporting Act. Much of it was forced upon them. After my cover story on privacy and the credit bureaus appeared in *Business Week* in 1989, Congress set to work reforming the credit industry. Hearings were held at which highly charged testimony recounted dozens of stories of horrors inflicted on consumers by the credit bureaus. Then hundreds of magazines, newspapers, and television shows across the country ran every variation they could come up with on the suddenly chic subject of privacy.

Initially, the credit bureaus reacted unilaterally with disdain for all of this unwanted attention. Typical were the comments of Walter Kurth, president of the Associated Credit Bureaus: "The credit bureaus are doing a very good job. Any reforms of the industry can be accomplished by industry initiatives. We don't welcome or need any outside help from Congress or consumer groups."

Soon after, though, the Big Three's solidarity was rent apart. The first defector was Equifax. Unexpectedly, in 1990, Equifax senior vice president John Baker became an outspoken voice for change in the credit industry. He admitted publicly at venue after venue that perhaps the credit bureaus were wrong. Maybe they should be more responsive to consumers and privacy advocates, he said. And Baker called for compromise and rapprochement, which have never been a part of the contentious battles between consumer activists and the Big Three.

To prove that Equifax was giving more than lip service to this issue, the credit bureau took an $18 million charge against its earnings, virtually wiping out profits, during the first quarter of 1991 in order to implement new initiatives. It built a huge telecommunications network so that consumers could call in toll-free to order their credit reports and receive them within forty-eight hours, get instant advice about data on their reports, and correct inaccuracies.

At the same time, Equifax cracked down on the activities of information resellers like the one that sold me Dan Quayle's credit report. Under the new arrangement, Equifax, and not the reseller, cuts the deal directly with the credit-report buyer. Equifax certifies him through an extensive series of visits and interviews to make sure that his reasons for buying credit data from the reseller are legitimate.

And to ensure that Equifax is attentive to privacy concerns each time a new product is developed or the company enters a new market, it created an office of consumer affairs to act as an ombudsman for consumers. Equifax also put on retainer a veteran civil liberties activist, Columbia University professor Alan Westin, and a longtime individual-rights legal counsel, Robert Belair, to advise on privacy questions.

The importance of these new initiatives to Equifax's identity was best summed up by CEO Jack Rogers when he told shareholders, "Our goals of market leadership and technological innovation must be balanced with a commitment to protect our most important asset— the confidentiality of information."

At first, TRW derided Equifax's new stance. TRW officials whispered cynically that Equifax's consumer initiatives were just a marketing ploy, a calculated corporate positioning. In effect, TRW said, Equifax had found a way to make privacy pay.

But soon the heat from consumers, the media, and politicians for the other credit bureaus to follow Equifax's lead grew too hot. So TRW gave in and imitated Equifax—at least in a limited way. It also set up a toll-free number to advise consumers on credit file problems, though it refused to guarantee that a trained credit consultant would be on the other end of the line, or that a credit report would be sent in a timely fashion. Then TRW went Equifax one better: it offered consumers one free credit report each year.

Trans Union, which is owned by the painfully shy Pritzker family of Chicago and isn't a public company, doesn't have to answer to investors the way TRW and Equifax do, so Trans Union continued to forge a hard line. The credit bureau argued that it couldn't afford to take the steps that TRW and Equifax have. Instead, Trans Union said it would continue to keep its real customers—credit report buyers, whether financial institutions, retailers, employers, or information resellers— and not consumers, well serviced.

Initially inspired by altruism or not, Equifax and TRW admit that they hoped that, as a by-product of their outreach to consumers,

Congress's enthusiasm for amending the FCRA would dim. It almost did. Although three bills were introduced in 1990 to revamp the credit industry, even their backers conceded that none had a chance of getting out of committee. Says Representative Richard Lehman (D-Calif.), former chairman of the House Banking Committee's Subcommittee on Consumer Affairs and Coinage and a sponsor of one of these bills, "It's so easy to stop a bill in Congress. Especially when you're facing down three powerful companies with affiliates in every community in the country. That puts a lot of pressure on local Congressmen not to do anything."

What's more, adds Lehman, considering TRW's many connections in Congress as a longtime defense and intelligence contractor, "we had a pretty big armada against us."

As Lehman predicted, these bills failed. Then suddenly in mid-1991 the tide turned. The Federal Trade Commission disclosed that credit reports had become the biggest subject of consumer complaints: there were nine thousand in 1990, as opposed to just six thousand the year before. At about the same time, a Wyoming man sued TRW when he was turned down for a car loan because his credit report was incorrectly peppered with data pertaining to his father, who was less financially stable. The jury ruled against TRW and awarded the plaintiff $290,000. Then TRW made its embarrassing blunder in Norwich, Vermont, tagging every citizen in that hamlet a tax scofflaw. And attorneys general in fourteen states took TRW to court claiming that its database is rife with inaccuracies.

Eventually, in late 1991, TRW settled with the attorneys general. Under the agreement, TRW said it would attempt to beef up the amount of identifying information included in each credit file to ensure that credit data is posted to the appropriate file—thereby minimizing the number of credit report errors. Among the information TRW will try to attach to all credit files are full first and last names, middle initials, full street addresses, dates of birth, and other identifiers. TRW also promised to simplify the language of credit reports, which is virtually incomprehensible to most laymen. For such a well-publicized and highly charged case—during which TRW was repeatedly branded an arrogant company maintaining a database so riddled with mistakes that it was an insult to consumers—this settlement was remarkably soft. Even TRW appeared to be surprised and relieved by how light it was. The changes included in the settlement "are either current business practices or things we expected to do," says John McGee, a TRW spokesman.

Still, despite TRW's attempt to downplay the turmoil surrounding it, the company's problems sullied the entire credit industry, because to many TRW *is* the credit industry. And with so much bad press the credit bureaus finally caved in. TRW and Equifax practically begged Congress to amend the FCRA—if for no other reason than to create the impression that the credit bureaus have been punished for their misdeeds, and that new laws would make them "consumer-friendly." "The time for legislation is now," said D. Van Skilling, general manager of TRW's credit reporting business.

With the credit bureaus "signing on to the concept," as Equifax VP John Baker puts it, odds are that FCRA amendments will be adopted in 1992. Unfortunately, this is no cause for jubilation. The proposed new rules miss the mark badly. They do little to narrow the fundamental and growing conflict between privacy and high technology in modern-day America. During the original writing of the FCRA, Senator Proxmire was unable to get the credit bureaus to agree on limiting the customer base for credit reports, and that failure haunted Representative Esteban Torres (D-Calif.) two decades later as he drafted the FCRA amendments, packaged as the Consumer Credit Reporting Act (CCRA). Recalling Proxmire's problems, and fearful that the credit bureaus would drop their support for the legislation if it was overly restrictive and affected their business, Torres produced a bloodless law. Like all U.S. privacy legislation, it soothes a wound, but ignores the more profound injury.

Put simply, the CCRA tackles only the limited problem of credit report errors. To make sure that consumers are aware of mistakes in their files, it requires the credit bureaus to give consumers one free copy of their credit report each year. It also makes it easier to sue the credit bureaus when they fail to delete erroneous data. And it provides for civil remedies against credit grantors that give the credit bureaus inaccurate account information about an individual.

But the CCRA is silent on the question of who may legitimately access credit reports and on the confidentiality of credit data. In effect, it reendorses the broad permissible-purpose rule, which has already made credit data an unrestricted commodity. No mention is made of stemming the activities of companies that serve as data middlemen, which recklessly resell credit information to virtually anybody, or of limiting credit report sales to, for instance, only banks and legitimate credit grantors.

What's more, the CCRA does nothing to let consumers reclaim control over the information the credit bureaus maintain about them. Such activities as segregating people by their credit data, demographic analysis, and computerized forecasting, as well as the subsequent broadcasting of this privileged information, are virtually untouched by the CCRA.

Credit errors are a serious problem, and perhaps the CCRA will lessen their impact on individuals. But privacy of credit records is even more critical in a computerized society, and Congress has clearly bypassed a chance to legislate it—especially when Congress had the credit bureaus on the ropes.

Unfortunately, it may be too much to ask Congress to wrestle with a deep-seated ethical and moral dilemma such as privacy in the age of technology. But Congress's failure to do so adds poignancy to Senator Proxmire's sad commentary about the Fair Credit Reporting Act, spoken five years after he fought so hard to get it passed: "I'm afraid that in writing the measure in the present law we gave away too many of the elementary protections consumers need to control the use of personal information about them."

3

The Man Who Knows Too Much

I might have been a
goldfish in a glass bowl
for all the privacy I got.

H. H. Munro (Saki)

I had just gotten to sleep when John Branch called me. He was angry, the tone in his voice bullying. "I hear you've been snooping around for information about Dan Rather," he said.

"I got some already, but I'm still looking for more," I answered.

"From where?"

"I can't say."

"Okay—well, I want to know what you're up to," Branch said abruptly. "So I have to see you. Soon."

We made an appointment to meet the next day.

I knew about Branch, though we had never spoken before he telephoned. Branch is one of the key figures in the nation's little-known information underground—a subterranean network of information resellers who freely traffic in sensitive data, no matter how personal or private, or how illegally obtained. For the right price, there is virtually no piece of information about a person—any person—that can't be obtained from these info-peddlers.

The most visible habitués of the underground are some of the superbureaus, such as the one I bought Dan Quayle's credit report from. These companies receive information from hundreds of legitimate and illicit data sources, among them the major credit bureaus; federal, state, and local government databanks; and confidential private information suppliers at, for instance, banks and insurance companies. Then they resell this data at a substantial markup, sometimes as high as 500 percent, to subscribers of their own. They're one-stop gateways, usually via any personal computer, into databases that most of us don't know exist (though we may be well represented in them) or, at least, would have no idea how to gain access to through any other means.

And when something is too touchy for these superbureaus to handle—the IRS records of a celebrity, for instance—or too difficult for them to obtain, they tap the expertise of dozens of shadow enterprises, publicity-shy companies adept at penetrating sensitive information channels. These companies buy and sell custom data about people as if it were just another commodity, like pipe fittings or chewing gum. They're insular, one-man shops—John Branch runs one of them—that are far more secretive than the superbureaus and usually extremely careful about whom they deal with. They sell everything the superbureaus do, and more. And if you gain their confidence and are discreet, they'll fill your request for information—no application required, and no questions asked.

Perhaps what's most alarming about the information underground is that it is virtually unmonitored. Credit bureaus and the government are at least in principle constrained by legislative restrictions and oversight bodies. Companies and individuals in the information underground, by contrast, are barely known to the authorities. And no oversight agency has the staff, funding, or expertise to conduct a lengthy and expensive investigation to figure out the workings of the underground network, or to produce enough evidence that companies in it are breaking the few privacy laws that exist.

"We know they exist and that they're far too lax," says Jean Noonan, until recently the associate director of credit practices at the Federal Trade Commission, "but there's really nothing we can do about them right now."

The information underground taps into legitimate data sellers—they're highly active customers of the credit bureaus, motor vehicle agencies, and real estate databanks, for instance—and also buys data from illicit suppliers, such as bank and medical networks. Straddling the two makes the underground an exciting, deliciously dangerous place to work. As a result, generally the companies in it are run by lifelong thrill seekers such as former private investigators, law enforcement veterans, and retired intelligence operatives.

The contacts I made in the underground offered me free rein to use their nationwide data network on the condition that I never reveal their identities. I readily agreed. What's more, the superbureau I used as a conduit into the information underground, which I call the U.S. Investigative Network in this chapter, is also a pseudonym. I wasn't asked to hide the name of this superbureau (indeed, the company that operates it would probably have preferred the publicity), but I don't want to encourage readers to seek it out for data joyrides. Providing a recipe for finding old girlfriends, errant spouses, people who have run off without paying debts, or biological parents is not my purpose. My only aim is to demonstrate the existence of this vast web of information buyers and sellers, and to provide a sample study of how easily and deeply the network intrudes upon personal and confidential information.

I chose Dan Rather as my test case, because I was told the stoic, tight-lipped CBS anchorman has taken numerous steps to guard his personal information. With this in mind, he seemed like a perfect subject to assess the limits of the underground.

Rather has good reason for being wary. During Richard Nixon's paranoid Presidency, he was the subject of unwarranted investigations by numerous federal agencies, from the FBI to the IRS. He's also a highly visible target and extremely vulnerable. To right-leaning crazies and other liberal-haters, Rather is the embodiment of TV's tilt to the left. It was only a couple of years ago that he was mugged on Park Avenue by an assailant who repeatedly asked, with insane urgency, "What's the frequency, Kenneth?"

Because Rather has taken special steps to guard his personal data, it required some more persistence to obtain data on Rather than it took to get Dan Quayle's credit report. But in the end it only involved extra keystrokes on my computer, and patience. I still received most of what I asked for from the information sellers.

I started with Dan Rather's credit report, because that's the simplest bit of confidential information to obtain. But to get that I needed his complete address, and preferably—but not necessarily—his Social Security number. So I began by requesting from the superbureau Rather's credit report header, which contains biographical data taken from credit bureau files and is usually available by just typing in a person's name. The header provides a lot of useful raw information for further investigation.

(My keyboard input is in **bold**; the text in plain type is queries and responses from the computer.)*

*Actual information has been disguised to protect Dan Rather's privacy.

Looking for . . . .
Credit Report Header

Last name: **Rather**
First name: **Dan**
Address: **New York, NY**

Press [cr] to continue

Response . . .
HEADER REQUEST
Dan Rather
XXX [New York Street]
New York, NY 10000
Spouse: [Name]
Year married: 1964
Date of Birth: [Date]
Social Security No.: [Number]
Employment: CBS News
Employed Since: 3/62

Now that I had Dan Rather's address and Social Security number, getting his credit report was virtually assured.

Rather's credit file confirms what most of us would suspect about him, based on the personality that comes across the television screen: he's frugal. His million dollar-plus annual salary has enabled him to live virtually debt-free.

Looking for . . . .
Credit Report

Last name: **Rather**
First name: **Dan**
Social Security No.: **[Number]**

Press [cr] to continue

Response . . .
Credit Highlights

Name: Dan Rather

Social Security No.: [Number]

- Rather has two credit cards—one from a department store and the other from a bank—with a balance greater than $100. His monthly payment for these credit cards is less than $600 per month.
- Rather has six other credit cards—four from department stores and two from banks—that are either unused or have a balance of below $100.
- In August, 1980 Rather took out a $200,000 mortgage to purchase his New York apartment. The loan was retired as fully paid in October, 1985.

- END OF REPORT -

It's hard not to be envious of a clean credit report like Rather's, depicting someone who is not only paying his bills on time but has so few bills to pay each month. However, delving further into Dan Rather's electronic alter ego offers a slightly different perspective on him. The credit report, as is often the case, doesn't tell the whole story.

By asking the superbureau for his actual credit card bills, I obtained a list of the stores he shops at and how much he spends at them. With that data, another Dan Rather emerges.

I found out that although Rather may not pay finance charges, he still makes heavy use of his credit cards each month. He just usually pays them in full before any interest is tagged on. I also learned that Rather doesn't spend a lot on entertainment. Shopping seems to be more his speed. Apparently the man who wears inexpensive-looking vest-sweaters on camera does his share of buying at trendy clothes stores off camera.

The credit card bills I received on my computer came in this format:

Credit Activity (Highest Use Card)

Name: Dan Rather

Social Security No.: [Number]

Period: April 14, 1991 to May 14, 1991

Category: CLOTHING

Date	Merchant	Amount
4/16	XXXXX Department Store	$ XXX.XX
5/06	XXXXX Boutique	$ XXX.XX
4/18	XXXX Men's Wear	$ XXX.XX
4/10	XXX Clothier	$ XXX.XX
Subtotal:		$ X,XXX.XX

In all, seven categories of merchants frequented by Rather were included on the bills: Clothing, Restaurants, Sporting Goods, Travel, Luggage, Jewelry, and Art. Total expenditures that month were in the mid-four figures—and he paid the entire amount when the bill arrived. He shopped at five clothing stores—all high-toned—and ate at only two restaurants, both ethnic. Rather spent ten times more on apparel than on dining out.

Now I was hooked. I wanted to see how much deeper I could wade into Dan Rather's private life without leaving my computer. Unfortunately, that's when the trail grew cold. I had hoped to get his unlisted home phone number and then access the toll calls that he made during a recent month—information that I have gotten without any difficulty from superbureaus and other databanks when the subjects were not celebrities. But Rather spurned my efforts, covering his tracks too well.

Looking for . . . .
Unlisted Telephone Number

Last name: **Rather**
First name: **Dan**
Address: **XXX [New York Street]**
City, State, Zip: **New York, NY 10000**
Social Security No.: **[Number]**

Press [cr] to continue

Response . . .
Number not available without an apartment number.

- END OF REPORT U.S. INVESTIGATIVE FILE -

Gas and electric bills usually contain apartment numbers. So I went back into the databank and attempted to access Rather's Con Edison files.

Looking for . . . .
Con Edison Bills/New York City

Last name: **Rather**
First name: **Dan**
Address: **XXX [New York Street]**
City, State, Zip: **New York, NY 10000**
Social Security No.: **[Number]**

Press [cr] to continue

Response . . .
Subject unknown at that address.

I learned later from sources who know Dan Rather that his gas and electric accounts are billed to CBS News—precisely to prevent snoops from finding out exactly where he lives. But though the databank was unable to provide me with the information I requested, it didn't leave me empty-handed. It turns out that Dan Rather may have succeeded in safeguarding his own privacy, but his neighbors weren't as lucky. Without my asking, the superbureau provided the name and apartment number of everybody who lives in Dan Rather's building and has an active Con Edison account billed to that address. The superbureau did this, a note on my computer screen said, as an aid to my investigation. Then I was asked:

Any other Con Edison Bills/New York City requested . . .
No

- END OF REPORT U.S. INVESTIGATIVE FILE -

This was a crushing dead end, but it was tempered somewhat by a note I received via electronic mail the next night when I again logged on to the U.S. Investigative File system:

Heard you were trying to locate Dan Rather's phone number. Sorry I can't help you with that. But for what it's worth I was doing an investigation for a client a few weeks ago and while running through the unlisted telephone number database, I came across Vanna White's. Not sure if it has any value to you or not, but her phone number is [number].
Good luck.
Colonel Lewis

I never found out who Colonel Lewis is. But I called Vanna White's number and got her answering machine. I left a message explaining the way I obtained her telephone number. I told White to return my call if she wanted to know more about this incident or the book I was working on. I never heard from the "Wheel of Fortune" queen. When I telephoned her again two weeks later, her phone number had already been changed.

Branch Breaks

John Branch's telephone call came at the tail end of my search for data on Dan Rather. I was excited about meeting Branch. Though overall he's kept a surprisingly low profile and isn't well-known, several of the sources I came into contact with spoke of his exploits and hijinks.

For example, in the mid-1960s, after a revolutionary regime came to power in a Latin American country, an American company needed help repatriating some equipment, including a sophisticated electronic device the size of a small house, and a safe with millions of dollars in cash.

Branch and others put together a team that in broad daylight drove a convoy of tractor trailers into the center of the capital city, broke down the massive equipment, and loaded it piece by piece into the semis, along with the safe. Then the trucks implausibly rumbled slowly out into the countryside, across the border into a friendly country, before dropping the bounty onto a ship destined for the United States.

"The company paid us next to nothing up front, but over a million when the mission was accomplished," Branch says. "It really wasn't that hard to do. The infrastructure was in upheaval. We hit at the perfect time, well before the regime solidified control. When we were there things were so haywire that the presence of some workers tearing down electronic devices didn't raise a lot of suspicion."

Branch is a surveillance-equipment fanatic. He got his start selling snooping devices to the police, who came to him with fat grants from the federal government to beef up their wiretapping and surveillance capabilities. The government grants are not what they once were, so Branch has expanded. The cops aren't his only market anymore. And while exotic electronic audio and video devices still account for a large portion of his sales, they're not his only product line: now he also sells illicit data. And he pitches this treasure trove to corporate security departments, criminals, information joyriders, and anyone else who wants it.

Typical of Branch's recent clients were the security personnel at the nuclear energy plants owned by the federal government. They carried out of Branch's warehouse millions of dollars' worth of listening devices and a wiretapping network that could eavesdrop on two hundred phones at once, although it was illegal for them to possess or use such equipment without a court order. When caught with this contraband, the security forces claimed that they needed it for covert surveillance and counterintelligence programs to protect the plants against terrorists.

But according to a half-dozen current and former employees at these plants, the purpose of these devices was to keep close tabs on the workers there. For instance, Gary Lekvold, an engineer at the Hanford nuclear plant in Richland, Washington, claims that he was suspended after telling officials that intrusion-detection devices installed at the site to protect plutonium from theft would never work. And since then, says Lekvold, "I've been trailed while driving and my phone has been bugged. I've worked in electronics for thirty years. I can recognize audible evidence that something is intruding on a phone line. I'm well acquainted with the clicking and hollow sounds."

John Branch says that Lekvold's suspicions are warranted. But that doesn't stop him, he says, from selling equipment to renegades. "I can't see a difference between the good guys and bad guys, between the police and criminals, and between the thugs and the meek— they're all the same," says Branch, "all loyal only to their own personal agendas. So I'll sell to anybody that can pay for it."

And more and more people, it seems, find it necessary to come up with the bucks.

There was the forty-four-year-old father of two young children out-side of Los Angeles suddenly arrested for dealing drugs. "I never even heard of some of the drugs the indictment said I was selling," he told me, still obviously agitated every time he thinks of the Kafkaesque incident, in which he was dragged in handcuffs from his home mo-ments after he sat down on the couch with his five-year-old son to watch the Lakers game.

But the complaint was filed by somebody he knew well. It was a bookie with whom he had gotten into an unfortunate dispute earlier in the year. Before the situation was resolved it had degenerated into a messy argument.

"I didn't know how well connected the bookie was," the man says. "But I found out. He had pictures of me that he claimed showed me peddling drugs to his children. And the police, who obviously knew him well, believed him."

So the father hired Branch to get all he could on the bookie. Branch went all out: he wiretapped the bookie, had him followed, and ran his name through every conceivable databank to find out everything he could about him. "By the time Branch was finished we had so much dirt on the guy that we were able to scare him into dropping his complaint," the man says.

That's the good side of Branch's million-dollar business. But there's a vile aspect to it also. The contraband equipment that Branch and others quietly sell and the data they supply more often than not provide buyers with knowledge and information for a far less savory purpose: to compromise a victim's privacy. Illustrative of the huge privacy breach an ill-advised data search can leave in its wake is the case involving Procter & Gamble and *The Wall Street Journal.* In the summer of 1991, the Cincinnati-based consumer-goods giant sus-pected that a current or former employee was leaking confidential corporate information to the newspaper's Pittsburgh correspondent, Alecia Swasy.

Unauthorized disclosure of trade secrets is illegal in Ohio, so P&G convinced local fraud squad detective Gary Armstrong, a moonlighter at P&G since 1977, to conduct a computer search of the phone records of every resident in Cincinnati and parts of Kentucky. The aim was to identify who called Swasy's home, office, or facsimile machine during an eight-week period starting March 1.

That fishing expedition cast a net over nearly one million telephone numbers and covered forty million toll calls. And its tentacles spread even further than that. In at least one instance, when the investigation of telephone databanks found that someone had dialed Swasy's home from the Westin Hotel in Cincinnati using a calling card, Armstrong dug deeper to identify the holder of this credit card.

P&G was red-faced when the databank sweep turned up fewer than fifty callers to Swasy's numbers—and none of them were connected with Procter & Gamble. It was a serious blunder, a random invasion of so many people's privacy with no headline-grabbing arrest at the end. P&G's general counsel, James Johnson, quickly wrote a note to *The Wall Street Journal* saying Procter & Gamble "regretted" the incident and promised in the future to "notify you in advance where legally permissible" before beginning such an investigation.

But such an offhand admission of corporate remorse is not enough for some, because the company's actions were worse than P&G is willing to admit: ethically they were reprehensible, and legally they were dubious. Peering at hundreds of thousands of people's phone records when there is a serious crime to be solved may be legally justifiable, says Columbia University's Alan Westin, but when there's no clear indication that a crime has even been committed, it "raises the question of whether technological capacity has gone over the line in terms of what is a reasonable search and seizure."

That case became public, says Branch, but there are numerous others like it occurring every day that nobody hears about. He was involved in one, he says, in which a boss had an inkling that an employee was sharing internal information with the competition. Branch obtained the list of telephone calls the employee made from his home and gave it to his boss. On this piece of paper was the fact that at precisely seven o'clock every night the employee did indeed phone the owner of the competition. Called on the carpet the next day, the employee had no satisfactory explanation for these phone calls. As a consequence, he not only lost his job but was blackballed from his industry.

Branch readily admits that he takes no sides. "I'm not anybody's conscience," Branch argues. "It's none of my business what my clients do with what I sell them. Man by nature wants to know the truth, but doesn't easily find it often. I offer avenues through which to look for it."

Branch didn't want to meet me at his San Francisco showroom, where customers and colleagues might see me. Instead, we talked in an old red barn he had converted into his "safe office" near a ramshackle deserted farmhouse miles from the Bay Area.

He picked me up about seven in the morning. I climbed into his Cherokee and we lit out over fifty miles of Northern California freeway into the deep valleys of parched ranchlands, down one dirt road after another. The big wheels of the Jeep kicked dust into the caked morning fog, tingeing the brown clay soil floating in the disturbed air around us with a silver glow.

I may as well have been blindfolded. Branch made so many sharp turns and sudden shifts in direction that, with the sun covered by a thick layer of clouds, for most of the ride I didn't have a clue what direction we were traveling in—which is probably the way Branch wanted it. Finally, about thirty minutes after the last road sign I saw—it said Livermore, California—we arrived at a desolate hundred-acre tract. After heading up a three-hundred-foot winding driveway, we were at the big, red, Dutch-gabled barn.

On the way, Branch revealed a lot more to me than I did to him. "I know you bought Rather's credit report and phone records from a databank in Tennessee," Branch said, an unfiltered Camel dangling from his lips. "They were nervous about giving it to you. They thought you were working for the FBI, trying to catch them doing something illegal. So they did a background check on you, found out you were a journalist, and said, what the hell, they have no love for Dan Rather anyway, may as well give you what you're asking for. You know, they're one of the few that can get something as sensitive as that."

Branch's explanation made sense. The superbureau I initially dialed in to for the Rather material was near Helena, Montana. But unlike Dan Quayle's credit report, none of the data I asked for on Rather appeared instantly on my computer screen; it took weeks to get. Each night I booted up the machine, to be met with the same frustrating message:

REQUEST BEING PROCESSED. NO NEW INFORMATION.

The delay, as Branch explained, was because the Helena databanker was laundering my request by funneling it through a dozen or more different information resellers. Because of Rather's sensitivity about his privacy and his privileged position, private information about him resides on data channels that require top-secret security clearance to access. Consequently, my request bounced from one computer to the next like a ball in a pinball machine, slapping against a bumper that wanted nothing to do with it, getting thrown clear across state lines to another computer, sliding into what looked like promising holes, then being tossed back out unceremoniously, until it finally hit pay dirt.

That was in Tennessee. The information reseller there had friends in high places and was able to supply the Rather information I asked for; he sent the data back to my computer via my original Helena contact.

My conversation with Branch was stopped short by a driver who must have been going ninety miles an hour when he cut us off, forcing Branch to put on his brakes quickly—otherwise we would have careened off the side of the road and over a hundred-foot precipice.

"Shit, I'm going to get that bastard," Branch said as he threw his cigarette out the window.

He picked up the car phone and called his office: "Get on the computer and run a DMV on this license plate: California ABC123." It took about a minute.

"This is when what I do becomes fun," Branch said to me.

"Write this down," Branch barked at me as his secretary came back on the line. "Joel Lancaster. 2328 El Camino, San Luis Obispo. Unlisted number? Okay, thanks."

Branch made another call. "Hey, Irv, run this name and address through your computer. He's unlisted. I need the number fast." He passed me the phone and asked me to read the information on my pad to Irv. While we were waiting for a response, I asked Branch, "Who is Irv anyway?"

"Just somebody I know at the phone company," Branch replied.

Moments later, Branch was dialing Joel Lancaster's phone number. A message machine came on and Branch spoke into it: "Listen, you bastard. I know who you are. I know where you live. I may even be watching you now. And you know me. You cut me off this morning on a two-lane northeast of San Francisco. And if you ever do that to me or anyone else again, I'll break your bones"—and he hung up.

Branch was laughing uncontrollably. "Imagine the fear running through that guy's body when he walks into his house and hears that message. Now, that's power." He was puffed up like a banty. Self-inflated by self-inflicted macho.

Inside the barn, Branch showed me some of the equipment the manufactures and sells:

- A pinhole lens: a tiny electronic eye about an inch wide and maybe three inches long—"smaller than my dick," as Branch puts it—that can be mounted on a wall, a ceiling, or even a sprinkler head and never be noticed. Perfect for observing and taping indelicate liaisons, or employees trying quietly to make off with company property.
- An envelope compromise spray: this turns an opaque envelope translucent for about thirty to sixty seconds before it changes back again. "It lets people see what's inside a letter undetected," says Branch."You could be looking for a letter bomb or checking on who's sending someone money and how much money is involved."
- A bionic ear: essentially a high-powered microphone that feeds conversations, or any other nonbackground sounds, from as far as three hundred feet away into a pair of headphones.

  Sounds suspiciously like a bugging device, which is supposed to be sold to no one but the authorities. And they're supposed to use it only when they have a court order. But that doesn't deter Branch from selling the bionic ear openly.

  "For something like this, though," he says, "you have to ask me for it the right way—otherwise I won't sell it to you, because it's illegal to do so."

  What's the right way? Branch offers: "You tell me you need this bionic ear to use while hunting. You want to hear the deer's footsteps even before you see the animal. Okay. Can't argue with that. Give me $150 and you got it. Simple as that."

What's not so simple is figuring out how people like Branch end up the way they are, suffused with the kick-everybody-in-the-balls attitude they have. "You have to be a closet anarchist," Branch says.

Ironically, he became one because of the government, in particular the FBI. Less than ten years ago, Branch had a small business distributing prerecorded videotapes to stores. But, as Branch tells it, the big distributors in his area, who had tie-ins to the studios and tape producers, felt that smaller competitors such as Branch were a nuisance they'd rather do without. So they pressured the FBI to begin an investigation of videotape counterfeiting and suggested that Branch's would be a likely company to target.

"I was no virgin—I knew how to finagle a buck out of a deal—but I wasn't counterfeiting," Branch claims.

Still, the FBI apparently wanted to find out for itself and Branch became the target of a huge investigation, which included raids on his offices, surveillance and tails, and even bugging of his telephone.

Branch fought back hard. He put together what he says was a "secret police force" of five people and turned the tables on the feds. Using scanners, they tracked the movement of FBI cars. And when the agents pulled into Branch's parking lot, he and his boys went out to bother them and show them the exit.

They also followed the feds to their headquarters, a storefront with opaque smoky glass that kept anyone from seeing inside. It bore the name Statewide Tracers Management, Inc. Branch's team surveilled FBI activities there, both to find out the agents' next moves and to build up a case for charges of purposeful harassment of Branch. Then, on the legal front, Branch's attorney, armed with the information Branch was providing, had the FBI in court almost on a daily basis to protest the agency's treatment of his client.

"It cost me $600,000 to fight them, but it cost them $10 million to take me on," Branch says proudly. "I was a pain in the ass. And I fought them to a draw. They never got anything on me."

Branch gained from this experience. In fact, it redirected his life. For one thing, he realized that he was in the wrong business. It was clear now that his forte was information gathering and making equipment for covert investigations. So he quit selling videotapes and switched to bugs and data.

"Let me show you a picture," Branch says, and he sifts through a packed file cabinet for a folder labeled "FBI.1." "Here's a shot of my equipment store in San Francisco. Look at the sign over the door."

It doesn't carry the name of his business. Instead, it says Statewide Tracers Management, Inc., the same name used by the FBI for its front during the Branch videotape investigation. "That's to constantly remind me that the good guys can be just as evil as the bad guys, so there's no point in trying to figure out who's black and who's white," says Branch. It's also meant as a reminder to the FBI about the investigation it should never have started.

"Want to know the main thing I picked up from scuffling with the

FBI?" Branch asks. "Privacy doesn't exist, so why waste your time trying to protect yours and everybody else's?"

He reached into his drawer and pulled out a white sheet of paper. "Here. This is what you've been waiting for. This is what you really came to see."

John Branch was right. This paper was exactly what I was looking for. On it the dismal fate of privacy in this country was embodied. The consequences of the proliferation of computers and the uninhibited reach of tangled, interconnected databanks were given shape. What I was looking at was a simple list that detailed exactly what information Branch can obtain, and at what cost. Such items as

> *Bank Account:* Given the person's name and current address, we will turn over the subject's bank account and balances. Cost: $200
>
> *Credit Charges:* Given a person's name and credit card number (obtainable from a credit report), we will provide the subject's most recent Visa, MasterCard, or American Express charges. Cost: $150
>
> *Nonpublished Numbers:* Given an address, we will show the phone number or numbers at that location. Cost: $100
>
> *Post Office Boxes:* Given a person's post office box number, we will provide a street address. Cost: $100
>
> *Social Security Earnings:* Given a person's Social Security number, we will pull his Social Security report with the historical records of the subject's earnings and employers. Cost: $150
>
> *Safe Deposit Boxes:* Given a person's name and address, we will provide the location of his safe deposit box and what's in it. Cost: $200
>
> *Phone Calls:* Given a person's phone number, we will provide the numbers the subject has called for the last sixty days. Cost: $200
>
> *IRS Records:* Given a person's Social Security number, we will provide a subject's complete tax forms for the past three years. Cost: $550

There were numerous other elements to the list, a bald-faced roster of personal information proving there's nothing that can't be revealed.

Knowing that Branch could net virtually every piece of personal data he fished for just confirmed my deepest suspicions—and ratified Branch's contentions—about privacy: there is none anymore.

But how do you do it? I asked Branch.

"Each case is different," Branch explained. "In fact, the biggest surprise about it is that this so-called private data is available through dozens of arteries, not just one. So you can never block access to it. Shut one channel down, ten others open up."

That sounded familiar. Two nights earlier, after hours on the fortieth floor at the headquarters of a New York bank, Joseph Van Winkle, a security VP, had taken me on an eye-opening journey.

Van Winkle had come a long way since his days as an FBI agent. It would have taken him many years and a lot of major busts to ever get a large, well-appointed office like this working for the feds. There was a deep-vanilla couch on one side with a pair of plush leather high-backed chairs facing it. At the other end of the room, a good twenty feet away, was a massive mahogany desk. Outside, visible through huge wraparound windows that enveloped the corner office, the dark city was a mass of twinkling lights.

Van Winkle is one of many former agents who gave up the life of the G-man for the perks of the private sector. Now he is supposed to make sure that corporate computer operations are safeguarded from hackers and other data thieves.

Van Winkle was seated behind his desk. I was in the visitor's chair across from him. We talked about the security business for about thirty minutes. But when the thrust of my questions kept bringing us back to the subject of data privacy, he started tapping at the computer keyboard on his desk. "Come around behind me," he said. "Watch over my shoulder. I'm going to show you why it's so easy to get people's bank records. Do you mind if I look up yours?"

I said that would be okay. "Now I don't know where you bank," Van Winkle said. "All I have is your name and address. So I'll start with a credit report."

Van Winkle pressed a button on his computer and the modem dialed into a databank. A few passwords and keyboard entries later, my credit file was on the screen. Scanning the data, Van Winkle said, "I see that your bank account is at First Citizens Bank. That's good. I know the password to their computer system. And there's your Social Security number. I may need that also."

He wrote down the Social Security number, hung up the modem, and immediately dialed another number through his computer. The instructions on the screen asked Van Winkle to input the network node he wanted to access and the password. He did and the system welcomed him to the First Citizens Bank network.

Van Winkle typed in my Social Security number. Seconds later my account balance, last deposit, last few checks, and other extraneous items were displayed. Total time elapsed: five minutes.

Van Winkle said getting the password for First Citizens' network—or any other bank's, for that matter—isn't very difficult. Heads of security at banks and stores know each other pretty well; many of them worked together in law enforcement. And they're feverish information junkies, even to the point of sharing intimacies about each other's computer systems. And when that doesn't happen, as most private investigators know, bank-system passwords are for sale, compiled by information resellers who purchase the codes from bank employees.

But even if he didn't have the bank's password, there are other ways to get at the data, Van Winkle explained: "Most likely you have a MAC-system ATM [automated teller machine] card in conjunction with your First Citizens account. I have access to the MAC system through *my* bank's ATM network. So all I need to do is dial into the MAC computer through my bank, and through the MAC system access First Citizens' computer, where I can call up your account."

I was perplexed. "Why are you telling me all of this?" I asked Van Winkle. Few bank security managers have been willing to talk so freely to me about the warts deep inside their business.

"Because I don't like it," he answered. "And I want you to write about how bad it is. Every time we build another computer network, private information is compromised even more; dozens of new lines of data communications are opened up. I don't like it. But I don't know what to do about it."

I tell Branch about Van Winkle's illuminating demonstration. Not to be outdone, Branch says computers are nice, but there are ways to get the same information without going high-tech. To obtain my bank balance, for instance, he would place a cold call to First Citizens— "it's best to telephone during lunch hour," Branch advises, "because that's when the neophytes are at the bank desks"—and tell the bank clerk that he's from H&R Block, that he has a check to mail to the Internal Revenue Service today to cover my quarterly tax return, and that he needs to make sure that there's enough money in the bank account to cover the check.

"And I ask the clerk, 'What identifying data do you want from me?' " says Branch. " 'His Social Security number? His account number?' And nine times out of ten, if I press just a little, she'll not only tell me whether you have enough money in the account, she'll also tell me the exact amount you actually have in your account. And the best part is, nobody will ever find out that she leaked this information. In fact, *she* doesn't even know she did.

"Now do you need anything else from me?" Branch asks.

"Yeah, I'm having trouble getting a recent bill for Dan Rather's CBS American Express card. It's not listed on his credit report, because he apparently doesn't have a personal account with American Express. But I assume he has a corporate account through CBS."

Branch smiles. "I can make that happen, but it'll cost you $150—up front." I gave him a check. The meeting was over. John Branch, I realized, had accomplished his mission that day flawlessly: he had made a sale.

Nazis in Size 6 Dresses

Branch isn't a big fan of the superbureaus. "They offer their wares too recklessly," he says. "I'm far more discreet. I only deal with an exclusive word-of-mouth clientele."

Branch's criticism of the superbureaus is appropriate in many cases. Most of them openly mail brochures to thousands of information-hungry people such as private investigators, attorneys, intelligence operatives, marketers, retailers, and insurance companies, as well as to people like me, wide-eyed observers of the wild shenanigans in the bustling information marketplace. And if you can afford the sign-up fee—frequently a hefty $500 or more—they will issue a password and unveil the family jewels.

Tracers Worldwide, a superbureau based in Elmhurst, Illinois, is a good example. Its latest service guide, which I received in the mail, promises to supply telephone records, mobile phone records, credit card usage reports, workmen's compensation records, earnings reports, names and addresses of employers, Social Security numbers, and reports of bank account searches—"just a few of our more than 100 services," says the superbureau.

And this isn't some fly-by-night operation. After all, as the service guide points out, the superbureau "is the only private company ever selected by the U.S. government as experts in locating missing persons." And the company's founder, whom the sales literature never names, "has appeared on numerous radio and T.V. programs including *The Donahue Show,* and has been featured in *Playboy Magazine,* in major newspapers, and in syndicated news columns such as *Jack Anderson.*"

Not all superbureaus are like this one, however. Some take pains to point out that they don't traffic in sensitive information, and go to great lengths to fight the image of being privacy Rough Riders. What's more, they say they reject any customers who appear to have less than honorable intentions.

Joseph Ferrari, president of Buffalo-based Ferrari-"International Information Brokers," which offers online access to nearly 150 databases of personal information, says, "We screen requests for new memberships very carefully."

And when subscribers ask for information that under the law requires an individual's consent before it can be made available to a third party—such as a credit report—"an actual signed release for that data has to be mailed or faxed to us before we supply the information," says Ferrari.

That's good, but Ferrari's praiseworthy diligence only highlights how much information in this country is afforded absolutely no legal protections. A look at the vast menu of instant information that Ferrari provides—all of it, as Ferrari noted, public—reveals some remarkable items for sale that many of us would probably object to seeing revealed.

Through Ferrari, by typing in a person's name on a home personal computer anyone can obtain his Social Security number, driving record, criminal record, employer's name, welfare files, and marital history. That's for starters. Probe a little more and information will appear about the car he owns, his home, and the size of his mortgage payments.

"This type of information," says Vincent Brannigan of Georgetown University, "is, perhaps unfortunately, clearly public information. No one can argue with that. But what protected it from widespread abuse in the past was institutional inertia: it was stored on paper in some bureaucrat's file cabinet."

The number of clerks who had to be convinced you needed a particular piece of information, and the time it took to find it, prohibited sorting through other people's private lives. What's more, there were always numerous forms that had to be filled out before a clerk agreed to pull a file from an overstuffed cabinet. Those forms left behind an audit trail detailing exactly who looked at what.

"If something went awry," says Brannigan, "the authorities could find the culprit." Not anymore. Computers have eradicated the safeguards.

And allowed even those superbureaus that stay within the law to sell some pretty bizarre data. By juxtaposing information from numerous legitimate sources it's possible to produce remarkably strange psychographic depictions of individuals. There are superbureaus, for instance, that offer databanks providing the names of American Nazi sympathizers with a lot of available credit to spend on additional anti-Semitic icons. And there are others that supply the names of women who wear size 6 or smaller dresses, are over the age of forty, and support the Irish Republican Army.

In the world of superbureaus, with information nothing but a commodity, packaging is often what makes one piece of data more valuable than another. Even relatively tame Ferrari boasts in its sales literature: "We will try anything new for a $10 fee."

A Dangerous Web

A few days after our meeting, John Branch telephoned me. "I got the information you wanted," he said. "Turn on your computer and dial in to the Helena databank. It's waiting there for you."

We talked a few more minutes while my computer called the databank. And before we hung up, the bill for Dan Rather's corporate American Express card—laying out details of his charges (the amount, where, and on what date)—was on my screen.

That short phone call was the last conversation I had with Branch. But it provided me with a view of Branch that I never saw during my many previous sessions with him. His warning to me as we hung up belied for the first time all the layers of macho and true grit in the face of danger that he seemingly worked so hard to impress me with. Unexpectedly, there it was, a kink in his virile armor, which had been so impervious before. "Remember," he said emphatically in a voice colored with trepidation, "if anybody asks, I had nothing to do with getting you this information."

That phrase is heard more and more these days among databankers who are well aware that the level of information they're trading in is as explosive as shrapnel, and as antithetical to individual privacy as asking a person at knifepoint to turn over every personal paper in his possession. They're involved in a dangerous game. A wealthy information peddler can lose all that he has attained, and wind up as nothing more than a jailhouse gossip, if the authorities find out that the data was supplied to harm someone.

That's not to say that chasing down out-of-bounds databanking activities is a high priority for U.S. law enforcement authorities. It's not—and it doesn't really have to be. Accessing private records is generally done silently. Most of the time, no one even knows that it has occurred. It's usually never made public by the perpetrator. And the embarrassed victim—if he ever learns that he's a target—is likely to keep this fact quiet too. Generally, invasion of privacy claims do not result in monetary awards unless the victim is financially damaged, so a victim has little to gain by making an issue of it.

Newark-based U.S. Attorney Michael Chertoff says he's grown increasingly uncomfortable with this "see-no-evil" stance taken by law enforcement authorities. So in December 1991, Chertoff culminated an eighteen-month investigation by announcing the arrest of eight information undergrounders in five states, nabbed for obtaining and selling confidential government data from Social Security Administration and FBI computers. "These people," says Chertoff, "peddled the citizens' right to privacy to the highest bidder."

All eight have pleaded innocent to the charges against them.

The arrests came after an elaborate sting operation. According to sources, Chertoff and a team of special agents enlisted the help of former FBI agents who had become private investigators after leaving the agency, as well as information undergrounders who were avoiding prosecution by cooperating with the government. This group canvassed data resellers, saying that they wanted to purchase criminal histories and employment and earnings records on people they were investigating.

Many turned them down, usually, they told me, because they smelled a trap. But those who agreed to provide the data were pumped for more and more confidential information. Conversations were taped, and subsequent transactions, such as correspondence over facsimile machines and bank deposits and withdrawals were monitored and carefully documented. In all, authorities say, the indicted information resellers supplied dozens of employment records by paying Social Security workers to pull this data from government computers and friendly Texas cops to turn over information from the FBI criminal database.

I had become familiar with each of the InfoUnderground 8 while researching this book and found a couple of the indictments particularly ironic. One that stood out was the arrest of Ned Fleming, who runs Super Bureau, Inc., in Monterey, California. Fleming, whose thirty-one-year-old daughter and Super Bureau employee, Susan, was also indicted in this bust, wrote me soon after the publication of my *Business Week* cover story "Is Nothing Private?" in late 1989. In the article, I described the most visible tier of the information underground as "superbureaus," a term common to databankers but never before used in a national publication. Fleming said in his letter he was disturbed "to find my company name used as a generic word in a feature that created a negative image of what we do." And he added, in sentences that eerily jarred my memory when I heard of Fleming's arrest: "As in any business, there are those who do and do not live by its rules or laws. We do—and perhaps more so than the Big 3 credit bureaus."

The arrest of George Theodoreakopolous also was curious. Theodoreakopolous is the reclusive head of Tracers Worldwide, the company whose brochure openly offers to sell the most confidential data at the same time it proudly boasts that its founder (unnamed in the sales literature) is a government consultant and a media darling made prominent on "Donahue" and in the pages of *Playboy.*

Considering that those indicted, if convicted, face millions of dollars in fines and dozens of years in jail, it's striking how little money it took to entice them to risk throwing their lives and careers away— perhaps an indication of the slim value they place on individual privacy. Social Security data was sold for only about $200 per record and criminal histories for a mere $100 each.

The confidentiality of government records is protected under the Privacy Act, but few prosecutors have ever been able to make privacy indictments stick. With the laws enunciating privacy mostly weak-kneed, it's a nebulous and subjective concept to build a case around. However, Chertoff hopes to try these successfully chiefly not by arguing that the defendants invaded individual privacy but by painting them as racketeers—that is, people who trafficked in stolen property. In this case, that means information illegally obtained from the government.

Ultimately, Chertoff hopes that there will be still more arrests. "The information that resides in government databases is not a commodity in which government employees should traffic and from which others should profit," he says. "We will continue to use the investigative and prosecutorial tools necessary to help maintain privacy."

Few doubt Chertoff's sincerity in this matter—nor his ambition to make an issue out of such a hot topic. The politically astute, quick-witted thirty-nine-year-old prosecutor has a penchant for highly charged cases that are magnets for publicity. Recently he was the lead counsel, for instance, in the trial of Jersey City mayor Gerald McCann, which resulted in McCann's conviction for savings and loan fraud and tax evasion. And a couple of years ago, Chertoff successfully tried Genovese family consiglière Bobby Manna and his lieutenants for racketeering and murder.

But though this promises to be a juicy trial, the defendants are mostly small-time data renegades. Typically, those especially well connected and active on the underside of the infotropolis, those in possession of extremely sensitive information, are left alone, the fear being that unmasking their activities in a loud and contentious public trial would blow the lid on the unnerving extent to which information peddling occurs in this country. And show that it goes far beyond accessing simple employment and criminal records. Indeed, such a courtroom confrontation would only highlight the impotence of law enforcement authorities in the face of the seething information underground.

Indeed, this fear of public disclosure is apparently what motivated authorities to pursue and agree to an out-of-court settlement in a disturbing hushed-up incident in the state of Washington recently. The prosecution and other principals involved won't discuss it. Databankers, however, are still buzzing over it, because it clearly indicates that those trafficking in extremely sensitive data still hold the upper hand.

According to very deep sources and internal court documents, in late 1988 a veteran high-level secret-information seller based in Seattle—a consummate pro so mysterious to the hoi polloi of his industry that most other information resellers have never actually seen him in person and don't even know his name; they just call him Jim—committed an uncharacteristic blunder. After years of avoiding the wrath of authorities, even while working relatively in the open as a key national conduit for sensitive information of any sort, he approached a clerk working for the Internal Revenue Service—one he thought he had developed a rapport with and could trust—and offered to pay him top dollar for someone's tax records. This clerk, it turned out, could not be compromised. He took the money from Jim, told him he'd see what he could do, and then immediately informed his superiors of the dirty dealings. A short, quiet IRS investigation ensued, and Jim was arrested for attempting to blackmail a federal employee and conspiracy to traffic in illegal information.

It figured to be a quick trial, with Jim on the losing end. He would serve a short sentence, pay a minimal fine, and be told to get out of the business. But Jim had a trump card up his sleeve that government prosecutors never expected. It turns out he had been a pretty busy information gatherer during the preceding few years, with a roster of clients that included some of the mightiest in Hollywood and the intelligence establishment. He had obtained for these people—and still had in his possession—intimate information, such as IRS and Social Security Administration records, financial files, phone records, and credit transactions, on such luminaries as Sylvester Stallone, Julia Roberts, General Richard Secord, boxing promoter Don King, and boxer Michael Spinks, among many others.

And Jim threatened to use any trial as a showcase—more like a circus, thought the government—to disabuse the public of the naive notion that the authorities are vigilantly guarding our privacy. Jim also said cunningly that it was frightening to imagine the litigious free-for-all that would result from the revelation of the names of his powerful clients in court—and, therefore, in the press—and the discovery by the celebrity victims that they were marks.

He didn't have to say much more. By early 1989, federal prosecutors were anxiously pushing for a deal with Jim. And what was eventually agreed upon in August of that year was remarkably cushy.

To start with, for twelve months Jim could not violate any law. Secondly, according to the settlement papers, "for a period of six months," Jim had to "provide full and complete cooperation with the IRS and the FBI with respect to any unauthorized disclosure of, and/or access to, taxpayer information or confidential investigative files of those or other federal agencies." Meaning, in simpler terms, that Jim had to rat on others.

To Jim, it was a deal made in heaven. The feds were not shutting down his business. At the same time, he was given carte blanche to put his competitors effectively out of commission by notifying the authorities of their underhanded hawking of contraband information. Consequently, during his six-month stint as a stool pigeon, Jim tattled on those he had a score to settle with and those who had clients he coveted. In short, he purged the industry of those that were in his way.

Then, when his period of acquiescence with the authorities was over, Jim went his own way again. In spades. "He's back doing what he did before," says one now-docile information reseller who was fingered by Jim and is under constant threat of indictment by federal authorities. "If you want to find out any piece of information, no matter how sensitive, he's the man to ask. His sources and resources are amazing. And from where I sit, he seems to be an untouchable."

Odds are, Dan Rather wishes the same could be said about his credit records and personal information.

4

Bull's-Eye

You go through life dropping little bits of data about yourself everywhere. Following right after are big vacuum cleaners sucking them up.

Evan Hendricks, editor of *Privacy Times*

It was a telephone call that Karen Hochman would rather forget. Hochman, a New York City direct-mail consultant, had just arrived home one night when she received an upsetting phone call from a salesman who wanted to sell her long-distance service from ITT. At first the telemarketer used the soft sell, but Hochman wasn't buying it. "I told him that I didn't make many out-of-town calls, so thanks anyway," she recalls.

Then he threw down his trump card. "I'm surprised to hear you say that," he responded. "I see from your phone records that you frequently call Newark, Delaware, and Stamford, Connecticut."

Hochman was "shocked and scared" by the salesman's obvious invasion of her privacy—and his detached demeanor when informing her of it. "Where the hell did you get my phone records from?" she asked, and then threatened legal action.

The salesman made a quick retreat and hung up. "If people are able to find out who I call, what else could they find out about me?" says Hochman.

ITT doesn't like the sales approach of its salesman any more than Hochman does. "It's sleazy," says a company spokesman, but, he adds, ITT has "very little control" over the thirteen telemarketing companies working for it.

The telemarketer wouldn't discuss the matter, but information industry sources did. "It's obvious where he got the phone records from—the same place that I could get them from," says a vice president at a leading seller of personal data. "He has a contact at AT&T, MCI, Sprint, or some other long-distance supplier, who typed into his computer a search request for the phone records of all active long-distance users that make calls to certain states and spend above a certain amount of money doing that. Hochman's fit the bill."

Perhaps what's most disturbing about this incident is that it's not particularly unusual. Variations on it occur constantly these days. During the past few years, direct marketing has become an aggressive, extremely competitive business—and the privacy of individuals is more an annoyance than a concern to most companies sending junk mail or making junk phone calls.

As businesses increasingly shun mass-marketing techniques such as broad-based magazine, newspaper, and TV advertising in favor of micromarketing, which is predicated on knowing something about each consumer before deciding which ones to pitch to, databases with confidential information are prized for the intimate details they provide about our characteristics. And they're used for what they reveal about our likes and dislikes based on private choices we have made.

It's a Madison Avenue cliché that fifty cents of every advertising dollar is wasted on people who don't have the slightest interest in the product. But which fifty cents? The proliferation of databanks gives marketers a way to look for answers to this question before spending the dollar. Computerized databanks have ignited an explosion in the number of lists that our names appear on. Virtually every move we make is collected in one computer or another, and marketers crunch this data endlessly to form psychographic profiles so detailed that people are often amazed by how much outsiders know about them. According to estimates, the most desirable names—for instance, of affluent individuals with expensive homes, two luxury cars, and product-happy teenage children—may be rented by databankers and list makers to promotion-hungry companies tens of thousands of times each year. "During the last five years I would guess the lists available have increased about tenfold," says Rose Harper Kleid, chairman of the New York–based Rose Harper Kleid Company, a direct-marketing firm, "while the number of names that are rented each year has grown ten to fifteen times." No wonder that Americans receive sixty-three billion pieces of junk mail and twenty billion unsolicited telemarketing calls annually.

There are few areas of our lives not touched by marketing mania. For instance, each time you book a flight with a travel agent, the information pertaining to this trip—including your name, address, credit card number, and where and when you are going—is entered into a computerized reservation system owned by the airlines. This data is then collated and sold.

Rental car companies buy this data to promote summer and holiday specials to families that prefer flying when going on vacation. And *Business Week* recently confirmed that it purchases from the airlines for subscription mailings the names of people who frequently travel on business.

Widespread dispersal of this information concerns some travel agents. "It violates traveler's privacy," says Richard Cieciuch at Rich-Bern Travel Service, located in Oyster Bay, New York. "But there's nothing in the contract that says this data may not be used by the airlines any way they choose."

Walter Freedman of Chicago-based IVI Travel worries more about the effect it can have on business and even the safety of travelers. "You can bet there are six or seven competitors who would like to know where IBM's executives are going. It can tell them a lot about the company's plans. And with this kind of data automatically disseminated to hundreds of thousands of computers worldwide literally as the bookings are made, the thought of how easy it would be for terrorists to get their hands on it and use it to plan kidnappings or worse makes one shudder."

Despite the dangers, it's hard not to be impressed—albeit grudgingly—by how efficiently list makers winnow seemingly valueless data from public and private computer files and turn it into a profitable product. Typical is the success of Dateq, a company located near Atlanta. Dateq was founded in 1985 by two former employees of the credit bureau Equifax. It already has annual revenues approaching $40 million. Early on, the company sold driver's license and automobile data to insurers, but it has moved beyond that service. Says Robert Stanley, the president of Dateq, "These days, marketing is an increasingly important part of our business."

The most delicious plums Dateq plucks from motor vehicle records are birth dates. "We're selling a lot of 'happy birthday' lists," says Stanley. "These lists let our customers mail birthday cards to people they've never even done business with yet. To a consumer, that's impressive—and almost magical." Some retailers, says Stanley, prefer even more specialized lists, choosing, for instance, to buy the names of people reaching "turning-point ages: eighteen, twenty-one, thirty, or even forty—impact birthdays that compel consumers to go out and splurge."

Mimicking the achievements of its "birthday bank," which has swollen to about fifty million names, Dateq is now isolating heights and weights on driving records, and reselling them. Recently a petite women's apparel shop bought the names of thin women from Dateq, and a big men's store purchased a list of tall men.

This may be wizardry by Stanley's reckoning, but many consumers object. A whopping 87 percent of respondents to a recent *Time*/CNN poll said that companies selling information should be "required by law to ask permission from individuals before making the information available." Stanley dismisses this as unworkable, and rejects any suggestion that the list marketing business needs reform. "We don't hear of any abuses," Stanley says curtly. "How else," Stanley asks, with his arms outstretched as if he's embracing an unbounded universe of information, "could you compile a list of everyone in Atlanta in the zip code 30076 that drives a Mercedes, is fifty years old, is over six feet tall and under two hundred pounds, and has blue eyes?"

We have little choice about the data we provide to state departments of motor vehicles—and we have no say in how it's used. But we *can* control the amount and type of information we share voluntarily with direct marketers. Often, however, the information is collected so imperceptibly that we are unaware we've disclosed anything about ourselves.

The telephone is one of the stealthier data-gathering devices. Each time a person responds to an offer from an 800 service, the caller's phone number is recorded by the long-distance carrier. The phone number is compared against cross-directories to identify the caller's name and address. This data is then sold by the telephone companies to marketers, who use it as the basis for promotions, or to other databanks, which add the subject matter of this call to the individual's existing profile.

As an example, callers who innocently phoned a toll-free number that provides the pollen count by zip code soon started getting junk mail and coupons promoting antihistamines, ragweed pills, and allergists. And when people by the thousands dialed an 800 service last Thanksgiving for tips on cooking turkey, their mailboxes were immediately stuffed with Thanksgiving-related junk mail from companies ranging from RJR Nabisco, promoting Reynolds Wrap, to local poultry farms, selling fresh-killed birds.

"Direct marketers pay a lot for these lists because they're considered 'fully qualified,' the theory being that a consumer has to be extremely interested in a subject or product to make a call to find out more about it," says Ken Phillips, chairman of the Committee of Corporate Telecommunications Users and a teacher at New York University and the Massachusetts Institute of Technology. "I'm extremely leery of this from a privacy standpoint."

In Europe, Phillips adds, it's illegal for the phone companies to disclose who's calling whom. "Churchill insisted on this," explains Phillips, "after discovering that the Nazis obtained details about phone usage from the telephone companies, and targeted for harassment people calling places the Nazis frowned upon."

This bit of history should be instructive, says Phillips. Considering the difficulty of stemming the flow of data after it enters a computer and begins to travel virtually unattended from one databank to thousands of others daily, Phillips wonders how long it will be before callers of 1-800-POLLEN find a notation that they are allergy-prone in their files at medical-records databankers like the Medical Information Bureau (see chapter 8).

It takes some work to short-circuit objectionable telephone data marketers: before dialing an 800 service find out who runs it, and ask this company point blank whether it is more interested in selling your name for profit than in providing information. However, sometimes the use of telephone data by marketers involves more sophisticated activities than promotion campaigns built around lists culled from calls to toll-free numbers. Take the sales effort devised for the MCI Friends & Family program. With this service MCI customers provide a list of other MCI subscribers they call frequently, and then get discounts each time they telephone them.

To promote this program, MCI quietly, without prior notification, sifted through its customers' phone bills for the telephone numbers of people they called who subscribed to its competitors—AT&T or Sprint. Then MCI mailed promotional pieces to these non-MCI subscribers implying strongly that a friend or relative—the MCI customer—felt it was in their best interest to switch long-distance services and take advantage of the deep discounts at MCI.

Some customers were offended by this exploitation of their names to peddle an MCI product. "MCI used me to promote its service without ever asking if I approved," says Paul Ferris, a venture capitalist in New York. Ferris was particularly upset when he found out that MCI sent Friends & Family mailings to people he called who were potential investors in a new enterprise he was underwriting, and with whom he was involved in sensitive negotiations. "It totally recast their perception of me, and might cost me the deal," Ferris says. "MCI's mailing made me look like some shoddy huckster who just made a dollar turning over their names to MCI."

Of course, there's one way to take a stand against that type of unauthorized activity. Do as I did: drop your MCI account.

It won't be long, say most experts, before the United States will be a mostly cashless society. Check-debit cards—better known as ATM cards—are being planted in the wallets and purses of virtually every bank account holder in the country now. And it's not just because banks want to make it easier for consumers to get money after daily business hours and on weekends. Systems are already being installed to allow customers to use these cards for purchases of everyday items such as food, pharmaceuticals, gas, and household goods at supermarkets, drugstores, convenience outlets, and gas stations. Indeed, when these computerized checkout networks are ubiquitous, most retailers are likely to discourage the use of cash and checks completely, and probably even offer discounts to those paying with check-debit cards.

When that occurs, details about every purchase an individual makes—the name of the item, the quantity bought, how much it costs, what time the shopping was done, and so on—will be cross-checked against personal financial and demographic information maintained by the banks—how much is in the individual's account, how much he earns, how old he is, where he lives, how much his home costs, and the makeup of his family.

That kind of data is extremely desirable to marketers such as consumer food giants, supermarkets, and oil companies, which will follow up by mailing coupons and money-saving offers targeted directly to the tastes, lifestyle, financial demographics, and specific buying habits of each individual.

You can imagine getting a note from Coke, a day or two after you buy ten twelve-packs of Pepsi for a party, asking you to mend your errant ways and consider the Real Thing for your next barbecue.

Or you might expect a letter from Frito-Lay saying, "Congratulations on your promotion and raise! But we noticed you didn't buy any Doritos last month, although you've been a loyal customer during the previous five months, buying more than 100 bags. What's wrong? We'll call you in a few days to discuss this."

"It's odious," says Mary Culnan, an associate professor at Georgetown University. "It's an invasion of a person's right to make purchases privately, without someone looking over their shoulders or passing judgment on what they buy or gaining commercially from what should be a confidential decision. It's all part of the ongoing enumeration of the individual's personality and choices. And in an age when so little is private, will the joy of shopping without being monitored be taken away also?"

Quietly, that joy is already being eroded. American Express, for instance, recently spent upwards of $10 million for two Connection Machines, the world's fastest computers, to begin a massive analysis of customer buying habits. And less ambitiously, many companies are lining their databanks with as much information about purchasing behavior as they can get in order to be ready when the debit-card computer systems can fill in the missing pieces in consumers' electronic profiles.

Dominick's supermarkets, a huge Midwestern chain, gave its customers a foreboding insight into the future recently in a letter that said mysteriously, "We have been confidentially recording the purchases you make when you pay by check and use your Dominick's Check-Cashing Card at the register. We are studying this data and will soon make a decision on how to use it."

Citicorp has already made up its mind. Ultimately Citicorp plans to integrate supermarket data it owns with more sensitive banking information, but until then it's doing the next best thing: selling the information, as is, to as many marketers as possible. Citicorp began to accumulate this data a few years ago when a handful of supermarket chains accepted the bank's offer to install computer systems at their checkout counters. In exchange, Citicorp was given carte blanche with the "consumer purchase behavior data" (Citicorp's term) automatically scanned into the store computers each time a customer shops.

It has taken a bit of time to aggregate the information, but now, according to Citicorp's latest ads, the bank's "consumer database" contains the names and addresses of 334,345 Cosmetics Buyers, 1,112,351 Coupon Clippers, 456,779 Fancy Food Buyers, 902,992 Make and Bake at Home Consumers, and 511,227 Weight Conscious Consumers. Each of these people, the ad continues, is primed "for all kinds of direct mail offers."

Supermarket scanning systems are not the only way to obtain this type of data. The savings and loans have pioneered a data-gathering strategy in which customers' checks are constantly monitored for whom they're made out to and, based on the notations that often appear on the memo lines of the checks, what the money is being used for. "The S&Ls determine people's income from payroll deposits, and sell that [information] to marketers along with what they've learned from the checks about where people like to shop and what they tend to buy," says Benjamin Dixon, a director at the federal government's Office of Thrift Supervision.

Borrowing a page from the S&Ls, banks are eavesdropping on home-equity credit line checks. "We spot-check the drafts as checks clear to see if the customer is using the money to pay for college tuition, hire a contractor, consolidate his debts, or buy a car," says William McGeevy, Chase U.S. Consumer Services vice president. So far, adds McGeevy, "we're not doing anything with this information, it's just sitting in a database somewhere."

Until when? McGeevy won't say. But Evan Hendricks, editor of *Privacy Times,* thinks he has a clue: "Will this information find its way into marketing lists and other databanks before long? Ask yourself the question about what a bear does in the woods."

Secondary Purpose

Ed Burnett says that the first time he heard about it he was shocked. Burnett runs Ed Burnett Consultants in Englewood, New Jersey, a supplier of fairly tame mailing lists containing the names of people who, for instance, subscribe to *Fortune, Forbes,* and *Business Week,* buy books published by Simon & Schuster, and give money to the American Heart Association.

So when Burnett saw the article in a trade magazine a couple of years ago about the credit bureaus offering data from credit files to junk mailers and telemarketers, he was stunned. "I thought credit data was confidential information," Burnett says, "I couldn't imagine how they thought they could get away with this."

Burnett admits that his reaction was inspired by more than ethics and moral principles. Jealousy also played a role. "Lists like those can wipe out the legitimate guys like me," Burnett says. "The credit bureaus can offer details about people that no other list supplier has. They have an unfair advantage."

Other direct marketers agree wholeheartedly with Burnett. "It's a big problem when the credit bureaus begin to act like direct marketers," says Ron Plesser, an attorney who has counseled the Direct Marketing Association, an industry trade group.

But this criticism hasn't altered the credit bureaus' strategy of increasing revenue not only by increasing sales to existing customers, such as credit grantors, but also by selling credit data to new, controversial markets. "Two billion dollars a year is spent on direct marketing and $800 million is spent on credit reports," says Richard D. C. Whilden, former executive vice president and general manager of TRW Information Systems Group. "Who wouldn't want to move from our traditional business to that one?"

Especially when it's so inexpensive to do. The credit bureaus already maintain the data for credit reports in their big mainframes. Rejiggering it to meet the needs of direct marketers can be done by just pressing a few buttons. These are incidental costs for incremental revenues, especially since virtually all the overhead costs to produce these direct-marketing lists were paid out when the data was gathered and the computer systems were developed. So profit margins for these products run astoundingly high. "They can turn forty percent margins on direct-marketing lists as opposed to about twenty percent on selling credit reports," says Louis Giglio, an analyst at Bear, Stearns & Co.

A good example is TRW's Highly Affluent Consumer database. With it any customer—a catalogue company, a telemarketer, or a fringe political group—can buy names, addresses, and telephone numbers of people categorized by income; by whether they have bank cards, travel-and-entertainment cards such as American Express, or credit with retailers such as Bloomingdale's; by how much credit they have available; and by how often they use their credit cards. What's more, TRW will screen out of this list those who have been delinquent on their credit payments and those who, according to computer models, are likely to go bankrupt.

Credit bureau lists are very desirable because unlike typical mailing and telemarketing lists, which tend to be static—made up of people who subscribed to a magazine twelve months ago, for instance—

credit bureau files are constantly updated, literally week by week, with information that provides a clue as to exactly how much money a person has to spend. Each time a consumer uses his credit card, the credit bureau adds to its files to present an immediate and timely snapshot of the individual's current buying potential. For that reason, only the credit bureaus can offer a product such as Trans Union's Bankcard Hotline, which contains names of individuals who have used their credit cards recently, how much they spent, and their available credit.

It may be good business, but list selling violates the intent of the Fair Credit Reporting Act, says *Privacy Journal* editor Robert Ellis Smith. "It's an example of credit information being used for secondary purposes—purposes different from the one for which the information was initially gathered," notes Smith. "The credit bureaus are supposed to be in business solely to collect data that enables credit grantors to assess a person's creditworthiness, not to constantly broadcast little tidbits about each of us."

The credit bureaus disagree with Smith's assessment, arguing that they've been selling lists practically since the FCRA became law twenty years ago—and few have complained. In fact, the Federal Trade Commission (FTC) has actually endorsed the practice.

Although they began to supply lists based on credit files to clients that do not grant credit, such as direct marketers, only recently, the credit bureaus have for many years sold lists of names to banks and retailers—legitimate customers for credit reports under the FCRA. This complex activity is called prescreening.

Prescreening allows a lender to comb credit records to locate individuals who meet specific criteria. For instance, a bank may ask a credit bureau to identify New York State residents earning at least $50,000 a year who haven't been more than thirty days late with a credit payment in the last two years and have an unused balance of more than $10,000 on their credit cards. The credit bureau, in turn, finds all the names in its databank that match this profile—and sends this list to the credit grantor. The credit grantor then mails credit applications to these people.

When prescreening began, nearly two decades ago, some in Washington objected that it violated the Fair Credit Reporting Act, which had just been passed. So the Federal Trade Commission conducted a lengthy investigation to determine whether prescreening, which occurs without the consumer's knowledge and without the initiation of a business transaction with a lender, is permissible under the FCRA.

The FTC was hopelessly deadlocked on the issue and finally came up with a Solomonic compromise: the agency said prescreening is allowed as long as it leads to a "preapproved" offer of credit to the people whose names are fished out of the credit bureau database. Although consumers do not give credit grantors that buy lists through prescreening authorization to look at their credit records, the FTC asserted that these banks and retailers are making an honest attempt to do business with individuals who meet specific credit standards.

But these preapproved offers of credit, which millions of people are receiving these days, are not always what they seem.

Representative Richard Lehman (D-Calif.) tells about the solicitation he got from the FCC National Bank offering him a Visa card with a preapproved credit line of $2,000 and no annual fee. In the mailing, the word *preapproved* appeared about half a dozen times. And in a Q and A section, this question was posed: "But I don't have to tell you my salary and my credit history?" The answer: "No! You're preapproved for this Visa card with a generous credit limit. That means all you have to do is return the Request Certificate . . . which should take less than a minute. No lengthy applications procedures or personal questions."

Then in the fine print, barely large enough to read, was the disclaimer: The bank "reserves the right to obtain a current credit bureau report and to cancel its offer if adverse information appears on such report, if it is unable to get a report, or if we are not able to verify any of that information."

"That's deceptive advertising," says Lehman. "It can be harmful to unsuspecting consumers who, thinking they're preapproved, may go out and make an investment or purchase something with the credit line that has been promised them in this mailing."

This example is so egregious that even the credit industry couldn't defend it. After hearing of it, Kenneth E. Hoerr, chairman and chief executive officer of USA Financial Services, representing the nation's lenders, admitted that "it's clearly a misleading solicitation in that it is subject to significant additional checking and this is not clearly and prominently disclosed."

But even full disclosure in bold letters is not enough for some experts, who say that the FTC erred badly in approving prescreening.

But though they're under attack for it, the credit bureaus refuse to discuss altering prescreening. "It represents a significant amount of activity for us," says Equifax senior vice president John Baker, "about twenty percent of our annual revenues from credit sales." Because of that, lawmakers who tried to outlaw prescreening a couple of years ago failed. The amendments to the FCRA currently under consideration in Congress leave prescreening virtually intact.

Credit bureau solidarity, though, falls apart on the issue of selling credit data to nonlenders. The FCRA restricts credit report sales to customers "with a permissible business purpose," such as lenders, employers, landlords, private investigators, and attorneys with clients involved in litigation. Marketers, by contrast, are not using credit data for business or legal transactions, but to rank potential consumers by their financial credentials. In 1991, after considerable internal soul-searching, Equifax quit list marketing (though not prescreening). On making the announcement, the credit bureau said, "It is not socially responsible to continue to sell data from credit files" to marketers.

Equifax's action came on the heels of an embarrassing incident for the company. In 1990, Equifax and Lotus Development Corporation teamed up to develop Lotus Marketplace: Household, a huge database containing profiles of 120 million people in the United States, obtained from census records, public files, and mailing lists. Included were the age, gender, marital status, household income, and buying habits of each of these Americans. Equifax planned to sell the database at a relatively inexpensive price to small businesses via a new medium, the CD-ROM, a compact disk that can be inserted into a desktop computer system and can store and provide vastly more information than any floppy or hard disk.

As soon as Marketplace was announced, privacy advocates were up in arms. Typical was the response of Marc Rotenberg, director of the Computer Professionals for Social Responsibility: Marketplace, he said, "poses a particular threat to personal privacy because they place the actual data in the hand of individuals and beyond the control of even the responsible information brokers. . . . Once this information on our lifestyles, buying habits, and the other most intimate aspects of our private lives is sold to strangers, our ability to control the disclosure of personal information is diminished and our right to privacy is undermined."

The Wall Street Journal, The New York Times, and *The Boston Globe,* among others, echoed Rotenberg's words on Marketplace. This riled up consumers, and Equifax received more than thirty thousand telephone calls and thousands of letters of complaint. As a result, in February 1991 Equifax canned the product. But it is questionable whether privacy advocates actually won a victory with Marketplace's demise. In contrast to the marketing lists still being sold by TRW and Trans Union, there was no personal credit data included in Marketplace. And all of the information about so-called lifestyle and buying habits contained in it was statistically derived numbers, computer-generated predictions of what people earning certain salaries and living in specific zip codes might do and buy.

Nevertheless, the furor over Marketplace left Equifax red-faced—and it pulled the product. Meanwhile, TRW goes a lot further, without embarrassment, baring confidential credit files to unauthorized customers. TRW argues that it complies with FCRA rules since it never lets the list buyer see the names he's purchasing. Instead, these names are sent directly to a disinterested third party, such as a mailing house, usually in the form of labels. There, envelopes are stuffed with the sales materials and slapped with the labels—and the list is then destroyed.

But that's no protection at all, argues mailing-list supplier Ed Burnett. "Who pays this so-called third-party mailer anyway?" says Burnett. "The direct marketer does, not TRW. If a direct marketer tells his mailing house to make a copy of the TRW list and send it to him for his files, you can be sure he won't risk losing this business by some misplaced allegiance to TRW's rules."

What's more, as a *U.S. News & World Report* editor found out, TRW doesn't always follow its own guidelines. The editor, Alicia Mundy, called up a TRW salesperson and, identifying herself as a researcher, asked to buy the names, addresses, and telephone numbers of five thousand credit card holders with credit lines of $3,000 and annual incomes between $100,000 and $125,000. The salesperson asked what the list would be used for.

"I told her I was doing 'sort of a survey,' " says Mundy. The sales rep agreed to ship the list. Total cost: $450. This wasn't an isolated incident, according to Mundy: a half-dozen other TRW salespeople offered to sell her similar information.

Insiders of the credit industry say that's not surprising. "This is a marketing environment with extreme pressure to sell names in order

to meet base monthly sales goals and maximize your commissions,"
a TRW sales rep says. "The rules about who can see and who can't see
a list are not followed all that closely."

Red Line, Green Light

Deluged by junk mail and dinner-hour telephone solicitations, the
average American might welcome living someplace free of direct-
marketing appeals. That's the situation of the people living in lower
East Point, a downtrodden neighborhood in this small Georgia town
on the outskirts of Atlanta. It's far different for their neighbors up the
road in the trendy Upper Point: their mailboxes are stuffed and their
phones don't stop ringing.

Residents of lower East Point are bypassed because they live on the
wrong side of town. Their credit files, financial standing, purchasing
behavior, and lifestyles are not what most marketers look for when
they tap databases for new customers. That's not to say that nobody
is interested in the people of lower East Point. Bankruptcy lawyers
contact them all the time, as do charlatans with schemes to beat the
lottery, and people who claim to fix bad credit. "These people are so
disenfranchised that they don't even get good junk mail," says a local
civil rights worker.

Living with the knowledge that they're "below the curve," as micro-
marketers indelicately call them, is bad enough. But lower East Pointers really hit the roof recently when the homes in Upper Point received
offers for big discounts on furniture at a new store in town and they
weren't given the same opportunity.

The problem occurred when a local newspaper—a weekly free
"shopper"—purchased data about the town's residents from a company that specializes in providing breakdowns of the economic status,
personal tastes, and buying patterns of clusters of homes—sometimes
as few as eight—in every U.S. city and hamlet.

Companies that sell this kind of information—chiefly Claritas NPDC
in Alexandria, Virginia, and National Decision Systems (NDS), an
Equifax affiliate based in Encinitas, California—buy statistical and raw
data about individuals from numerous sources, among them the Census Bureau, real estate databases, motor vehicle files, supermarket
scanner systems, product warranty cards, consumer surveys, polls,
and even the credit bureaus. Computers crunch this data against
national and regional models to produce sketches that portray the

likely political leanings, tastes, and lifestyle of each American by his address.

"Tell me someone's zip code, and I can predict what they eat, drink, drive—even think," says Jonathan Robbin, target-marketing specialist and founder of Claritas, expressing the credo of his profession.

In contrast to the list suppliers, Claritas and NDS don't sell names, just neighborhood profiles. These are valuable road maps for retailers scouting the appropriate location for an upscale boutique or a tattoo parlor. They're also invaluable to salesmen, such as insurance agents, who are looking for the next group of houses to call on.

These profiles are fascinating reading. For instance, according to Claritas, residents of the nation's wealthiest homes—known as the "Blue Blood Estates," which make up about 1.1 percent of U.S. households—buy computer equipment and tennis balls, visit Europe, invest in U.S. Treasury notes, and drink Irish whiskey. They don't, however, use Tupperware, go bowling, purchase pregnancy tests or groin irritation remedies, or chew tobacco. They read *Barron's* and *The New York Times,* but not *1,001 Home Ideas* or *Hot Rod.* They drive Rolls-Royces and Jaguars, but rarely a Dodge Diplomat or Chevy Impala. In food, their tastes tend toward bottled water and cold cereal, not canned meat spreads or powdered fruit drinks. And they watch "Late Night with David Letterman," "60 Minutes," and "20/20" instead of quiz shows and the Christian Broadcasting Network. Politically, they're conservative. Where are these homes? Beverly Hills; Potomac, Maryland; Scarsdale, New York; and Bloomfield Hills, Michigan, among other places, says Claritas.

In sharp contrast to the "Blue Blood Estates" are the homes Claritas calls "Shotguns and Pickups"—about 1.9 percent of U.S. households. Residents there buy wood-burning stoves, have vegetable gardens, can tomatoes, and travel in truck-mounted campers. They don't have valid passports. They watch bowling and auto racing on TV but hate Ted Koppel and Financial News Network. They read *Grit* and *Four Wheel & Off Road,* not *Tennis* or *Audio.* They buy powdered soft drinks, dry soups, and whipped topping, but can't stomach pumpernickel bread. And they drive Plymouths, not Jaguars. These homes are located in crossroads villages like Molalla, Oregon; Zanesville, Ohio; Monroe, Indiana; and Moravia, New York—towns where it's not uncommon for the business district to consist of bars, grocery stores, and tackle shops.

Interesting sociology, but to lower East Pointers data mills like

Claritas can be dangerous. The people there took offense at being classified as residents of "Tobacco Roads," where asthma relief remedies and room heaters are more prevalent than electric shavers and live theater; where *Southern Living* is read, but not *Ms.;* where Chevy Impalas are driven, but nobody owns a Saab; and where people watch "The Arsenio Hall Show," then change the channel when "Joe Franklin" comes on.

Not only was this characterization insulting to lower East Pointers, but it became an economic stigma. Relying on this neighborhood data, the local shopper began to print customized editions—often with different advertisements and articles—for each cluster of homes in the circulation area. Soon after, residents living in Upper Point's "Furs and Station Wagons" homes received copies of the newspaper with an ad inviting them to sign up for credit at the new furniture store and get 25 percent off on their initial purchases. The local merchant wasn't as generous to lower East Pointers: the furniture store's ad didn't appear in their edition of the paper.

Because Upper Point is predominantly white and lower East Point is mostly black, the Southern Christian Leadership Council (SCLC), a civil rights organization, issued press releases denouncing the demographic advertising as racial discrimination. Lower East Pointers and the SCLC may have correctly assessed the indignity they suffered, notes Denny Hatch, editor of the newsletter *Who's Mailing What!,* but they missed the real meaning of the incident. "This wasn't a onetime occurrence. Don't they understand? All direct marketing is redlining," says Hatch, alluding to the practice in which banks refuse to issue mortgages to buy homes in poorer areas.

Hatch has a point. With private, sensitive databases now the primary criterion for most critical marketing decisions, people with few blemishes on their computerized files, who meet high standards of lifestyle and status, are hungrily sought after by marketers. Opportunities for "undesirables" are more limited. A privileged class has emerged that is offered new credit cards, travel promotions, shopping club memberships, and educational programs for the children—in short, chances to improve themselves and enjoy a better lifestyle. The data-disenfranchised, meanwhile, are ignored. Residents of "Money & Brains" and "Blue Blood Estates" may find junk mail to be a nuisance, but receiving a letter saying that they have been preapproved for credit is an inconvenience that few lower East Pointers will ever experience.

It's not something that the information industry addresses willingly, but a statement by TRW vice president of direct marketing Edward Freeman provides a hint of how discriminatory databases can be. "It is now feasible, using the array of data we have—credit information complemented by other public or demographic information such as age, driver's license, and zip codes—to identify consumers based on interests and economic capacity, so that the stuff you call junk mail will not be junk mail anymore," says Freeman. "Rather, you, as the consumer, will receive mail centered around the things that you are interested in, as demonstrated by your lifestyle and interests in our databanks."

In other words, if your mailbox is empty, you're a nonentity in the age of electronic information and direct marketing—a person with either no interests or no "economic capacity" to enjoy them. Even more frustrating to society's disadvantaged is the fact that each day new morsels are added to their electronic image. Bereft of opportunities, it is virtually impossible for these people to improve their profiles.

5

A Trace Left Behind

Once privacy is invaded,
privacy is gone.

Supreme Court Justice
William O. Douglas

When I spoke to her on the telephone, Christina Danvers had a warm, full-throated, gentle voice. She sounded engaging and winsome. And in trouble.

Her husband of a dozen years had run off not long ago, leaving thirty-five-year-old Christina with a trail of debt, including an IRS lien of nearly $60,000. She took up the matter with the New Jersey courts, which made the obvious decision: Michael was responsible for half of the debt, the judge said. Christina owed the other half.

But Michael was nowhere to be found. So a bench warrant was issued to apprehend him and force him to pay his share. With this, the case was, in essence, closed. When somebody runs off, no matter how many judgments against him are pending, the courts generally wash their hands of the matter until he surfaces.

They have no choice. There aren't enough investigators at the judiciary's disposal to shadow people who are purposefully making their path cold and erasing their footprints with every step they take. And if the police spent their time looking for every errant husband, small-time embezzler, and common criminal on the lam, it's not likely that they would do a very good job of protecting the local populace.

That leaves people like Christina Danvers in a bewildering no-man's-land. The authorities were on her side and sympathetic to her plight, but besides verbal support they had little to offer. They encouraged her to find Michael, but didn't provide any resources or help in the effort. Once he's located, though, they assured her, they'll take steps to put him under lock and key. That was little comfort for Danvers. It meant nothing but day after day of frustration and emotional paralysis. She didn't have a clue where to begin.

That's why she called me. A few days before she telephoned, Danvers had watched a television program on privacy on New York's WABC-TV, in which I conducted an experiment to prove that unrestricted databanks can in a flash furnish crucial tidbits about practically any individual's whereabouts and closely held secrets. The premise was that by simply piecing together entries found on the invisible computer networks snaking throughout the nation now, it's possible not only to locate someone but also to sketch an accurate portrait of that person.

To dramatize this, the producers at WABC got a willing couple to serve as guinea pigs. Then they gave me only the name of the husband, Ted Darling. Relying solely on my computer, I was asked to find out as much as I could about Ted and his wife.

To do this, my plan was to access databanks maintained by super-bureaus and more legitimate electronic public records. First, I dialed an online directory—a computerized version of the white pages. With it, I learned the name of Ted Darling's wife, and the couple's address and telephone number.

(My keyboard input is in **bold**; the text in plain type is queries and responses from the computer.)

Looking for . . . .
Last name: **Darling**
First name: **Ted**
Region: **Northeast**

Press [cr] to continue
Response . . .
Ted Darling
21 Flagstone Road
Scarsdale, NY 10583
914-472-XXXX
Spouse: Alice
Length of Residence: 2 Years

- END OF REPORT U.S. INVESTIGATIVE FILE -

Knowing the Darlings' address, I ran a request for their credit report header, following the same line of investigation I used to obtain information on Dan Rather.

Looking for . . . .
Credit Report Header
Last name: **Darling**
First name: **Ted**
Address: **21 Flagstone Road**
        Scarsdale, NY 10583

Press [cr] to continue

Response . . .
HEADER REQUEST/TRW

Ted Darling
21 Flagstone Road
Scarsdale, NY 10583
914-472-XXXX

Social Sec. No: 073-XX-98XX
Date of birth: 12/18/43
Employer: Darling and Garner, Esqs.
Attorney
608 Tremont Avenue
Bronx, NY
Salary: $125,000 +

Spouse: Alice

Social Sec. No: 073-XX-68XX
Date of birth: 01/25/43
Employer: McLaughlin Group
Television Producer
1210 8th Street
New York, NY
Salary: $75,000 - $100,000

Former address:

280 West 95 Street
New York, NY
Reporting 1989

- END OF REPORT TRW AND AFFILIATES -

I had spent a scant five minutes on the investigation so far. In that short time, I unearthed from actual data and educated deductions that my subjects, Ted and Alice Darling, live in a comfortably expensive home in upper-crust Scarsdale, New York; that Ted's an attorney in the Bronx and Alice is a television producer in Manhattan, working for John McLaughlin, the host of the popular syndicated current affairs roundtable "The McLaughlin Group"; that they're in their late forties; and that a few years ago, before their salaries reached the six-figure level, they lived in a semigentrified neighborhood—the Upper West Side of Manhattan, on Ninety-fifth Street.

The next step was to download public records and a full credit report on the Darlings. With these, I found out that the couple's three-bedroom home cost $320,000 when the Darlings bought it in 1989 and that their mortgage runs $1,500 monthly; that they drive a gray Mercedes and a white Jeep, which they lease for a total of $692 per month; that they used to own an '85 Volkswagen and an '84 Porsche; that Alice is an old-fashioned girl: she has no credit cards in her name and even uses Ted's Social Security number in all her business dealings; and that two months ago they bought a computer from Radio Shack.

Finally, a superbureau databank provided a list of the long-distance calls made by the Darlings recently.

Looking for . . . .
AT&T Toll Calls/Northeast Region

Last name: **Darling**
First name: **Ted**
Address: **21 Flagstone Road**
        Scarsdale, NY 10583
Social Security No.: **073-XX-98XX**
Telephone No.: **914-472-XXXX**
Period Requested: **December, 1990 - January, 1991**

Press [cr] to continue
Response . . .
RE: DARLING 914-472-XXXX

TOLL CALLS
12/28/90 THROUGH 1/28/91

305-937-XXXX
305-935-XXXX

313-342-XXXX
201-567-XXXX
201-827-XXXX
202-457-XXXX
201-585-XXXX
203-322-XXXX
202-628-XXXX
301-576-XXXX
305-921-XXXX

- END OF REPORT U.S. INVESTIGATIVE FILE -

Running these telephone numbers against a computerized cross-directory that supplies a person's name, address, and household makeup from just a phone number, I learned that Ted's parents as well as Alice's live in Florida; that Ted's sister lives in Detroit; and that Alice's employer, John McLaughlin, spends part of his time in his Washington, D.C., offices, but to unwind he prefers his Hollywood, Florida, home on Buchanan Street.

My attempt to turn over the Darlings' personal life began with just one name. After less than an hour at the computer keyboard I knew more about the Westchester couple and their circle of intimates than many of their friends do. Interestingly, the only item I couldn't discover from databanks was something immediately evident when you meet Ted and Alice face-to-face: the Darlings are black. But the computer never thought to tell me that. Most databanks, it turns out, for all their faults, have in at least one way a not inconsequential edge on people: they're usually color-blind.

Predictably, when the Darlings were confronted—on camera, of course—with the profile I had assembled, they were flabbergasted. "It's shocking," said Ted Darling. "People that can get personal information like that so easily can use it to con others. You've even found out what we purchase. You know what we have in our house."

Television at its split-second-reaction best. It was a minute or so of broadcast time, but millions saw it and instantly were made to understand, in one sublimely epiphanous moment, the impact on the individual of forty years of computerization in America. What began as a revolution in business machines, in which corporate systems such as payroll, accounts receivable, and billing were simplified and made less labor-intensive, has restyled the way information about Americans is collected, maintained, bought, sold, and circulated in this country. And because we used real people and real information on WABC to show how skillfully databanks reveal the hidden picture of a person's secret self, the frightening effect the computer potentially has on personal rights was clearly laid bare.

Indeed, the Darlings regretted ever giving WABC permission to use them for its experiment. Soon after the segment aired, the couple received numerous abusive phone calls from viewers who chose to invade the Darlings' privacy even more. Because of this, the Darlings begged WABC not to repeat the show as had been planned. WABC agreed without hesitation.

"I was moved, scared, and amazed by that demonstration," Christina Danvers was telling me on the phone, as if she were complimenting Penn and Teller for sawing a woman locked in a see-through Plexiglas box in half. "And I need your help. I need you to find my husband."

It was hard not to have sympathy for Christina Danvers. It's one thing to be concerned about the misuse of computers, about machines that wind up in the wrong hands, about unrestricted databanks containing far too much personal information, about crimes committed as a result of computerized networks, and about subsequent invasions of privacy. These are undeniable hazards. But desperate cases like Danvers's lend a different perspective. Indeed, there are millions of others in the same boat as she—not only divorcées, but thousands of small businessmen and individuals abandoned by clients or acquaintances who are ignoring court judgments to pay for the services they received or the loans they were generously given. And when you hear of these, the realization hits that among the debris overly intrusive databanks have rained on society, there is at least something positive.

Without these online information sources, tracking down people who have done wrong and have probably gone off to upend the lives of still others is an extremely tedious pursuit—and not one that the law in most cases, let alone everyday people, is likely to attempt without truly compelling reasons. The cost in time, money, and manpower makes it virtually prohibitive. But the ability of databanks to find anyone in an instant—and, conversely, the inability of anybody to conceal himself for long these days from the voracious reach of computers, which record without bias the minute-to-minute meanderings of the good as well as the bad—makes it easy to tail even the most shadowy figure, for those who know how to do it.

I told Danvers I wasn't a licensed private investigator, but I knew of one who handled computers even better than I do. I referred her to him, and asked if I could follow the case. She agreed. And I called Bob Lesnick, who runs Gamma Investigative Research in West Paterson, New Jersey.

Lesnick—midforties, average height, slightly overweight, his best feature a shock of wavy salt-and-pepper hair—doesn't fit the part of the typical television PI. He's not graceful, well dressed, tall, built like a hunk, or a womanizer. He doesn't drink much and his offices—nothing but a series of walk-in closets in which two people can't comfortably pass each other without bumping—are located on the second floor of a ramshackle, distressed building in a low-rent business district. The town, West Paterson, soured decades ago when the rural mountain people fled, replaced by hillside developments and not enough jobs, especially when the silk manufacturers deserted nearby Paterson.

But outward appearances mean nothing when picking the right private investigator. Lesnick plies his trade better than most. That's because even with his less-than-dashing cut, he's the very model of a modern, even avant-garde private eye. He's come to a conclusion that few other PIs are sufficiently bright or open-minded to reach: that the old sole-on-concrete, gumshoe approach to uncovering information is rapidly going the way of the LP record. Computers, Lesnick says, have the capacity to revolutionize investigating. They hold practically all the answers. You just have to know where to look.

Lesnick embraced computers to enhance his arsenal. "It's the most modern weapon we have," says Lesnick. "Few people, even criminals, can evade a databank." What's more, says Lesnick, computers are transforming the nature of crime these days. Databanks, Lesnick says, "are extremely potent. They carry information that is used more and more for deliciously conceived, clever, and spectacularly injurious crimes. It's always been my view that you can't be a worthy adversary to something you don't understand."

Money Machine

A case that investigators frequently cite to illustrate Lesnick's point about the enormity of electronic crime is the one involving Mark Koenig. Were it not for databanks and desktop computers, Koenig would still be what he really is: a nondescript computer nerd, adept with chips, circuits, and machine language, living an ordinary life. However, easy access to an extremely private databank changed all that for Koenig. It made it possible for him—as it has for many others—to shed the commonplace yoke and commit a crime that, as one Secret Service agent put it, "danced on the edge of brilliance."

Koenig is in jail now. But he might not be were it not for a slip of the tongue. And although he failed, Koenig stands out as one of the more inventive perpetrators of a modern-day crime spree that is rapidly spreading unchecked. Criminals using databanks as weapons, says a high-ranking FBI agent, are creating "an uncontrollable technocracy." And like a new strain of bacteria, this agent adds, these crimes are taxing the limits of conventional techniques to fight them.

Mark Koenig was a twenty-eight-year-old GTE Corporation consultant in 1989 when he cooked up his scheme to defraud Bank of America ATM customers of millions of dollars during a long holiday weekend. The plan was so well devised that it still has federal authorities and California banking regulators clucking over what might have been had he gotten away with it. Koenig's take, they say, would have been enormous—"between $7 million and $14 million," according to Carolyn J. Kubota, an assistant U.S. attorney in Los Angeles.

To put the crime into motion, Koenig devised a strategy to capture account information and ATM code numbers (so-called personal identification numbers, or PINs) of BofA customers at the very moment they were being used by unsuspecting cardholders at money machines—and to download them into his personal computer at home. Koenig then made counterfeit ATM cards out of cardboard, gluing VHS videotape on each of them to emulate the black magnetic stripe on the back. And with a homemade electronic device connected to a data encoder, he automatically programmed the account data from his PC onto the ersatz cards. In all, more than six thousand ATM cards were counterfeited in this way.

Koenig had access to this privileged information because a few months earlier he had installed a series of Plus network ATMs—the kind that Bank of America uses—for his employer, GTE, at supermarkets and other stores throughout California. These ATMs, like all large computer systems, come with a so-called manufacturer's default key, essentially a common password an installer can use to test the system during the installation phase. Typically, the system owner changes this password to a proprietary one after the computer is plugged in.

As he was tightening the nuts and bolts, splicing the wires, and breaking in the machines, a brainstorm hit Koenig. It occurred to him that by leaving the default password on the system but telling the system owner that it was removed, he could eavesdrop on the bank network anytime he wanted to. In effect, he would have his own password, a secret passageway into this vast databank, that was completely concealed from everyone else. All he had to do was dial in to the system through a modem attached to his PC and nobody would even know he was eavesdropping.

That night when he returned home to his tiny apartment in the Ladera Heights section of Los Angeles, Mark told his wife, Jackie, what he had in mind. He knew she'd be shocked at first, but he was pretty certain that gradually he'd wear down her resistance. He pulled out all the stops, touched all the hot buttons that made things happen in their relationship. With a mixture of boyish charm and a dreamer's naïveté, Koenig convinced her of how important this heist was to him—and, indeed, to them.

They had to take the risk, Koenig said. This was the chance of a lifetime, that moment when opportunity and destiny intersect. They'd never be able to purchase that expensive home they had their eyes on with their menial salaries, he said. Now, with financial independence finally staring them in the face, for the first time they could actually take seriously the thought of living in it. Before long, Jackie was convinced. She always followed Mark's dreams without reserve, and usually without regret.

Mark wanted more people involved, so the couple enlisted Mark's brother Scott; a friend, Robert Hussey; and Hussey's wife's sister, Bobbi Jo Bobby. At the first meeting of Koenig & Co., Mark laid out the plan. They would fan out across the country, he said, wearing disguises to conceal their true identities on the videotapes made at ATM kiosks, and use the cards at hundreds of money machines for six straight days before and during the upcoming Presidents' Day weekend. For orchestrating the scheme, Mark would get half the cash they hauled in. The rest of the money would be shared among the other four.

The plan had *foolproof* written all over it. For one thing, Koenig downloaded data only from Bank of America accounts. This was to confuse the authorities when the crime was discovered, to make investigators think it was an inside job at BofA. What's more, Koenig had already field-tested the bogus cards with three trial runs, without a glitch. Only a small amount was taken during these tests.

The hustle probably would have worked, but a friend of Jackie Koenig's spoiled it. One day, a couple of weeks before the big pinch, Jackie was talking to an old chum. During the conversation, Jackie excitedly spilled the beans about their plan. Her friend was shocked at what she was hearing, and at the ease with which Jackie had taken to this massive, multimillion-dollar crime. Outwardly, though, Jackie's friend kept her calm. In fact, she covered up her true emotions so well that Jackie asked her to participate. "She described it as a get-rich-quick scheme," the friend says. "Perfect and undetectable."

Perfect, thought her friend, if you want to spend the rest of your life in jail.

"I knew it was bad news," Jackie's friend says. "Conscience-stricken," she ran to the Secret Service to tell the agency what was afoot. To thwart the scheme, the government asked her if she was willing to cooperate by wearing a concealed tape recorder to a meeting at the Koenigs' apartment on January 27, 1990. She readily agreed.

At the meeting, Mark Koenig proudly told Jackie's friend—and the government through the tape recorder underneath her blouse—every detail of his complex plan. He spoke freely of his motives and his aspirations. He showed no remorse over the innocent people whose financial affairs would be thrown into chaos. He didn't seem to care about the checks that would bounce, the bills that would go unpaid, and the food that couldn't be bought as money these BofA customers thought was in their accounts would suddenly disappear. And there was no guilt about the larceny he was about to visit on Bank of America.

The tape was pure dynamite, and the Secret Service moved in quickly. On February 4, as the phony ATM cards were being encoded, agents raided Koenig's apartment and arrested all five suspects. Seized in the raid were 1,884 counterfeit cards completely encoded with Bank of America account information, 4,900 partially completed cards, and the machine used for encoding.

The government was lucky this time, says Bob Dawson, Bank of America vice president and managing director for credit risk management: "Were it not for the informant, we never would have stopped the crime." Dawson estimates that ATM fraud like this costs financial institutions about $60 million a year.

Koenig and the others pleaded guilty to conspiracy and counterfeiting. They received sentences ranging from eighteen to forty-one months.

This was a clear-cut case of what the dark side of technology can bring, says Alan Michaels, chief financial officer of Applied Communications Inc. of Omaha, Nebraska, the company that had loaned Koenig to GTE to install the ATMs. "Koenig had access to data," says Michael. "He chose to use it in an illegal way."

George Burns's Revenge

Bob Lesnick admits to a healthy respect for Mark Koenig—especially his high-tech panache and classic ingenuity. "I'd love to have had him working for me," says Lesnick. "With his knowledge, he probably could make my computers sing."

Lesnick hasn't done a bad job of it himself. A former liquor-store and laundromat owner whose computer skills are self-taught, Lesnick has souped up his IBM PC with an array of complex programming and detailed instructions that enable him in a microsecond to propel himself devilishly from one databank to another, from one tiny buried piece of information to another, with just the click of a mouse.

It's dizzying to watch Lesnick at the keyboard. Type in a number, get back a name. Move the mouse. Go to another source. An address appears on the screen. Connect to a different databank. See a bank balance. Window to the credit bureau. Double-check the information. Then, bingo. Lesnick turns and smiles. I know, he says, where the subject has buried that $1 million he's keeping from his business partner.

He takes this kind of stuff personally. When the information isn't there, Lesnick's mood turns disagreeable, as if the computer isn't cooperating, as if it's mocking him. It's daring him to find the hot button he hasn't located yet, to uncork just the right minuscule piece of silicon in some inconsequential chip below the motherboard—the computer's drivetrain—that's hiding what he wants to know. When Lesnick tracks down his bounty, though, without even leaving his office, pressing the Save button on his computer is as satisfying to him as hearing the jaws of a handcuff click closed on the wrists of a perp.

When I told him on the phone about Christina Danvers and her fruitless attempts to locate her husband, Michael, Lesnick immediately dove into the case. Often, with databanks, these kinds of investigations can be wrapped up in a matter of minutes. Lesnick hoped this investigation was one of them.

"This Michael Danvers," Lesnick said. "Do you have his Social Security number? I want to do some preparatory work before we meet with the client."

Anticipating his request, I had asked Christina Danvers for Michael's "Social." I gave it to Lesnick.

Ten minutes later, Lesnick called me back. "I found him," he said, his excitement uncontainable. "I ran his Social Security number through a locator database and out popped an address in Clearwater, Florida."

Then, Lesnick said, he telephoned Directory Assistance, asked for Michael Danvers at that address, and "pay dirt—the operator gave me his phone number: 813-985-9862."

Lesnick warned me not to tell Christina that we already knew her husband's whereabouts. "If clients think all of this comes so easily, they don't like to pay a lot of money for it," he said.

We met Christina Danvers at a rest stop on the Garden State Parkway near Irvington, New Jersey. It was a warm afternoon in late March—Passover began the night before; the next day would be Easter—with the wind whipping gentle whirlpool-like breezes. We were sitting in McDonald's, sipping coffee. Her fetching telephone voice notwithstanding, Christina Danvers was a hard-edged woman, tall, thin, and short-haired with nervous birdlike eyes. Five long chains with thick gold crosses dangled off her neck. I found out their purpose later. Scars, seemingly from deep burns, crisscrossed her rough-hewn face.

Danvers told us all she could about her former husband. His date of birth, New Jersey driver's license number, height, weight, eye and hair color. His last known employer, and his previous addresses. She also gave us the name of a woman who she thought was Michael's latest flame. Christina proffered this information humorlessly, with little overt emotion, as if she were describing somebody she barely knew, not a person she had lived with for twelve years. "I don't care about him anymore," she explained. "And I don't expect to get any money out of him. He's probably penniless. I would just love to see him strung up by his short hairs."

"I think we can find him quickly," Lesnick said, patting her on the arm. "You've given us a lot of leads to start with."

"Oh, one more thing," Danvers said. Her eyes darted from Lesnick's to mine. An anxious look crossed her face. "He's been a drug abuser his whole adult life, been in trouble with the law in New Jersey many times because of that."

"What county?" Lesnick asked.

"You name it." She paused. "I don't want to tell you much more, because it's very embarrassing and personal, but—"

"We don't have to know any more," I interjected.

"Well, let me just say that he has '666' tattooed on top of his right hand between his thumb and index finger."

A devil worshiper. That's why Christina wore those crosses around her neck. To make sure that Michael and the malevolent lifestyle they shared—we since found out that the burn marks on her face were the residues of a lethal cult-infested night during their marriage—recede way into her past.

We were barely in Lesnick's car when he clapped his hands loudly together and said excitedly, "Pay dirt. We hit it. The address we have for him isn't on the list of addresses she gave us. That means we already have his new address. The one that she wants. Let's go to the office and double-check the information we have on some more databanks, then hold off until Wednesday before telling Christina."

Back at Lesnick's office, we ran Michael Danvers's credit report. That didn't turn out to be the mother lode Lesnick had hoped for. Indeed, suddenly the trail got extremely cold. The Clearwater address that Lesnick had uncovered just the day before was not his current one anymore, we learned much to our dismay. A notation on his credit report said that in August, seven months earlier, Danvers was evicted for not paying his rent. And there was no indication that he had given any of his creditors his new address.

"Shit," Lesnick said, hitting his desk with his fist. He looked panic-stricken, his optimism oozing away. He called the Clearwater telephone number for Michael Danvers that he gotten from Directory

Assistance previously. A message machine answered, with somebody named Karen saying that no one was home to take our call. The name Michael wasn't uttered in this message.

Lesnick telephoned Directory Assistance. This time, the operator contradicted what Directory Assistance had told him before: she said there was no listing for a Michael Danvers in Clearwater. Lesnick slammed the phone down in disgust. "Operators are so fucking illiterate," he said angrily. "Whoever I spoke to yesterday gave me the wrong information. There's no Michael Danvers there. What the hell was she talking about? We lost him now."

Lesnick was beside himself. Unexpected setbacks, especially those resulting from the mediocrity of others, enrage him. He started barking out orders. He told me to call every creditor on Danvers's credit report—all of whom had shut down their accounts with him—and, posing as another credit grantor, ask if they had a more recent address for Michael than the one in Clearwater. None did. They all said, though, that they would also love to get their hands on Michael Danvers.

Lesnick knew how they felt. He, too, was ruing the slipperiness of Michael Danvers. Indeed, frustrating Lesnick the most was the feeling that he had literally lost his prey. It's a unique property of electronic databases that for each slice of information accessed, there is the provocative sensation of peering in someone's window and watching him in his private, unguarded moments. There's an electronic communion that sparks a sense of intimacy between the hunter and the hunted, though the computer screen is as close as the two may ever get.

Though it's not clear why, through entries on a database one can "see" one's subject perfectly—something that, curiously, both Bob Lesnick and Rebecca Schaeffer's murderer, Robert Bardo, have experienced each time they've sat down at their computers, though they've been on opposite sides. Looking at this comically, it's the digital equivalent to what George Burns could do with the magical television set in the corner of his den on the Burns and Allen TV show in the 1950s, when he secretly watched Gracie, the two Harrys, and Blanche hatch schemes behind his back. Their one mistake: thinking that George couldn't see them. Databanks are usually less funny, but they produce the same result: they make it possible to visualize others without them ever knowing or suspecting.

For Lesnick, while Danvers was between addresses, the screen he stared at went blank. The tube was shut down and the curtain behind which Michael Danvers was hiding was opaque. Danvers was still somewhere out there, no doubt—in the vast datasphere, if you will. Now Lesnick had to find some new piece of online information to catch up with him again and bring him into view, to tune in the set.

That came on Monday morning. Taking a chance that Michael Danvers hadn't gone far from Clearwater and was still in Florida, Lesnick tried to access his motor vehicle records to see if a driver's license or an automobile registration provided a clue to his current whereabouts. At first he came up empty-handed. According to the records, no cars were registered in Danvers's name.

But there was a curious footnote to this file. A Michael Danvers with the same Social Security number and birth date as the one we were searching for had received a speeding ticket two months earlier in an automobile with dealer plates registered to Dodge City, a car dealership in St. Petersburg. That didn't give us Danvers's address, but at least we had spotted him again, and pinned down the fact that he was in Florida just sixty days ago and has some association with this Chrysler dealership. After all, he was driving one of its cars. Perhaps he was an employee, or a good friend of a salesman there, or dating the owner's daughter.

His driver's license report appeared on the computer screen next. Perfect coincidence stared us in the face. Just last Friday, the same day that Christina Danvers was telephoning me for help, ex-husband Michael, it turns out, was at a Florida motor vehicle office on the west coast of the state. He applied for a driver's license there—his old one had just expired—and he listed as his current address a tenement in a suburb of St. Petersburg.

Then Lesnick moved the mouse and jumped to an electronic white pages. He typed in the address we had just found for Danvers to pull down the names of those living at that location. Sure enough, the computer reported that Michael Danvers was listed as one of the tenants.

To double-check, Lesnick called Directory Assistance. He asked for Michael Danvers's phone number and gave his new address. The computerized voice responded: 813-573-XXXX. Lesnick called Directory Assistance again. He was given the same phone number. Then he asked me to call Directory Assistance. Just to make sure. Once more, we got the same number. That was it. We now felt certain we knew where he lived.

Lesnick was visibly sweating, not because of the exhilaration of the case and the quick workout at the computer as he raced to a positive outcome, but because of how close he had come to failing. It was a sheer pencil-thin line—a margin of just days—that separated successfully locating Danvers from having to spend hours roaming among entirely new, far more complex database connections than a simple motor vehicle report to find him.

"Do you realize if we had looked for him four days ago, instead of today, we would still be one step behind him, because he wouldn't have applied for his new license yet?" Lesnick said. "Then all we would have had to go on is this mysterious Dodge City ticket, which isn't much at this point."

The case was effectively solved, but Lesnick still wasn't satisfied. The Dodge City incident nagged at him. A perfectionist, Lesnick needed an explanation for the role that dealership played in Michael Danvers's life.

So Lesnick called up St. Petersburg's Dodge City. When the receptionist answered, he said he was from ABC Credit Services in New Jersey. Michael Danvers, he told her, was applying for a collateralized loan and gave "your auto dealership as a reference. Could you vouch for him and tell me what you know about about him?"

The receptionist turned Lesnick over to Dodge City's sales manager, who was more than happy to talk about Danvers. He's a model employee, the sales manager gushed, "one of my best salesmen for the past four months. The only thing bad I can say about him is he once got a speeding ticket driving one of our cars. But I wouldn't really consider that anything major."

"Bingo," Lesnick said, smiling broadly, as he hung up the phone—that word again; it's a favorite in his vocabulary. "Now we know where he works *and* where he lives. We also have popped a lot more that tells us volumes about him, like the bad debts, the eviction, the closed-out credit accounts. Funny thing is, we've never met Danvers, but we know more about what makes him tick than his employer does. I have to believe that sales manager at Dodge City doesn't have a clue about what Danvers is really like."

Christina Danvers was overjoyed two days later when Lesnick and I told her what we had learned. All that was left for her to do was get a New Jersey attorney with a Florida associate who could obtain a judgment in that state to garnishee Danvers's salary until the money he owes Christina is paid up. Or get a Florida bench warrant for Michael Danvers's arrest. Once that's done, Christina's fantasy might be fulfilled after all. It would be a perfect finish for her, she told us, if she could watch them hang high the gallows and pull Michael Danvers slowly up to the noose by the family jewels.

Bob Lesnick is a social realist. He doesn't fall neatly on either side of the political spectrum. He won't admit that, though. As an ex-Marine paratrooper who lost much of the motion in his left arm jumping out of a C-130 in Virginia in the mid-1970s, he says he's a gung ho conservative, a weapons lover who counts as one of his favorite books a dictionary of medieval methods of warfare, a fervent supporter of Accuracy in Media and subscriber to *National Review.*

At the same time, Lesnick understands the passionate thirst for privacy that most Americans express, and their antagonism toward databanks. He's well aware of the impotence people feel in the face of computers, and the harm these modern-day rumor mills can dish out, with no conscience and no remorse. And he even comprehends why privacy activists and the public through opinion polls inevitably articulate the desire to limit access to computerized information by the police, investigators like him, marketers, and the government. Still, Lesnick's sympathy for this position is tempered by a harsher reality that in his view overrides the rights of individuals.

That reality is the growing number of easy crimes facilitated by databanks these days. The high-tech rogues' gallery, populated by the likes of Mark Koenig, Robert Bardo, credit card fraud gangs, loan embezzlers, bank account manipulators, and numerous others, "should send a chill down our collective spine," says Lesnick. "It should make it obvious that law enforcement must be given increased access to databanks, not less."

Meaning, among other things, more sophisticated and widely available databases of criminals and suspects; ongoing monitoring of banking and credit transactions by government computers; proactive computer systems that surveil individuals and predict criminal activity; and letting investigators use databanks containing, for instance, phone records, Social Security files, asset information, and medical histories without having to tiptoe through gray zones of the law. There have been proposals for systems and policies like these, and in some cases they're being implemented (see chapter 6), but usually complaints from civil libertarians limit their scope.

"The vast amount of data and the computer's ability to draw conclusions from it rapidly should be looked at as a plus for law enforcement, not a venal temptation," says Lesnick. "Paradoxically, unless we adopt that view, the activities of criminals will ensure that what's left of privacy for many individuals and what remains of the right to control one's own destiny will dissipate even further."

It's an argument that, no matter how disturbing, has some merit. It underscores the dilemma that has resulted from our failure to impose limits and safeguards on databanks—that is, to define privacy in a high-tech world. Even now the absence of a centralized agency to establish societywide policies for computerized information stands out as a symbol of our neglect of this serious issue. With this as backdrop, it's no wonder that we're suddenly faced with discomforting questions. Among them: If we concede that computers have become an ally of a new breed of criminal—and the evidence points directly to that—can we continue to restrict their use, and the use of other means of surveillance, by law enforcement and investigators? Would we do that with any other newly adopted weapon?

"People are afraid of a police state emerging from the use of computers by the authorities," Lesnick notes. "But they should be concerned about the flip side: an uncontrollable computer-dominated crime wave led by dangerous criminals. That will be much more invasive."

As every man goes through life he fills in a
number of forms for the record, each
containing a number of questions. There are
thus hundreds of little threads radiating from
every man, millions of threads in all. . . . Each
man, permanently aware of his own invisible
threads, naturally develops a respect for the
people who manipulate the threads.

Aleksandr Solzhenitsyn

Hollow
Acts

It's a sobering thought: the IRS regularly scans taxpayers' credit
reports, supposedly, says the agency, to analyze their ability to
satisfy their tax liabilities. On the face of it, this may be an appropriate
use of modern technology. But there are opportunities for significant
abuse in the relationship of the IRS and the credit bureaus—two
dominant institutions that can independently, with one mistake, trans-
form orderly, regular existences into confounding and expensive
nightmares.

The computerized embrace of the IRS and the credit bureaus resulted in a hushed-up incident in the IRS's Southeast Region in 1989.
According to an internal IRS document, a disturbed employee there
peeked at "several credit reports" of people who "did not have an
open IRS case." When he found a credit report that was dotted with
delinquencies and late payments, tax-agency sources say, he sent it to
the subject's employers and business associates, hoping to impugn
the subject's character. Sometimes this was done on the IRS's letter-
head, other times anonymously. Eventually, the IRS employee's malicious activities were exposed when one of these checkered credit files
was sent to a state agency and a whistle-blower reported the episode.
The IRS employee was convicted and sentenced to two years' proba-
tion.

Unfortunately, other IRS staffers are seduced by the same tempta-
tions as this employee. An internal IRS survey soon after the incident
found that of every hundred credit reports accessed by IRS workers,

five are illegally obtained. That is, they are credit reports of Americans not under investigation by the IRS. And the agency admits that the survey results may underestimate the problem. "No audit trail exists to identify employees who access credit information," an IRS investigator wrote in an internal report on the matter.

The IRS incident isn't so rare. Despite public pronouncements by government officials who say this society is committed to protecting the rights of the individual, there's a little-understood antiprivacy underbelly in Washington, a D.C. data bazaar, as some insiders term it, which delights in collecting information on Americans and presumes that U.S. citizens are to be feared, not trusted. For the last thirty years, virtually every federal agency—including the Social Security Administration, the Department of Justice, the Internal Revenue Service, the Central Intelligence Agency, and the Secret Service—at one time or another has tried to sidestep privacy regulations as an inconvenience.

Typical is what has transpired since the passage of the Privacy Act of 1974. This legislation was adopted to "provide certain safeguards for an individual against an invasion of privacy." The law says the government may not maintain secret databanks, and mandates that all information the government collects about Americans be kept confidential. Under the legislation, people have the right to know about records pertaining to them, and they must be told who else sees them and how they're used. Further, without written consent an agency is prohibited from sharing an individual's records with anyone else and from using them for a secondary purpose.

The aims of the Privacy Act are noble, but its implementation has been horribly botched. After an investigation in 1990 the General Accounting Office (GAO) said that the government is a poorer and sloppier caretaker of personal data now than it was before the Privacy Act was on the books.

The reason has to do with technology. Prior to the passage of the Privacy Act, most government records were stored manually and on paper. But in order to abide by the Privacy Act, federal agencies were forced to quickly computerize their backward systems. They needed computers to index the data they collected and to provide a means to sort through it quickly. Otherwise, how could the government let the people know and view in a timely fashion what was collected in federal databanks, as the law required?

So the irony, says the GAO, is that the Privacy Act immediately accomplished the opposite of its sponsors' intentions: it hastened a surge in the number of sophisticated electronic files in Washington. And this, according to the GAO, has vastly "increased opportunities for inappropriate or unauthorized use of personal information, and made it more difficult to . . . safeguard individuals' rights."

The numbers are staggering. The 178 largest federal agencies and departments maintain nearly two thousand databanks, virtually all of them computerized and outsize, containing tens of millions of files each. Peppering these records are mind-boggling permutations of Social Security numbers, names and addresses, and financial, health, education, demographic, and occupational information—obtained from individuals themselves and from external sources such as state government files, the Census Bureau, the credit industry, and insurance companies. Remarkably, in clear violation of the Privacy Act, the public hasn't even been told about the existence of 11 percent of these systems, let alone what's in them.

Meanwhile, outsiders who have no legal right to know about these databanks or their contents are inexplicably given free access to them. Information in 56 percent of government databanks is examined regularly by private corporations and educational institutions, with few questions asked, according to the GAO. In almost all of these cases, the government doesn't even bother inquiring what the data is being used for.

Security for these supposedly private government systems is also embarrassingly lax. About a dozen agencies admitted to the GAO that there were "material weaknesses" in procedures for protecting confidential information in their computerized systems. Until last year, the Department of the Treasury, for instance, allowed its computer programmers free rein within agency databases containing personnel salaries and staff expense reports—far more information than these computer operators needed to do their jobs.

And even when employees are not purposely given the keys to personal data, poor internal security measures accord them the same latitude. Thirty-four breaches of sensitive federal computerized information systems were reported in 1988 and 1989. In one incident, an employee modified his own files to benefit himself financially; in two separate cases, unauthorized people gained access to computers using passwords others had disclosed to them; and in another incident, an agency's private contractor let dozens of other companies pull information out of a databank that was intended to be confidential.

Upon close examination, it shouldn't be surprising how lightly federal agencies take the Privacy Act—and, by extension, the individual's right to be free of secret government intrusions into their lives. After all, for more than twenty years Washington has been the surprisingly generous sugar daddy for a surveillance-equipment and information-gathering explosion that has rippled from one region of the country to another, and from one police department to another.

The government took on this role soon after the passage of the 1968 Omnibus Crime Control and Safe Streets Act, which outlawed wiretapping unless stringent conditions were met. To bolster conservative support for the bill, adjunct legislation was passed that year creating the Law Enforcement Assistance Administration (LEAA). LEAA's purpose was to provide federal money for fighting crime, in part by updating criminal justice systems in the cities and the states. An innocuous Great Society bureaucracy, it seemed, even to liberals.

But the agency turned out to be anything but benign. In short order, LEAA became the glue for an elaborate intelligence daisy chain that encouraged and supported the surveillance of thousands and thousands of Americans—and its impact continues to be felt today.

In its first year LEAA had a $63 million budget. By 1975 it was spending nearly $900 million a year—much of this money going to rearm outmoded American police departments with state-of-the-art surveillance equipment.

This huge influx of government funds started a cottage industry. Dozens of surveillance-equipment manufacturers, anxious to grab LEAA largesse, opened their doors for the first time. Before long, these companies would become the kingpins of the vast underground of information resellers described in chapter 3. During the 1980s, as computerized data became ubiquitous and extremely valuable, many of these companies expanded their businesses to include surreptitious data selling. But two decades ago, because of LEAA's big budgets, bugging and monitoring hardware were their most important products. And their wares constantly got more sophisticated, invasive, and pricey. After all, the government was picking up the tab.

Equipment wasn't the only thing the government paid for, according to sources. Apparently backed by CIA funds and headed by Agency personnel, a network of training schools, such as Bell and

Howell Communications in Massachusetts and the National Intelligence Academy in Florida, were started to teach the police how to use all this new LEAA-supplied hardware. As a former CIA agent who taught at Bell and Howell describes the relationship between the CIA and the supposedly private training schools: "I was the golden monkey, the icon with the CIA résumé who was brought in to attract students to the training operation. That would be okay if I was retired from the Agency. But that wasn't the case. I was assigned to this job by the CIA. I was still on the CIA's payroll."

Tuition and travel expenses for these training sessions were picked up by LEAA. And at the classes, says the former Bell and Howell teacher, "we taught U.S. police departments how to snoop on their local citizens," though the CIA is prohibited from doing so.

Some say that one American who got caught in the middle of this insidious interlock of high-tech stalking weapons paid for by LEAA and police training sponsored by the CIA was Kerr-McGee employee and antinuclear advocate Karen Silkwood. According to some sources, the Oklahoma City police department was one of many U.S. police forces with LEAA grants to attend National Intelligence Academy sessions. At these classes they were taught, among other things, how to keep tabs on local citizens. When their training was completed, the cops were taken next door to NIA's sister company, a surveillance equipment manufacturer called Audio Intelligence Devices. There they were allegedly stocked with state-of-the-art spy technology. In Oklahoma, as in many states, it's illegal for local police forces to own surveillance equipment.

But that didn't deter the Oklahoma City police, "who went back home itching to use their new surveillance toys," says Danny Sheehan, an attorney for the Silkwood family. "Their first victims: the only dissidents in their sleepy town, the Kerr-McGee antinuclear activists."

Inspired by the NIA classes, the cops were in the mood for action. But possessing for the first time the most sophisticated technology money could buy, they were in over their heads. And after they joined forces with Kerr-McGee's hot-wired corporate dicks, one bad deal led to another. Snooping with long-distance cameras was followed by telephone bugging, which was followed by breaking and entering, and that eventually led to Karen Silkwood's murder, argues Sheehan.

The Sheehan version of the Silkwood case may be exaggerated, but it and others that made the rounds, including tales of widespread

LEAA-supported surveillance of antinuclear protesters in New Jersey and black activists in Illinois by information-happy police, eventually killed LEAA. It was shut down in the late 1970s.

The demise of LEAA, however, didn't stop the government from pushing hardware and, later, data out to the hinterlands. The job of granting funds to local cops for surveillance operations was turned over to the Department of Justice's Office of Justice Assistance Research and Statistics (OJARS). OJARS quietly funnels about $10 million per year to the Regional Information Sharing System (RISS), a private organization whose membership boasts virtually every police department in the United States.

Many privacy advocates suspect that RISS money, like LEAA's before it, is being used to abuse the privacy of individuals. In one recent case, the Connecticut state police were caught illegally listening to and taping telephone conversations made at their barracks between suspects and their attorneys. One surveillance equipment manufacturer who admits to being involved in selling some of the hardware to Connecticut troopers says simply, "It was a RISS-backed campaign."

Databank Accounts

The prototypical government databank is the Federal Bureau of Investigation's National Crime Information Center (NCIC). At its inception in 1967, NCIC had about three hundred thousand records, mostly data about people involved in robberies, auto theft, and stealing license plates. NCIC has grown nearly twentyfold since then. It currently maintains records on twenty million Americans in more than a dozen categories. Included are murderers and drug dealers as well as missing persons and people of dubious character, at least according to somebody's judgment.

And although it has some severe faults, NCIC has always stuck to its original mandate and been a simple clearinghouse of criminal records. It may not stay that way for long. The FBI wants to implement the most massive NCIC expansion to date. New proposals would turn the computerized criminal records index into a monstrously huge national databank with tentacles that reach into virtually every information storehouse in the government and the private sector.

NCIC doesn't physically maintain much of the data itself. Instead, it can connect a policeman in, say, Florida who has arrested a local man on drunk driving charges with the suspect's criminal records in other states, where the suspect may be wanted on other charges.

It's a fast-moving electronic brokerage of criminal data over which information is exchanged by sixty-four thousand law enforcement agencies throughout the United States and Canada. NCIC responds to more than one million inquiries every day, or about 11.5 a second. Currently there's only raw computerized data available on NCIC. But soon police will be able to download into their NCIC terminals, many of which are in squad cars, fingerprints, photos, and descriptions of other physical attributes, such as tattoos, on the spot.

If NCIC only bartered in records of convicted criminals, it would be hard to complain about it—especially when big crimes such as drug deals are increasingly committed by people belonging to national networks. But NCIC goes much deeper. Not only does it provide access to records of criminals, it also supplies files on individuals in trouble with local authorities for any number of reasons: people arrested but not convicted of crimes, people with radical political leanings, and people whom local law enforcement authorities consider worth watching more closely because they're suspected of real crimes or because their behavior is erratic or eccentric.

Indeed, to add a person's name to NCIC, all authorities in any state, city, town, or village have to do is type it in. And because the database is such a wide-open, virtually unregulated forum of criminals and suspects, it has led to serious invasions of privacy based on mistaken identity and an unwillingness by many authorities to remove a name from NCIC once it's in there.

Terry Dean Rogan of Saginaw, Michigan, for instance, has been arrested five times for crimes he didn't commit. His wallet was stolen a few years back, and, until recently, when he was stopped by the police for a driving infraction or at a motor vehicle checkpoint, or when he filled out a government form, more often than not he was apprehended, handcuffed, and taken to the station house at gunpoint.

That's because it was a murder suspect who filched Rogan's wallet, and the suspect subsequently used Rogan's identification cards. Thus, NCIC repeatedly coughs up data that says Rogan is wanted for a murder, although the felony was committed by someone else. Rogan screamed foul each time he was arrested. But it wasn't until Rogan sued Los Angeles, whose police department had inserted his NCIC entry, and won a $55,000 settlement that officials finally removed his name from the database.

Roberto Perales Hernandez ran into a similar problem. He's been mistakenly jailed twice in the last four years as a suspect in a 1985 Chicago burglary. Both times this was due to the same inaccurate NCIC entry on him.

And Sheila Jackson Stossier, a former Eastern Air Lines stewardess, was going through customs after a flight from Mexico recently when she was arrested on the spot. The reason: a routine NCIC check produced a "hit"; a wanted felon, it seems, has a name similar to hers.

Cases like these are bad enough, but now the FBI wants to reshape NCIC radically and expand it well beyond its original scope. Under the FBI's surprising proposals for a new databank, called NCIC 2000, the amount of data available through the criminal databank would grow immeasurably. Information would be added that encompasses virtually every aspect of our lives. NCIC 2000 would give law enforcement authorities, using the FBI as a conduit, free and unquestioned access not only to current NCIC criminal files, but also to databanks at airline reservation systems, car rental companies, banks, retailers, credit bureaus, insurance companies, and phone companies. In addition, through NCIC 2000 it would be possible to obtain computerized records at the Internal Revenue Service, the Social Security Administration, and the Immigration and Naturalization Service.

The FBI first proposed this massive NCIC overhaul three years ago. But Representative Don Edwards (D-Calif.), a former FBI agent whose House Judiciary Committee's Subcommittee on Civil and Constitutional Rights oversees NCIC, was dismayed by the antiprivacy implications of the databank upgrade. So he immediately formed a panel, made up of three members of the Computer Professionals for Social Responsibility, Janlori Goldman from the American Civil Liberties Union Project on Privacy and Technology, and Diana Gordon, a political science and criminology professor at City College of New York, to study the FBI plan and decide whether it's a good idea.

The report, issued in early 1989, pulled no punches. It was scathing in its criticisms of the FBI proposals, saying that if they were approved NCIC will be "used as a dragnet, sifting through huge volumes of information [in the private and public sector] to find both potential crimes and possible suspects."

For one thing, the panel said, links to other ostensibly private consumer and government databases were overly aggressive and bordered on the illegal. And, the panel added, NCIC already lacks sufficient accountability—that is, it's too error-prone and available to too many people with virtually no audit trail—so a more ambitious version of the databank could have disastrous privacy implications.

NCIC's inaccuracies are a big concern, according to the panel. It's because of them that Rogan, Hernandez, and Stossier, among others we don't even know about, have been ensnared in horrible webs of confusion and mistaken identity. In a 1982 study of NCIC's records by the U.S. Congress's Office of Technology Assessment—the last major survey of the databank—11 percent of the arrest warrants listed on NCIC were no longer valid, another 6.6 percent were inaccurate, and and an additional 15.1 percent were more than five years old with no disposition of the case indicated.

That's an old report, but more recent analyses seem to suggest that not much has changed. A few years ago, a Midwest prosecuting attorney conducted a review of all arrest warrants from his county listed on NCIC. He looked at cases that were between one and twenty-three years old. Taking into account the availability of witnesses and new evidence that had come to light, the prosecutor concluded that 73 percent of the cases he examined were no longer provable—and many weren't even open anymore. Yet NCIC still listed ongoing arrest warrants for the cases.

As a result of the House panel's report, the FBI pulled its retooling plan for NCIC off the table, and proposed a drastically scaled-back version of NCIC 2000. Under this new plan, the FBI will work on upgrading NCIC's software. It promises to put in systems to reduce NCIC mistakes. The only new databases that NCIC will link up with are computerized criminal records maintained by the U.S. prison system and Canada. Congress likes the idea and is providing $20 million annually for its development.

Some are still wary, though. "NCIC is relatively under control from a civil liberties standpoint now," says a source close to the FBI and the House Judiciary Committee, "but things like that have a way of reappearing in Washington when the noise dies down. For now, however, there are other efforts under way that need to be watched closely."

Among them, the one that's most worrisome to privacy advocates is an FBI project that critics fear may become a national identification system for Americans. This databank is raising eyebrows not only for its breadth, but also for its contents: it would keep tabs on Americans by inescapable signposts in our blood and tissues.

During the past four years, the FBI has quietly been spending a whopping $2 billion annually to create a databank that analyzes Americans' genetic architecture. Initially at least, three categories of people would be included in it: known offenders, such as those convicted of rape, homicide, and aggravated assault; parents of missing children; and individuals who cannot be positively identified, among them previously lost youngsters who were just found, as well as the unknown dead. Independently, random DNA samples from hair, semen, and blood taken from crime scenes will also be stored in the FBI databank.

The idea, of course, is to use genetic markers to identify crime suspects and missing people more accurately. It's nothing more heinous than that, says the FBI. "The computer databank is only an information management and screening tool," explains John Hicks, the deputy assistant director of the FBI laboratory.

And to prove that, says Hicks, the FBI is not testing the DNA it stores for "any known functional inherited trait or characteristic" or for "disease conditions." The sole purpose of the databank is to let a homicide detective who finds hair follicles on the rug next to a body compare the DNA in the evidence against the DNA of subjects in the FBI databank. If a match occurs, the FBI says, there's a reasonable chance that the local cop has his man.

Some scientists claim that assumption is flawed, or at least open to very serious debate. Among people DNA matches are far more common than is generally believed, they say, so just the presence of genetic similarities between evidence at a crime scene and information about someone in the FBI databank could in many cases raise undue suspicion.

And if the databank's value as a forensic tool is in question, then some wonder whether its development should proceed, considering the serious civil liberties issues it raises—issues that will grow in importance if its tentacles eventually stretch a lot further than initially proposed. Says Representative Edwards: "I've been concerned for a long time about the runaway situation in this country with regard to databanks, where you can put a Social Security number in your computer at home, push a button, and have it automatically connected with Social Security, Immigration, Customs. So the thought of building another ultimately easily accessible databank with all this very personal information, most of which is nobody's business but your own, deserves grave attention."

Others share that view and argue that once a databank is amassed, someone will suggest expanding it before long. Philip Bereano, a professor of engineering and public policy at the University of Washington in Seattle, feels certain that "in not too many years there will be serious proposals made to take a DNA print from the heel stick of every newborn baby along with other testing of the blood that is routinely done, and to put that information into the databank. The rationale for this will be, of course, that it's for the individual's own good as well as for the good of society. We have enough historical evidence to realize that these kinds of claims are not only inevitable but very dangerous."

The loser, critics add, will be the autonomy of the individual, as DNA privacy will gradually yield to a sort of genetic redlining and even social control.

Pessimistic claptrap? Not if recent incidents are a guide. Already cases are emerging that point at ways in which the FBI databank could be used to discriminate against whole classes of Americans. Not long ago a rape-murder was committed in an East Texas town of about one hundred residents, almost all of whom are black and related to each other. DNA from five suspects was compared with genetic data from semen samples found at the scene of the crime. A match was declared with one of the suspects and the jury was told that the chances of a match occurring at random was one in ninety-six million. On the basis of that, the accused was sentenced to death.

But the jury was given misinformation. In such a tight-knit homogeneous population, genetic matches occur far more frequently than the odds given at the trial. In fact, the convicted man and the victim themselves shared three out of six rare DNA bands. A sixth suspect left town before taking a blood test. How much of that person's DNA matches the semen sample found at the crime scene? ponders the inmate on death row, who continues to declare his innocence.

"DNA tests are by no means infallible," says Eric Lander, a Harvard University associate professor for biomedical research. For one thing, accurate DNA tests require a quantity of blood or semen that frequently cannot be recovered where a crime has been committed. For another, contamination, heat, or moisture can degrade even sizable specimens. "It's a little-appreciated fact that DNA test results are subjective," notes Lander. "What one analyst may call a match, another may find inconclusive."

Lander says he's heard forensic scientists during trials provide mind-boggling statistical probabilities of a match—as high as one in 4.4 billion. "The research on population frequencies to support these astronomical claims simply has not been done," argues Lander.

Which raises the possibility that the FBI databank in the hands of local authorities could become a discriminatory crutch that will replace full-scale investigations of crimes—and too often wrongly finger suspicious but innocent people. When the FBI computer finds a genetic similarity between a name in its files and a piece of evidence, even though the link may be scientifically tenuous, the case could be considered solved. "Subjects in the databank—initially mostly minorities and the mentally ill—may continuously be tried and convicted of crimes just because their DNA matches, even if they have a good alibi and lack a motive," says Paul Billings, a genetic specialist at Pacific Presbyterian Medical Center in San Francisco. " 'Round up the usual suspects' could take on a new and more sinister meaning."

Indeed, the deck gets stacked even higher against DNA databank dwellers because the FBI will at no cost testify for the prosecution about its DNA findings. Defendants, by contrast, must go to private laboratories for testimony that rebukes the FBI's claims. These companies charge as much as $490 per DNA sample tested and $1,000 per day for expert testimony, which often is unconvincing to a jury against an FBI agent's assertions. Few defendants can afford to pay those kinds of fees, even though doing so might be the only slim hope they have of avoiding incarceration or a death sentence.

Genetic discrimination (see chapter 8) is already a hazard. An expansion of the FBI databank into a populationwide DNA information pool maintained by the federal government could make today's limited but invasive use of genetic data seem innocent by comparison. It could usher in an era of wholesale discrimination and even attempts at social engineering, says Representative Don Edwards: "Analyses of DNA can yield information on family relationships and predisposition to disease. Ultimately scientists may even try to identify predisposition to violent behavior."

Edwards is worried that considering the appetite for DNA data already exhibited by many in the private sector, especially employers and insurers, there will be no shortage of people "eager to have access to DNA" records that identify everybody with genetic diseases or disposed to undesirable personality traits and occupational diseases.

"Certainly the trend with criminal history records has been toward greater non-criminal-justice access," notes Edwards. "It would open up an unprecedented realm of privacy intrusions to follow a similar path with respect to DNA files."

Representative Edwards isn't always successful at limiting the expansion of FBI databanks, but he's an extremely fastidious civil liberties watchdog and he keeps the agency on its toes. No attempt to widen the scope of FBI computer systems bypasses the close and public scrutiny of the House Subcommittee on Civil and Constitutional Rights, which Edwards chairs. But there are numerous other little-known databanks sprouting throughout post-Watergate Washington, like mushrooms after a rainstorm, and virtually nobody with the power to affect their funding is questioning the usefulness of these databanks, or asking whether they go too far in abridging individual privacy. As a staffer on the House Government Operations Committee put it, "Nobody with political clout is willing to challenge them."

FinCEN, which stands for Financial Crimes Enforcement Network, is a good example. FinCEN was set up by the Treasury Department in 1990 to catch money launderers. At its launch, FinCEN was met with wholesale approval on Capitol Hill. And President Bush bolstered FinCEN's stock by calling it a centerpiece of his national drug control strategy, drawing on the argument that money laundering is usually done to disguise illicit income from drug trafficking.

Money is often laundered by being moved among bank accounts across state and international borders. The aim is to spread the dollars widely in small amounts so that they are effectively mainstreamed and indistinguishable from the legitimate money supply. Only then can the money be spent. To try to brake this rampaging $100-billion-to-$300-billion-a-year problem, FinCEN monitors all banking transactions in the United States that exceed $10,000, and it tracks hundreds of thousands of electronic funds transfers made at automated teller machines or over international money exchange networks.

With this transaction data, FinCEN creates files on financially active individuals; these files include names, addresses, and logs of banking activities. FinCEN files are then electronically overlaid with information on individuals taken from supposedly secure federal databanks, which FinCEN has immediate online access to, among them confidential databanks at the Customs Service, the Drug Enforcement Administration, the Securities and Exchange commission, the Secret Service, the Federal Reserve, the Internal Revenue Service, and a couple dozen other agencies.

Finally, by combining all this data, FinCEN creates computerized profiles depicting the backgrounds, demographics, lifestyles, and day-to-day activities of individuals and businesses. FinCEN continually examines these profiles for patterns of murky financial behavior. An alert is emitted when a person is discovered who, for instance, has an SEC history of defrauding investors in penny-stock deals, owns a small gift shop and reports a $100,000 annual income to the IRS, and makes a $500,000 deposit every month followed by $15,000 money transfers to numerous bank accounts around the world. As a result of FinCEN's suspicions, this person would be put under surveillance and shadowed—in the hope that he would eventually be caught in the act of attempting to launder some of his supposedly ill-gotten gains.

FinCEN officials boast about hypothetical cases like these as the reason for the database's existence. But their crowing can't drown out the whispers in Washington that FinCEN's only real accomplishment has been to invade the privacy of millions of innocent Americans by, without their knowledge, eavesdropping on their banking activities and, without justification, randomly peering into their files in sensitive government databanks. "Scrutinizing presumptively legitimate banking transactions, facially lawful transactions—the large percentage of which are in fact legal—raises a very serious problem," says a House Judiciary Committee staffer who has tried in vain to get Congress to investigate FinCEN. "In a free society, the surveillance that we engage in is supposed to be based upon particularized suspicion, not unfocused assumptions and random access to private databanks."

Moreover, in practice the patterns of dubious financial behavior identified by FinCEN are often so obvious that the same result could have been achieved without a massive computerized free-for-all that invades the privacy of everyone just to catch a few. The case of Stefan von Metzger, who ran a plastics brokerage firm, is illustrative of this, and of the way money-laundering convictions are typically obtained.

Von Metzger was tried and found guilty of laundering money for Colombian cocaine traffickers based partially on evidence from a Treasury Department computer scan. The computer noticed that time after time von Metzger shipped huge sums of cash to Panama immediately after making a large deposit in his bank account. But though the computer earns high marks for helping to convict von Metzger, it wasn't the computer that first noticed something awry about his behavior. A tip from observant officials at von Metzger's bank alerted Treasury investigators to his curious deposit and withdrawal activities, and that led to the in-depth computerized probe by the databank.

The course von Metzger's case took is the norm, not the exception, admits David Wilson, head of financial investigations for the Drug Enforcement Administration. Analyzing millions of current banking reports without some prior concerns about an individual, says Wilson, "rarely produces fresh leads."

And when errors creep into databanks such as FinCEN, as inevitably happens with big, unfocused computer systems, the few leads that are produced may point straight at innocent people. FinCEN hasn't been in existence long enough for any clear-cut assessment of its effectiveness or accuracy, but considering the track record of the FBI's NCIC, another open-ended databank, critics say it's Pollyanna-like to think FinCEN is any different. Especially when it was revealed recently that a key source of FinCEN data, another government database, TECS II, is apparently far from reliable.

TECS II (Treasury Enforcement Communications Systems, version two) was developed in 1987 by the Customs Service, an arm of the Treasury Department. Its main task is to determine whether someone entering the country has committed previous customs violations or is wanted by other law enforcement agencies. To do this, each time an individual's name or license plate number is entered into the computer by Customs Service inspectors at nearly three hundred ports of entry into the United States, TECS II immediately searches through its database of nearly one hundred million records as well as those maintained by other agencies, such as the Drug Enforcement Administration, the FBI, and the Defense Department. If no record containing any derogatory information is found, the person or car is cleared to enter the country.

The General Accounting Office conducted a secret survey of TECS II in 1990—secret, say TECS II critics, because its conclusions were not what anybody wanted to hear. GAO looked at sixty-nine TECS II computerized records, and found errors in 59 percent of them—including numerous misspelled names and physical descriptions that were incomplete, inaccurate, or simply left out. These errors, the GAO report said, were sufficiently egregious to result in "known or suspected law violators entering the United States undetected and innocent persons stopped and intensively inspected at the borders for offenses."

In addition, according to GAO sources, the report found security problems at the TECS II data center in Newington, Virginia. Computer printouts containing sensitive information were strewn willy-nilly, and a suspended employee was openly scanning the database using a supervisor's password—with the supervisor's permission. Nothing prevented this employee from entering more inaccurate data into TECS II, the GAO noted.

Yet despite the concerns raised about FinCEN and TECS II, and dozens of other databanks with equally intimidating acronyms, no one has been able to stimulate any Congressional enthusiasm for taking a hard look at these suddenly ubiquitous computer systems in Washington—databanks that barter sensitive government information among themselves with the nonchalance of someone plugging a toaster into a wall. "The agencies running these big networks come up to the Hill each year with charts showing the number of convictions ostensibly obtained from the work of the databanks, and nobody is cynical about these claims or about how many innocent people's files had to be looked at to get these convictions," says a House Judiciary Committee staffer. "The question of whether these convictions could have been gotten some other, better way is never even considered. The nation has lost interest in the rights of innocents."

And that's a loss that could be seriously damaging to a democracy, privacy advocates argue. "We're not talking about credit reports in the private sector; we're talking about someone being thrown on the sidewalk with a gun to his head because of an overly aggressive person in authority taking cues from an overly aggressive databank," says Marc Rotenberg, director of the Computer Professionals for Social Responsibility. "If you've got the wrong person, you're talking about a serious civil liberties question."

Where Have You Gone, Joe Califano?

Databanks used for law enforcement and the sharing of government information for criminal investigations are exempted from the Privacy Act, so these areas are relatively untouched by legislative oversight.

Only the vigilance of Congress, which can restrict their expansion by limiting their funding, acts as a check on such databanks.

By contrast, the confidentiality of information about Americans collected by all other branches of government that administer federal programs and provide services is ostensibly safeguarded by the Privacy Act—virtually the only law on the books that protects the public against intrusions of a central government. But the legislation has failed.

The late Senator Sam Ervin, Jr. (D-N.C.), the 1974 law's chief sponsor, warned that the Privacy Act would become "a hollow piece of legislative mockery" if it wasn't enforced word for word. This statement was remarkably prescient. Hardly had he uttered his admonition before some federal agencies began an assault on the Privacy Act, using any excuse they could find to rewrite it without Congressional approval, usually for political expediency.

In fact, the Privacy Act has been butchered so badly that now privacy advocates rue its very existence. Having the Privacy Act on the books, they say, has fostered the mistaken notion that privacy is, indeed, protected by the government. And this sentiment has dimmed "Congressional interest in privacy in recent years," says David H. Flaherty, a professor of history and law at the University of Western Ontario. "It doesn't matter that many of the most fundamental problems of protecting personal privacy that have emerged since 1974 are not at all addressed under the existing statute. The lack of interest in the enforcement of the Privacy Act has discouraged its revision."

Perhaps the most vicious assault on the Privacy Act is a little-known activity called computer matching. Developed in 1977 by Joseph Califano, Jimmy Carter's Secretary of Health, Education, and Welfare (HEW), computer matching has quietly ensnared supposedly confidential data about Americans in the nets of an ongoing fishing expedition that shows no signs of abating fifteen years later.

Computer matching is a simple concept: its purpose is to put the government's computers to work to rid the nation of deadbeats. As Califano explained it when Project Match was introduced, the technology exists to take the files of welfare recipients and the files of those on the federal government's payroll and instantly match them. Anybody appearing on both lists is double-dipping, ripping off precious taxpayer dollars, and should be prosecuted, Califano said.

That was just the beginning. After welfare cheats, Califano said, computerized matching would track down student loan defaulters, and doctors with their hands too deep in the Medicare cookie jar. And once the program shifted into high gear, there were dozens of more illegal activities that computer matching could unmask.

Initially, few argued with Califano's plan. After all, who could complain about using the millions of dollars in computer equipment that the government owned to catch welfare cheats—especially those infamous on-the-dole women wearing fur coats, driving Cadillacs, and living in Fifth Avenue hotels whom the local news shows parade before the cameras every few years?

"Anything that promises to catch welfare cheats doesn't get a lot of objections," says a House staffer who led a series of hearings during the 1980s examining the impact of computer matching.

But since Califano opened the floodgates with his high-tech attack on the welfare system, computer matching "has become an industry in Washington, D.C.," says a House Government Operations Committee staffer. "Any two computer tapes that will stand still for five seconds, they'll match."

And it's still growing unchecked. By 1986, a decade after Califano initiated Project Match and the last time anybody bothered to count, there were already 127 computerized matches conducted by the federal government, according to the U.S. Congress's Office of Technology Assessment.

That figure may be low. In 1982, Thomas McBride, then inspector general of the Department of Labor, said in hearings before the Senate Committee on Governmental Affairs that there are "roughly five hundred, more or less, routine recurring matches going on."

But whichever estimate is right, it means that, at the very least, an astonishing seven billion personal records about Americans were transferred from databank to databank in Washington, D.C. No wonder, with this avalanche of personal data cascading throughout the government, that getting access to an IRS record is mere child's play for some.

And it's only gotten worse. "You strip a hornet's nest when you look at these activities today," says a senior source at the Office of Management and Budget (OMB) who is closely involved with Privacy Act implementation. "The potential for invasions of privacy and the misuse of personal data are increasing each time we match one database against another."

Some matches seem frivolous: the Selective Service Administration has compared its files with birthday lists kept by chains of ice cream parlors, looking for eighteen-year-olds who haven't registered for the draft.

But most matches are a lot more serious. The Internal Revenue Service allowed Selective Service to look at taxpayer files for draft dodgers. Those who were found received an ominous letter *from the IRS* saying that they faced prosecution if they didn't register.

The Credit Alert System at the Department of Housing and Urban Development lets private banks check HUD records to see if mortgage applicants are in default on Federal Housing Administration loans. Other agencies share with the credit bureaus files on people who owe the government money.

And the Internal Revenue Service matches the income Americans report on federal tax forms against lifestyle databanks that detail where people live, what kinds of cars they own, and how many credit cards they carry. The purpose is to nab anyone who claims to earn only $10,000 a year but lives in a $500,000 home, has five gold Master-Card and Visa cards, and drives a Mercedes.

Match mania is clearly epidemic, but these computerized dredging expeditions would be more acceptable if there were tangible benefits accruing from them. Few have been found. Instead, what have mostly come to light are cases in which computer matching has wrongly identified alleged embezzlers of taxpayer dollars, cases that have embarrassed individuals and showered them in public and social humiliation.

In September 1978, ten months after he inaugurated Project Match, a beaming Joe Califano held a press conference. At it, he read off the names of fifteen D.C.-area residents whom the computers found to be working for the government and taking welfare cash at the same time. They were being indicted on felony counts of defrauding the federal government of $1,200 to $9,900 in welfare payments.

Yvonne Jannifer was one of the names the HEW boss made public, but she never should have been on his list. A year earlier Jannifer, a thirty-two-year-old nurse, had quit her job at a local veterans hospital and gone on welfare after she contracted cervical cancer. Months later, with the cancer under control, she returned to work and tried to have the welfare payments stopped. But the checks kept coming.

At first, Jannifer sent them back with a note saying that she was working again and should be removed from the welfare rolls. But nobody bothered to pay any attention to her correspondence. Finally, she tired of arguing with welfare authorities and figured if they couldn't take her name off the list, that was their problem and not hers. Still, she never cashed the checks that continued to arrive like clockwork. Instead, Jannifer kept them in a drawer in her apartment.

By the time Califano publicly called her a welfare cheat in late 1978, she had half a dozen untouched checks to take to the judge to corroborate her tale of a system that wouldn't let her out of its grip. Jannifer was cleared of the crime, but not of the shame of being branded a welfare scofflaw.

In the end, three others of the Project Match Fifteen were also let go, while four pleaded guilty to misdemeanors and six to felonies. All of the convicted were indigent, and the most any of them repaid was $2,000.

"When you consider the court-appointed attorneys' fees, the salaries of those doing follow-up investigations, and the cost of court time, not to mention the pain and suffering of those mistakenly indicted," says Evan Hendricks, editor of the newsletter *Privacy Times,* who has conducted in-depth analyses of the costs and benefits of computerized matching, "this was not a very cost-effective match."

That's one example, but how about other other matching programs? Do they fare any better than Project Match? To hear the rhetoric, you'd think they do. In a 1983 circular Joseph Wright, OMB's deputy director, called computer matching "a spectacularly effective technique" that will "reap for the American public the savings that private industry has for many years been obtaining."

And the Grace Commission, which studied ways to reduce government inefficiencies, said in 1984 that "computer matching is an effective management tool for identifying fraud, waste, and abuse of government benefits, entitlements, and loan programs." Projected cost savings from it, according to Grace: $15.9 billion over three years.

Moreover, Richard Kusserow, inspector general of the Department of Health and Human Services (HHS), boasted in 1983 that an HHS match of Social Security files with Medicare death files "has led to about $7.5 million in recoveries to date," and predicted that "total savings over time will reach $25.2 million."

Unfortunately, none of these statements is grounded in reality. Few agencies, then or now, have done cost-benefit analyses to assess whether computer matching truly pays off—or whether it's yet another part of the complex house of mirrors that Washington has constructed to trick itself into thinking it's holding down costs. That's what the Office of Technology Assessment reported in 1986, when it found that "only eight percent of the agencies that reported participation in computer matching activities (3 out of 37) did cost-benefit analyses prior to computer matching."

What's more, those agencies that did try to weigh the benefits of matching against its costs did a poor job of it. According to the Congressional General Accounting Office in a 1986 study, "The methods that have been used for assessing the costs and benefits of matching projects were not well developed, well described or standardized."

One of the matching programs the GAO examined took place in 1985. The Social Security Administration (SSA) matched its files of the supplemental income Americans said they earned with what these people were telling the IRS they received in interest and dividends. This match cost $6 million to conduct. And, said OMB's Wright, "it identified 161,000 hits and $114 million in overpayments [to individuals from the SSA]. The match recovered $85 million."

But nobody in the government knows how the SSA came up with the $85 million figure. "That's not surprising," says a senior OMB source. "It's no better today. I get details of dozens of matching programs across my desk every month, but nobody can tell me whether they're working or not."

In one important respect—the only one that Joseph Califano really cared about when he created computer matching—they've worked exceedingly well. They're helping to justify new social programs. In virtually every piece of Great Society–like legislation there is a computer matching provision that says, according to a Republican Senate staffer, " 'Over the life of the program we're going to use matching techniques to find x amount of savings and hold down the costs of the overall project. So this $10 billion, five-year program is really only going to cost $1 billion after computer matching saves us $9 billion.' There may be skepticism about how well matching works—and whether these savings will ever actually be found—but this isn't really about costs and benefits, it's about furthering a legislative agenda."

Surprisingly, Califano agrees. His motives for developing Project Match, he now admits, were political, not fiduciary. Califano viewed computer matching as virtually the last resort to stop Congress and the

American people from shelving his beloved Great Society domestic program, which he helped design as Lyndon Johnson's assistant for domestic affairs a dozen years earlier. In essence, Project Match would be the justifier, the counterargument for the claims that these big government programs were being abused by most of the people taking money from them.

"If I hadn't come up with Project Match, these programs would have been in deep trouble politically in Washington, and with the man in the street," Califano says now. "By 1976 most people were getting tired of taxpayer dollars spent for helping people they suspected were probably getting money and support from some other place also. So with Project Match, the trade-off was clearly worth it. I wanted nothing else but to keep those programs alive. It wasn't even close."

The trade-off Califano speaks of so offhandedly was his blatant retooling of the Privacy Act, just three years after the law was passed. Califano knew Project Match went counter to the language of the Privacy Act and was on shaky legal ground, so to circumvent the act, Califano used the law's so-called routine use exception. That exception lets an agency release personal files without consent as long as the disclosure is for, in the Privacy Act's language, "a purpose which is compatible with the purpose for which it was collected."

Califano reasoned, with somewhat tortured logic, that federal databanks are maintained in part to protect the legitimate interests of the government. Therefore, sharing information from these databanks among agencies to catch government two-timers is compatible with the purpose of maintaining these records in the first place.

But that argument didn't sit well with others in the Carter administration, even in Califano's office. In an August 17, 1977, memo, the HEW attorneys warned Califano that in practice routine use had come to mean that information was disclosed only when there was an "indication that a violation . . . has occurred or might have occurred."

But in computer matching no such suspicion existed about individuals whose data was being pulled. Instead, Califano was proposing a dragnet that would grab up everybody's files, tramp pell-mell through them, and then hold on to those that were found to fit the match—a so-called hit—while disregarding the others. That type of arbitrary use of private records, the HEW attorneys said, clearly was not what Congress had in mind when it included the routine-use provision in the Privacy Act.

HEW counsel were not the only ones that felt this way. The Civil

Service Commission (CSC), which maintained the government payroll and personnel files that Califano needed for the welfare match, initially refused to turn over its records to HEW. Only after a top-level showdown between the CSC general counsel and the HEW acting deputy inspector would CSC officials agree to place their databanks under HEW's microscope.

That virtually ended any real resistance to computer matching. But the activity has continued to nag at Congressional sensibilities. The sheer scope of personal data being bounced with no oversight from one computer to another has always made computer matching so difficult to rationalize in a society that ostensibly believes so deeply in privacy.

So citing horror stories about matching in which innocent victims were finding themselves mistakenly caught in a loose-lipped conversation between computers, and noting the fact that "the cost-effectiveness of computer matching has yet to be clearly demonstrated," the House Committee on Government Operations pushed through a bill in 1988 called the Computer Matching and Privacy Protection Act.

It requires that before anybody is denied any benefits or is accused of double-dipping in the government treasury, information resulting from computer matching must be independently verified, and it mandates that anyone caught doing something illegal must be allowed to contest these findings. What's more, the bill calls for cost-benefit analyses to be done on all matching schemes, an exercise that had been virtually forgotten since the mid-1980s.

This law is just a Band-Aid and not a repeal of match mania, House staffers who worked on the bill admit. It's unlikely that the cost-benefit analyses are going to be rigorously done. And there still are going to be a lot of victims of incorrect matches caught in embarrassing and frightening messes—only now they have a bureaucratic maze to slosh through in order to extricate themselves.

But, says one House staffer, "At least we've thrown a monkey wrench into the process and made matching more difficult to do because we've beefed up the red tape. If that deters a few overly aggressive matches, perhaps we've accomplished something."

The European Gambit

The Privacy Act was Sam Ervin's last hurrah. In 1973, the seventy-seven-year-old senior Senator from North Carolina had already announced his intention to retire the next year. Ironically, after nineteen years in the Senate, Ervin's remarkably effective four-star performance as chairman of the Watergate committee had just made it obvious that the longtime constitutional watchdog was a national treasure.

And made privacy a highly desirable commodity. On the heels of the Watergate hearings there were numerous other revelations about government excesses and intrusions into people's lives. In fact, the Watergate break-ins were just the surface. Equally egregious Nixon-inspired activities that came to light included the retrieval of IRS records on supposed enemies of the President; the creation of huge covert government databanks on thousands of Americans for the purpose of keeping tabs on Vietnam War protesters, civil rights activists, and alleged political dissidents; and Nixon staff overtures to at least a dozen federal agencies to open up their computerized files to executive-branch lieutenants whenever they were asked to.

Worse yet, it was disclosed that similar activities had been undertaken by Lyndon Johnson, John Kennedy, the CIA, the U.S. Army, and the National Security Agency. That all of this could be done with virtually no fear of legal retribution highlighted the utter lack of laws on the books protecting people from the government in the looming computer age. In turn, this solidified Congressional support for legislation clearly defining, in a way that would keep the public informed, when and how the government would be allowed to collect personal data, and the procedures by which government agencies could share these files with others.

Equally important, many sensed a privacy law was needed to put Watergate behind us—and to stop the ceaseless conspiracy notions that suffused the United States then. Even respected think-tankers such as Daniel Ellsberg, a Nixon target himself who at one time had high-level security clearances within the Pentagon and government intelligence, were claiming that it was too late for the United States: Big Brother, they said, was actually already operating a menacing secret shadow government that kept dossiers on each of us for ultimately venal purposes. With tales like these circulating—none, time has shown, apparently were true—clearly legislation was needed badly, if for no other reason than to prove to ourselves that in a democracy privacy was still a just cause.

That there would be a Privacy Act was suddenly a foregone conclusion. But to ensure that the law's vigor was never diluted, Ervin argued that a Privacy Commission, an independent group of experts "charged with protecting individual privacy as a value in government and society," was essential to ride herd on the federal government to comply with the dictates of the Privacy Act. Without it, Ervin said, it would be impossible, even with a law on the books, to "protect people's freedoms from the incursions of the arbitrary exercise of government power and to provide for the fair and responsible use of this power."

But Gerald Ford, who had become President by this time, didn't like the idea. Ford was opposed to setting up yet another costly bureaucratic layer in Washington—especially at a time when inflation was ravaging the government's ability to square its finances. So Ford threatened to drop his support for the privacy measure if the creation of a Privacy Commission was included in the final bill.

The Privacy Act became law, but without the Privacy Commission. It was a bitter defeat for Ervin, one that continued to nag at him until his death seven years later. It presaged the failure of the law that was to become his legacy. "The Privacy Act, if enforced, would be a pretty good thing," Ervin told reporter David Burnham in 1980 for Burnham's book *The Rise of the Computer State*. "But the government doesn't like it. Government has an insatiable appetite for power, and it will not stop usurping power unless it is restrained by laws it cannot repeal or nullify. There are mighty few laws it cannot nullify."

Sam Ervin's dream of a Privacy Commission is not yet dead. It continues to reemerge yearly on Capitol Hill, mainly because Ervin's urgent warnings, which he uttered so often throughout his tenure, that a computer-dominated society is a constitutional problem are becoming harder and harder to dismiss—especially considering the activities of direct marketers, the credit bureaus, the information underground, the shadow data sellers, technocriminals, and the government. So, since 1984, first Representative Glenn English (D-Okla.) and now Representative Robert Wise (D-W.Va.), the former and current chairmen of the House Subcommittee on Government Information, Justice and Agriculture, have introduced legislation calling for the creation of a Privacy Commission. It has a new name now, though, the Data Protection Board.

It's also not exactly what Ervin had in mind, but it comes extremely close. Where it falls short is in the type of power it would wield. The board, a three-member, bipartisan panel appointed by the President, would have solely an advisory role, and, unlike Ervin's Privacy Commission, would not be a Privacy Act oversight or regulatory body. Still, in some crucial ways the Data Protection Board would achieve Ervin's aims and have a significant impact on information collection and dissemination. It would be charged with recommending and issuing opinions about new government and private-sector databanks; investigating Privacy Act complaints; and supporting research into the social implications of new computer and communications technologies.

This means, says Congressman Wise, that, for instance, the embarrassing brouhaha over Lotus Marketplace: Household, the product developed by the credit bureau Equifax and the software house Lotus Development (see chapter 4)—killed after, as the companies put it, an "emotional firestorm of public concern and consumer privacy"—could have been avoided: "A company planning a new information product could ask the Data Protection Board to help identify and address privacy issues before risking millions of dollars that could be lost in a consumer backlash."

Unfortunately, not enough members of Congress feel the same way. In the seven years the idea of a Data Protection Board has been proposed in Congress, it has yet to generate enough support even to get out of committee. Indeed, the level of backing has been so dismally low that now, as one Government Operations Committee staffer admits, "we don't even ask people to take a position on the board yet, because they'll say no and not be able to ever retreat from this position, lest they risk charges of issues waffling. So we're just trying to, through yearly hearings, move them in our direction slowly without making them commit themselves one way or the other."

That strategy has produced some small gains. With consumer and individual privacy concerns swelling rapidly in this country, a few enlightened corporations are softening their stand against a Data Protection Board, and suggesting that having one may not be such a bad idea after all. As a senior vice president at a major information reseller told me: "It could deflect some of the heat from us, show that we're open to recommendations about how we collect and resell information, and give the public a place, besides us, to vent its frustrations."

That kind of attitude among corporations toward a Data Protection

Board, however, is just in the gestation stage—and unlikely to spread to enough key companies to make a difference for quite some time. Nevertheless, even in the face of this, supporters of the panel are not glum. Quite to the contrary, lately they're suddenly brandishing a revivified sense of optimism. That's because they've recently gained unexpected newfound allies—ones with significant political clout in Washington—to join their call for an American privacy panel, namely the European political and diplomatic community. It's an unlikely source of support, but, as it turns out, this community has good reason to get involved in the fight in the States.

In Europe the notion of a data protection panel is not a foreign one. Great Britain has had one since 1984, and those in Germany and France predate England's by six years. Besides these, Austria, Sweden, Norway, the Isle of Man, the Netherlands, Australia, and Ireland all have permanent data protection agencies. And in North America, Canada has one that's nearly fifteen years old. While most of these Western commissions have in the past operated purely within their own borders—and have hardly ever interacted with Americans—indications are that their impact on the United States is soon going to be far-reaching.

With the decision to unite the disparate European marketplace and to eliminate intercountry trade barriers and border constraints on the Continent, new directives will be issued soon to establish unilateral policies for the unrestricted transfer of personal information in Europe. Their purpose: to remove any obstacles to data exchanges within the open-trade territory, impediments that could stand in the way of uninhibited transborder commerce. Rules will be promulgated to ensure that companies are able to access and send essential electronic records—concerning personnel, credit, banking, and other financial matters, as well as marketing and demographics—without compromising the privacy of individual Europeans in the process.

A draft of these new privacy directives is already circulating, and it's sending a chill through the American business community. Among other things, it requires that any company, European or foreign, transmitting data within the Continent adhere to rigorous rules respecting the privacy of personal information. These include restrictions on the transfer of personal information to third parties, procedures to inform individuals about data transfers and get consent before they're performed, and methods to let individuals access their own files. In one of the most stunning examples of how seriously European countries plan to discipline those that are not prepared to protect personal information, the French Data Commission last year prevented the automobile maker Fiat from electronically transferring employee records from Paris to Rome because Italy has yet to adopt a data protection law.

This is the kind of restrictive atmosphere that U.S. companies have never had to endure. But they have it to look forward to if they want to do business in Europe after 1992. Restrictions on information storage and dissemination in this country, except for the weak rules imposed by the Fair Credit Reporting Act and the Privacy Act, have typically been the result of industry ethics and gentlemen's agreements—for instance, the telephone companies have adopted internal policies mandating that records of who's calling whom are private and not for sale, but no law exists to ensure that these policies are never abrogated.

American companies may be comfortable with a laissez-faire approach to data privacy, but the Europeans disdain it, and now they feel compelled by the ambitious new trading and industrial community they're attempting to form to take an active stand against it.

The Europeans want to convince their counterparts in the United States to set up a panel that will serve as a peer group to their privacy commissions, one that could see to it that American data-protection regulations mesh with European rules and meet European standards. And one that could help thwart any uncomfortable episodes in which Europe has to step in and review the records-management practices of, say, General Motors before it allows the automobile giant's overseas subsidiary to access personal credit files in order to approve car loans and leases in Europe.

Potential scenarios such as this suggest that the Europeans could make doing business in Europe a nightmare for American companies, says Congressman Wise, unless the United States cooperates and shows that it, too, is serious about online information protection: "This could affect so many American companies—banks, insurance companies, credit grantors, computer service bureaus, direct marketers, pharmaceutical firms, and manufacturers. Any company whose business involves the transfer of any type of personal data could become subject to European regulation."

And in a free-market economy such as the one in the United States, that's unacceptable. So now American companies find themselves in the touchy position of having to decide which is the worse evil: leaving themselves vulnerable to the constant threat of outside interference and information-practices oversight as the price of doing business on the Continent, which for many, such as IBM, represents 50 percent or more of annual sales, or an internal advisory panel like the Data Protection Board. Increasingly, the answer seems to be a newly minted respect for a privacy commission. "Two years ago the business community listened politely to what we were proposing," says a senior staffer at the House Government Operations Committee. "Now companies are telling us they're willing to seriously examine this."

That's a 180-degree shift that nobody could have expected. And it indicates that quietly the Europeans may be accomplishing what august, highly respected, brash Americans such as Sam Ervin never could: they may be moving U.S. corporations away from their decades-old hardened stance against a Data Protection Commission and making it a distinct possibility that the United States will soon join much of the rest of the industrialized West in having such a panel.

Perhaps in time for the twentieth anniversary of the Privacy Act. In time to allow Sam Ervin finally to rest in peace.

Hard Work

Who steals my purse steals trash; 'tis
  something, nothing;
'Twas mine, 'tis his, and has been slave to
  thousands;
But he that filches from me my good name
Robs me of that which not enriches him,
And makes me poor indeed.

William Shakespeare, *Othello*, act III,
scene iii

Most of the time a stiff wind blows across the seas in the Gulf of
Mexico near New Orleans. Sometimes, though, a squall bursts
like an avalanche on the black water, creating rollicking tidal currents
that attack boats with a vicious draw and tug. But the roustabouts
usually take these ill winds in stride. Monthlong shifts spent offshore
on giant oil rigs can be so tedious that even breakneck gulf weather
is a welcome hiatus from the interminable boredom.

That's how Ernest Trent felt—until October 2, 1986. Early that wind-
tumbled morning the thirty-nine-year-old Pennzoil roustabout was on
a boat near Galveston Bay, riding fast and choppy seas. He was waiting for the mammoth steel-beamed crane on board to get into position
to lift him off the boat's main deck so that he could carry supplies to
a series of offshore rigs.

Trent was holding on to the crane's guide wire with his right arm
when suddenly the boat ducked into a bloated five-foot wave. The
spray blocked the crane operator's view. He lost sight of Trent, whose
grip had partially slipped. The operator shoved the handle of his
machine down swiftly and the crane's basket rocketed upward, with
Trent barely in tow. For a matter of seconds, Trent says, "I was dangling in the air by my hand."

Then, his strength dissipated, he let go and dropped to the ground.
His arm pulsated and shook as though it had come loose. Alternating
sensations of numbness and shooting pain coursed through it.

They still do today. Trent's doctors told him that he has a permanently stretched limb. Heavy labor is impossible. So, after fifteen years at Pennzoil, Trent went on workmen's compensation. And in that accidental tumble on the broken seas, the weekly earnings of the Bossier, Louisiana, father of nine plummeted from more than $400 per week to about $260, a 35 percent drop. "Now we're just existing," Trent says. "Our nostrils are barely above water."

Since then, Trent has applied for nearly two hundred jobs—everything from door-to-door sales to stocking shelves—but he's been turned down for all of them. It makes no sense. He has a high school diploma; he has successfully passed correspondence courses in building construction, accounting, and management; and he is taking credits at a local community college, where he's on the dean's list. So why the complete brush-off from employers who are hiring workers with less educational background and fewer skills than he? "I'm blacklisted," says Trent.

He found this out when, in desperation, he begged a friend who supervises construction crews for a job. "I asked him to help me out with anything, even something menial and low-paying," Trent says. "But he told me, 'Ernie I can't hire you. Nobody can. Your name's not worth much to anybody.' "

That's because Employers Information Service, Inc. (EIS), a Gretna, Louisiana, databanker, has a file on Trent that reads like a filthy rap sheet to virtually every employer in the Southwest. Trent's transgression: he collected workmen's compensation benefits due him.

In its vast mainframes, EIS maintains upwards of a million files on workers throughout the United States in oil, gas, construction, and other heavy industries. These records contain names of those who apply for workmen's compensation and those who sue their employers after an accident. What's more, they also note, with no explanation, whether an employer would consider rehiring an injured worker after he gets healthy.

That means if a ditchdigger loses his arm in a run-in with a bulldozer and, of course, would not be rehired because he lacks the requisite number of limbs to give his former company an honest day's work anymore, he is marked as an undesirable and unwanted employee on the EIS lists.

EIS sells information from its databanks to hundreds of member companies. What EIS knows is important to these employers because workmen's compensation claims are overwhelming businesses, particularly on the Gulf Coast. Some employers in Louisiana and Texas are paying 20 percent of their overall payroll toward covering workmen's compensation—at least double the rate of the rest of the country. They're charged this because oil and gas companies, which dominate the region, have the highest accident rate of any industry in the United States.

So with this in mind, using EIS makes sense and even smacks of good business judgment—except for one thing, claim dozens of unemployed workers with stories similar to Trent's: many of these EIS subscribers, they say, are improperly rejecting job seekers solely on the basis of EIS reports that say they were injured on the job and collected benefits. Their present desire and ability to work doesn't matter, they assert; if EIS says they ever took money from the workmen's comp pool, there's no job for them. Period. That's a weighty allegation and, on the face of it, would seem hard to prove. However, surprisingly, some employers do concede, without much hesitation or embarrassment, that the workers' suspicions are justified.

King Fisher is one such employer. He's president of King Fisher Marine Service, Inc., an offshore rig supplier in the Southwest that, he says, is "the biggest homegrown company in this county." King Fisher is a charter member of EIS, a subscriber since 1966, when the databanker was founded as a nonprofit corporation by a group of local high rollers, including Zapata Oil Corporation, then run by George Bush.

Fisher is an old-timer full of brawn and bluster. His friends say they don't remember him backing down from a fight in his lifetime. That's evident in the way he manages his business. Fisher's knack for gutty survival has steered his fifty-year-old company through, he says, "three of these depressions in my lifetime." During that time, Fisher adds, he's learned "when to operate strictly by the rules and when to operate on instinct."

And relying on EIS is one of those things that his gut tells him is right. "In these times, when finding a good, dependable, hard worker is more difficult than ever, I'm not going to hire the son of a bitch who's just sued somebody down the street," says Fisher. "And EIS can tell me who that SOB is."

This pull-up-the-pants-high-and-duke-it-out approach toward his employees has served him well, Fisher says, and he has proof: "We give out a diamond pin with twenty-five diamonds to each person that's given us twenty-five years of service. We've handed out twenty-five in the last twenty-five years. That's loyalty."

Hercules Offshore Company, near Galveston, Texas, has an attitude similar to King Fisher's. This came out loud and clear during an eye-opening deposition taken in September 1989, when Hercules personnel manager David Case was asked about his company's use of EIS data. Said Case: "[EIS] is a 1-800 number. You call the employee's full name in and at the same time give his Social Security number," and within minutes you get back a report on that worker. When Hercules looks at the EIS data, Case continued, it has one set rule: it hires only workers whose reports indicate that "everything is clean. That way you can keep the riffraff out."

> **Attorney:** Does Hercules Offshore provide information to EIS on its former employees?
> **Case:** Yes, anytime we terminate a person we go through the same procedure. There's a form we file with EIS and they enter it into their computer.
> **Attorney:** If [a worker's] report reflected that he had a previous injury and litigation had been instituted, would that . . . exclude him from hire under Hercules's policies?
> **Case:** Under our policies and procedures, yes.

But that stance—and King Fisher's—is illegal in many states. Although the federal Fair Credit Reporting Act lets employers use computerized background data on job applicants for hiring decisions, in much of the country they're not allowed to reject someone just because he previously filed for workmen's compensation. That would essentially be a kind of entrapment—penalizing a worker for taking advantage of a program that the state created for him to use.

For its part, EIS stresses that its purpose is simply to provide objective information, and not to make it impossible for workmen's compensation claimants to find work. "We have no vendetta against injured workers," says EIS counsel Rutledge Clement. Indeed, EIS clearly states this in its application, which all subscribers have to sign before getting access to its data.

What's more, Clement avers, EIS won't tolerate misuse of its database. "If any subscriber," Clement says, "uses EIS data for a blacklist or any other illegal purpose, it will never purchase another piece of information from us."

Perhaps, but there's some question as to how hungry EIS is to police its membership. Not long ago, Boh Brothers, a local contractor, gave injured offshore diver Bruce Buchanan $10,000 to settle a lawsuit in which Buchanan claimed that Boh had relied solely on a negative EIS report to deny him a job. Although Boh denied any liability, EIS never investigated the company.

That's not surprising, say local labor activists such as David Czernik, executive director of the Louisiana Consumers League, and Carl Crowe, assistant to the president of the Louisiana AFL-CIO. "It's the big and politically powerful companies in New Orleans that sustain EIS," says Crowe. "So EIS is not about to bite the hands that feed it."

Ernest Trent, by the way, finally landed a job in late 1989. He's a security manager and supervisor trainee with Burger King, a company that is not a member of EIS. He's not making as much as he earned when he suffered the injury at Pennzoil four years ago, but he's happy to be working again and "paying the bills on time." That's more than can be said for many other workers in the area.

Data Cowboys

What's happening to these injured workers is not unique to them or their region. Increasingly, U.S. employers are combing databases of all kinds to find out anything they can about job applicants. Via computer, fax, and phone, employers check credit files, employment and school records, and motor vehicle histories. They find out whether an applicant has collected large medical claims. And they learn things they're not supposed to know: for example, that a person has been arrested, even if he was later acquitted or the charges were dropped. Virtually nothing about a person's background is sacrosanct or unavailable when employers are considering whether or not to hire somebody.

Indeed, providing personal employee data to companies is a booming business now. "It's spiraled out of sight," says a personnel manager at a Fortune 500 company. It's hard to believe, but that's almost an understatement: sales of preemployment data are growing as much as 75 percent a year for some information companies. The larger and more established—the credit bureau Equifax, Fidelifacts Metropolitan New York, and Apscreen, among others—say it's not enough to provide just raw data as EIS does. In fact, they say, that's doing job seekers a great disservice, because it fails to give the full picture.

So instead, these companies gather, combine, and package information from various databases and produce easy-to-read, simple-to-understand summaries that describe applicants' financial conditions, criminal and driving backgrounds, and business relationships. And they always remind clients, says David Karas, Equifax's marketing manager for preemployment screening, that their "data is just one part of the preemployment investigation." The other, he says, is "creative interviewing to find out what makes an applicant tick."

A thorough background report from these larger preemployment screening companies can cost thousands of dollars—much too expensive for many employers with high turnover, or for those, such as retailers, that may hire hundreds of people a year. That's where cut-rate data sellers come in. For just a few dollars per report—EIS files, for example, are available for less than $5 each—these less reputable databankers compile raw, unchecked information from credit bureaus, motor vehicle agencies, courthouses, and other sources, and resell them in virtually the same form in which they get them. "The activities of these data cowboys worry me," says Apscreen president Thomas C. Lawson.

One reason for concern is that some of the information they offer may not be legal to use when hiring. For instance, one of the more aggressive databankers, Information Resource Service Company (IRSC) in Fullerton, California, offers a pre-employment criminal check service, which provides data on whether a person has been arrested, even if the arrest did not result in conviction.

When I reported in *Business Week* in September 1990 that IRSC provides arrest data, IRSC Chairman Jack Reed wrote a letter to the magazine denying this. But then he seemed to admit that, at least in some cases, IRSC did make this information available. Reed stated that IRSC provides information from over 7,000 databases holding public and private records nationwide—including "criminal indices from various courts." He added that, with some exceptions, a California statute prohibits employers from requesting or seeking arrest information about prospective employees. But according to Reed's letter, the company will apparently sell this data to the subscribers after they sign a contract saying that they have read the statute, a copy of which IRSC sends to them, and that they agree to abide by it. What's more, Reed claimed IRSC "has and will cancel privileges of anyone found violating" these laws.

Nonetheless, the sales literature IRSC sent me is less cautious. In a description of IRSC's "criminal history check," sample data is included for a California job applicant that lists eight arrests—but no convictions. Though the sales literature cautions that "the extent and format of the information will vary from state to state," it also boasts that "armed with this kind of information, an employer can select the best applicant for the job."

IRSC shouldn't be supplying this kind of information, says Thomas Norton, president and owner of New York–based IRSC competitor Fidelifacts, because it results in an immediate bias against the job applicant, though he hasn't done anything wrong under the law. "Any employer that would reject a person who has an acquittal in his past is leaping into the unknown and asking for a lawsuit," notes Norton.

José Millan, California's deputy labor commissioner, agrees. Arrest data when no conviction followed may be juicy and just what an employer wants to know about a job applicant, he says, but "it's illegal for employers to have."

IRSC won't say where it gets this arrest data from, but private investigators think they may know its origin. They say databankers quietly tap friendly sources in the law enforcement community to obtain such highly sensitive and private information. They speculate this may be true of IRSC president Jack Reed, a fast-shooting information junkie known for dabbling in data overkill. Others feel IRSC may have the ability to access information that is not readily available over public databases. This possibility makes them view Reed with a degree of envy.

Steve Mednick, general counsel at the preemployment databanker CDB/Infotek in Orange, California, an IRSC competitor, is irate over Reed's activities, especially when CDB, Mednick says, is taking important steps to improve its privacy policies. Among them, CDB recently stopped selling credit reports to customers for preemployment investigations. This action came after a bill was proposed in California (later vetoed as antibusiness by Governor Pete Wilson) making it unlawful for employers to look at credit reports.

CDB viewed the bill as a warning that privacy matters to the voters, if not to the governor, so the company bailed out of selling credit data to its customers entirely. "It's inevitable that a bill like that will be adopted before long," says Mednick. "And we wanted to get out of the business before someone else forces us to, on their timetable."

But, says Mednick, if CDB is being so careful about intrusions of privacy—to the point that it has stopped selling legal, though sensitive, data, and has lost legitimate revenue in the process—why is IRSC allowed to provide arrest information in full view of the authorities?

Mednick posed this question to some FBI agents—clients of CDB—who were visiting his offices. "They just shrugged," Mednick says, "and made some comment about how bureaucracies move slowly."

But they did speculate that there's just one place Reed could be getting data about arrests that led to no disposition or conviction. "They said that the FBI could be the only source for that information," says Mednick.

IRSC's raw arrest data is prized by employers. IRSC claims Bank of America recently became a customer and now purchases thousands of arrest records each month. A Bank of America spokesperson could not confirm or deny this claim. Perhaps to avoid becoming too obvious about its activities, IRSC apparently filters some of the requests for this arrest data through the National Fraud Investigation Center (NFIC) in Ambler, Pennsylvania. NFIC admits that it provides these records to IRSC and dozens of other customers. But despite what the feds told Mednick, NFIC won't concede that the FBI is its conduit for the data.

And because the information it provides is improper for most of us to have, NFIC counsels its clients on ways to use it that ensure avoiding scrapes with the law. Says NFIC principal Jim Kerins: "We tell our customers, 'If a person has an arrest record, you don't have to hire him. Just don't tell him that your investigation turned up an arrest five years ago on a case that was eventually dismissed. Don't say that's the reason you're turning him down for the job. Instead say that you've found a better candidate, and leave it at that.' Any other answer is tantamount to putting a gun to your head."

Even with a growing chorus of complaints against him, Jack Reed now seems to want even wider access to data. "Reed is lobbying friendly Congressmen to sponsor a bill that would give employers free and open access to the FBI's National Crime Information Center," says IRSC vice president Sharon Guenther.

This vast databank, as noted earlier, makes available the names and records of not only criminals, but also anyone that law enforcement authorities have questioned about puzzling or unusual behavior. If NCIC was available to all employers, someone convicted of trespass in a political demonstration, or a forty-year-old who was convicted of a minor infraction when he was eighteen, might find it difficult to get a job.

It's unlikely, though, that any legislator will risk the wrath of frightened constituents when Reed proposes making NCIC virtually an open book.

With so much data available about them, and with workers not knowing what's being said about them in the information employers receive, job applicants are at a distinct disadvantage. That's because, these days, any time the information is damaging, the would-be employee isn't hired, employment experts say. "Hiring decisions have become data-driven and not values-driven," says David W. Foerster, Jr., executive director of the Resource Center, an Atlanta-based employee counseling firm, who bemoans "the checklist mentality of so many personnel managers these days."

Especially those that use computer software like the CompuScore System from National CompuScreen, Inc., a company based in the suburbs of Portland, Oregon. CompuScore, claims its developers, can predict a person's propensity for extreme substance abuse, theft, or violence. It does this through an eighty-question survey that asks such questions as "How often do you put things off that you know you should do sooner?" and "How often are you dissatisfied with your performance?"

Interviewees respond to these queries with an electronic wand rubbed over a bar code, and these digitized answers are sent via modem to CompuScreen. There computers tabulate and evaluate the test, and transmit the results back to the employer within twenty seconds. CompuScore's conclusions are proven to be 96 percent to 100 percent correct, says National CompuScreen vice president William Johnston. "It even unmasks individuals trying to deceive the system by presenting themselves as ideal job candidates," Johnston adds.

CompuScore is attracting its share of followers. More than three thousand companies are using it already.

To David Foerster, the claims for CompuScore are hogwash. There's no way to prove its success rate, he says, without following thousands of people through their daily lives for years after they take the test—and National CompuScreen is not doing that. What CompuScore does show, says Foerster, is that most personnel managers have lost the ability to find out what they need to know about an applicant in face-to-face, heart-to-heart job interviews.

"Employers are so caught up in the technology, the databases, and other gadgetry at their disposal, that they forget what hiring is all about," Foerster says. "It's really about being open to the person across the desk and going beyond the obvious, the surface, and seeing what's going inside the person applying for a job—to make sure that he or she culturally, ethically, and humanistically fits into the company's mandate and purpose."

Foerster adds that people are turned down for jobs because of such wrong reasons as bad credit records, large insurance claims, unacceptable habits and lifestyles, or questionable past medical or psychological conditions. And they're given no chance to explain.

Indeed, they're not hired even if they've turned their lives around or this data has no bearing on the type of job they're being considered for. Says Lawson of Apscreen, "An applicant's chances can be weakened by data that's actually not negative, but that's just deemed negative by somebody's very subjective judgment."

And he can be penalized when the data is incorrect. That was the case with James Russell Wiggins. In December 1989, the thirty-six-year-old father of four landed a $70,000-a-year sales job at District Cablevision in Washington, D.C. But six weeks later, a routine background check showed that Wiggins had been convicted of cocaine possession. The next day, Wiggins was fired.

Cablevision claims it took this step not just because Wiggins had a history of drug use, but also because he hadn't told Cablevision about this conviction up front.

But Wiggins says he didn't lie to Cablevision: "I never went before a judge in my life."

Equifax, the company that investigated Wiggins's past for Cablevision, made a big blunder: it pulled the criminal record of James Ray Wiggins instead of the file on James Russell Wiggins—even though the two men not only have different middle names but their birth dates, addresses, and Social Security numbers also don't match.

The day after he was fired, Wiggins roared into Equifax's offices in McLean, Virginia. "I'm calling the cops," he screamed. "You're ruining my life."

For over two hours, Equifax managers argued back, telling him there was nothing they could do about what happened. Incomprehensibly, they even told him, says Wiggins, that as far as they were concerned they had no proof that any error was actually made.

"They stonewalled me," says Wiggins, "because it turns out that by then they had already rechecked and knew that they had made a big mistake by confusing my report with someone else's."

Equifax won't comment on the incident. Cablevision tells reporters Wiggins can have his job back. Wiggins says that's not what the company is telling him. He's suing Equifax for about $1 million in damages in a case that's still pending.

Job seekers have some legal protections against employers who use databanks overly aggressively and frivolously, but, like most federal privacy laws, these protections don't work very well. The key legislation they have on their side, incomprehensibly, is not a labor law, but a consumer financial bill: the Fair Credit Reporting Act (FCRA). Under this act, it's illegal for employers to obtain any personal data about job applicants unless the employee has given written permission to do so.

That, as it turns out, is a *pro forma* activity. Regardless of the position, anyone applying for a job must sign the bottom line of an employment application. The fine print just above it reads something like this: "Under the provisions of the Fair Credit Reporting Act, 15 U.S.C. Sec. 1681, et seq., notice is hereby given that an investigative consumer report may be made which may include information pertaining to your creditworthiness, character, general reputation, personal characteristics, and model of living, which will be used for employment purposes. An investigation into your workers' compensation, accident, medical, and psychological background may also be conducted."

Few would have the mettle not to agree to this, especially when it's implicitly understood that if the application goes unsigned, it's unlikely that it will be given consideration.

But there's another part of the FCRA that ostensibly provides more protection. "Employers also have to inform the applicant when a particular piece of data has been used in the decision not to hire him," says Lee Paterson, a prominent employment-law attorney with Sonnenschein Carlin Nath & Rosenthal. "And they have to clearly indicate in writing where they obtained this information from, just as a credit grantor has to tell a consumer about the credit report it used to denied him credit."

In theory, that FCRA provision should help, because it gives a job applicant the opportunity to ask the databanker to show him a copy of the file that led to the rejection of his application, and it lets him delete or correct any errors in this file that reflect negatively on him.

But this doesn't work because, admits Jean Noonan, a former associate director for credit practices at the Federal Trade Commission (FTC), which oversees enforcement of the FCRA, few employees ever tell job applicants what data they've used for hiring decisions, and who gave it to them.

"It's not the same situation at all as we have with credit grantors," says Noonan. "By and large, credit grantors follow the FCRA to the letter. They've memorized the rules to a T, respond to thousands of applications a month, and have incorporated into their policies the kinds of written responses they must send to everybody who's applying for credit."

Employers, on the other hand, Noonan explains, have to comply with a lot of state and federal labor laws—they're inundated with mammoth paperwork and bookkeeping obligations—and their FCRA responsibilities often get lost in the shuffle. That is, when they're even aware of them. "We need to do a better job of educating employers about what they have to do when they buy data about a job applicant," Noonan says. "Ordinarily when we find a large number of companies committing a small number of violations each, then it's an education problem."

As a result of my discussions with the FTC on this matter in 1990, a broad investigation involving dozens of companies was initiated. Finally in 1991, the first settlement emerging from this investigation occurred. Electronic Data Systems (EDS), a subsidiary of General Motors, was found to have turned down about 150 people for jobs since 1989 in part because of poor credit reports. But EDS never told the job applicants that. In settling the case, EDS agreed to notify prospective employees about the credit data it used to make its hiring decisions and to give them the name of the credit bureau that provided the data so they could obtain copies of their reports.

There's more to come. "Several companies, both large and small, have been notified that they are the subject of inquiries involving the same question," says Barry Cutler, director of the FTC's Bureau of Consumer Protection.

Compounding the problem is the fact that it's extremely difficult for anybody to prove that an employer has denied him his rights of notification under the FCRA. It's tough to be certain that a specific piece of data an employer obtained was actually used in the hiring decision.

Attorney Lee Paterson recalls one case in which a client requested a routine preemployment report on someone even though "he already made the decision to say no to the job seeker." In this report, the employer found out all kinds of dubious things about the applicant's character that he had never asked for—and didn't need to know. His mind was already made up to hire someone else, so he never told the prospective employee what he learned, because it wasn't a factor in his negative decision.

"The [applicant] argued that the employer failed to live up to his FCRA responsibilities," says Patterson. "But he didn't have a chance in court. In the first place, in this case it wasn't true. The employer was not bound to tell him about the data he obtained, because it had no bearing on the decision he made not to hire the applicant. What's more, even if it were true, where could the applicant ever find the evidence to convince a jury that it was?"

At this point, many employment experts say, the real dangers from the excessive use of data in making hiring decisions are yet to be felt, but they will be. These activities, they argue, are already setting in motion trends that will ultimately shock the U.S. system and American society. Because of them, the have-nots will eventually have even less. Says David Foerster of the Resource Center, "The fallout from all of this is that we're creating a large group of unemployable people. It's not because they're bad and don't want to work, but because they don't meet the data criteria that [are] set as a standard for all new hires."

For instance, people in lower socioeconomic groups tend to have worse credit reports than people who are employed. Without a weekly salary or a financial cushion, it's impossible for them to keep up with monthly credit payments. So, asks Thomas Lawson of the employee-data firm Apscreen, "How can you reasonably deny a person employment solely on the basis that their credit record isn't spotless? That's what they need the job for: to clean up their credit records."

But it happens often. Admits a personnel manager at an electronic-components company that buys employee data, "Many people are punished even if they sincerely want to rehabilitate themselves."

This is a uniquely modern problem—another technological defeat for privacy. In the predatabanking age, there were natural safeguards that kept employers who wanted to be overly intrusive from succeeding. Previously, because record systems were "inefficient"—that is, they weren't computerized and information wasn't freely, automatically, and rapidly available to every desktop just for the asking— people who had been to prison, got into bad financial straits, or even went fist to fist with their bosses in a courtroom could get a fresh start someplace else. Indeed, in the very old days, moving from one frontier town to another just thirty miles away meant the opportunity to begin again, with nobody mentioning your past, because nobody had a clue about it.

But this traditional freedom is now gone. Bad news on today's electronic wireless, the ubiquitous PC, follows everybody like a dark cloud and is impossible to shake loose. With databanks, "the past is haunting," says Sanford Sherizen, president of Data Security Systems, Inc., in Natick, Massachusetts, a computer security consulting firm. "There is no second chance anymore."

Eye Spy

Surviving the rigors of data mania to get a job may be difficult, but even tougher for some workers is what they have to put up with once they're working. It's a disturbing and surprising truth, but employees have virtually no privacy rights in the workplace—and increasingly, companies are taking advantage of this.

All a company needs is some legitimate suspicion—for example, it thinks an employee is stealing or it suspects there's a saboteur in-house leaking new product plans to the competition—and it may arbitrarily rifle through desks, bug offices, and tramp willy-nilly through employee property. What's more, it can do all of this secretly, without ever notifying targeted employees that they're under suspicion and without telling these workers what was heard, witnessed, and discovered, even after the snooping has ended.

It sounds sleazy and devious, not something that blue-chip companies would be involved in. But that perception is dead wrong, says William P. Callahan, president of the private investigation agency United Intelligence, Inc., in New York. Lately, Callahan says, his business is mushrooming, with prestigious corporate clients acting more like "Spy vs. Spy" characters than an executive elite. "It doesn't matter if they have $3,000 suits," says Callahan. "They still want me to do everything from installing listening devices in workers' locker rooms to tailing employees."

And there's not much that makes them flinch in embarrassment. General Electric says it occasionally hides tiny fish-eye lenses behind pinholes in ceilings and walls to watch employees suspected of crimes. Du Pont says it monitors its loading docks twenty-four hours a day with hidden cameras for theft, drugs, sex, and "other forms of rock and roll." And Chicago-based Management Recruiters, Inc., one of the nation's leading headhunters, says its bosses quietly peer at their employees' computerized schedules to see who interviews the most job candidates.

"The electronic sweatshop is here," says Data Security Systems' Sherizen.

That may be true. At the same time, it's difficult to condemn any company that is concerned with worker productivity, protecting company secrets, and safeguarding its inventories for using the latest technology to ensure profitability and corporate survival. But sometimes what seems rational to the rational can lead to overzealous, patently wrong—and wrongheaded—activities in the hands of more aggressive employers who end up taking advantage of the wide latitude of the law to justify improper actions.

A 1987 incident at Holy Cross Hospital in Silver Spring, Maryland, is a case in point. Dangerously hot narcotics with a street price in the six figures for relatively minuscule amounts were disappearing from the hospital in alarmingly large batches. So Holy Cross quietly installed video cameras at a few key sites throughout the campus, hoping to catch employees in the act of pocketing the drugs. But the hospital botched the wiring on its new in-house television network badly and transmitted the images it captured via closed circuit to dozens of TV sets in Holy Cross, in patients' rooms, administrators' offices, and even some staff lounges. "It was like 'Candid Camera,' " says a Washington, D.C., lawyer who worked for Holy Cross at the time.

But it wasn't funny. One morning a nurse walked into a patient's room and caught him watching her colleagues undress on television as the camera slowly panned up one aisle and down the next of their locker room. That quirky silver box with red lights hanging on the wall—the purpose of which nobody knew, though everybody suspected it was up to no good—was a camera.

The nurse screamed bloody murder—and threatened to sue. Holy Cross immediately pulled the plug on its television network. Still, the hospital says it didn't really do anything wrong. "It was a minor mistake, and it only went on for a day or so," says a Holy Cross administrator. "But there was nothing illegal about our attempt to monitor these workers to stop the narcotics trade at the hospital. We just erred in how we went about it."

It seems, he says, that Holy Cross meant only for the hospital's security chief to be privy to what the camera picked up. Cold comfort for the nurses: the security head was a man.

Recently, a rash of incidents has come to light involving corporate electronic mail systems that, at least in the sheer numbers of employees potentially victimized, make long-distance videotaping seem innocent and controllable.

Electronic mail systems (commonly known as E-mail) are computerized messaging networks prevalent at just about every company in the United States now. Put simply, E-mail is one desktop talking to another. A worker types in a note on his computer screen, presses the Send button, and instantly his message appears on someone else's computer screen. Electronic mail, says E-mail expert Walter Ulrich, "opens up lines of instant communication that cut through the corporate hierarchy. They actually allow everybody to communicate with each other as an equal."

For instance, it's easier to tell the boss via computer that the company has lost its soul and is a joyless place to work, as dozens of IBMers told CEO Jack Akers in 1991 on the E-mail system, when you're a safe distance away and not forced to stare into his eyes.

Employers like E-mail, too, although for other reasons. To them, it's a productivity improver. Chitchat is cut to a minimum. Electronic messages tend to be short and curt, and full of substance in small packages—unlike phone calls or in-person conversations, which can last longer, even though no more than a few minutes are taken up with business-related matters.

But E-mail has changed. As employees have grown more comfortable typing into a keyboard what they once communicated orally, electronic mail has become less formal and rigid. Indeed, at some companies what's transmitted from one circuit board to another tests the limits of corporate propriety. Love notes, sexy pleas, ribald jokes, and bawdy gossip crowd out requests for purchase orders and new design specs. Increasingly, for many workers the blinking signal on their computer that they have a message pending is a pleasant, potentially titillating, break in an otherwise dreary day.

That apparently is what was happening at Nissan Motor Corporation U.S.A. in 1990. The E-mail network there, according to company executives, had turned into a chat line and a dating service. "Evening trysts were planned online, even between supposedly happily married employees," says one Nissan senior VP. "And flirtatious messages full of earthy language that even commented on the other party's private parts were not uncommon. Very little work was getting accomplished on those computers."

The E-mail network had become a rogue communications system, sponsored and paid for by Nissan. Before long, management had had enough, and the ax swung down on two information specialists, Bonita B. Bourke and Rhonda L. Hall, who were fired for unprofessional work habits, including "misuse and personal use of the E-mail system."

Nissan knew about the online indiscretions of Bourke and Hall because unbeknownst to the two women—and, indications are, to all the other workers at the company—supervisors were regularly monitoring employees' electronic mail messages to keep tabs on what they were saying to one another and to monitor how well they were doing their jobs.

Bourke and Hall don't deny Nissan's claims about their E-mail activities—indeed, their attorney admits that "some of the messages they were sending were pretty slimy." But Bourke and Hall are furious. Until they were let go, they assumed the E-mail system, which requires anyone who wants to log on to enter a series of passwords, was private, "like telephone conversations and the mail," says Bourke.

The Nissan incident comes on the heels of a similar one earlier in the year at Epson America, a manufacturer of computer printers. In that case, Alana Shoars, who ran the company's electronic mail system, says she was shocked one day when she walked into her supervisor's office and found "the printer chugging away, typing out for all to see every single message being transmitted on the E-mail network."

She complained to corporate higher-ups that this was an invasion of the employees' privacy and something that none of the workers there were aware of. But apparently she blew the whistle too loudly. Soon after, Shoars was fired for insubordination. Epson denies that Shoars's dismissal was related to electronic mail, and says it reserves the right to eavesdrop on employee E-mail whenever it feels it's necessary. Shoars, Bourke, and Hall sued their companies for damages.

Noel Shipman, the attorney for all three women, says he's fed up with the principle that the "employer is the big bad cat and the worker is the prey in the fishbowl." To accept it without resistance, he says, "you may as well just leave your bedroom door open at home and let your boss see if you do it on top or not. Even in the workplace each of us deserve a reasonable expectation of privacy, and it's about time the courts start to enforce that."

In response, Nissan and Epson contended that they have the right to know what their employees are saying to each other via a company-owned internal communications system. And they claimed that they are allowed to dismiss employees who are wasting time using E-mail frivolously, just as they would be allowed to fire someone for spending hours on the phone with his bookie instead of tending to the paper-work on his desk.

Eventually the cases were settled out of court for an undisclosed amount. Shipman had leverage primarily because California is one of the few states that includes the right to privacy in its constitution. And California's Penal Code 630, inspired by the state's constitution, says that people must be protected from new technology, even equipment not yet invented, that "allows people to invade our lives in ways not like before."

Mindful of this, some companies in California are taking steps to shield themselves from E-mail privacy lawsuits. Hewlett-Packard, for instance, recently sent out an internal memo that said starting immedi-ately it will add a warning to its electronic mail system, which all workers will see when they turn on their computers in the morning, saying that E-mail messages are monitored by department supervisors. The reason: to avoid tangling with employees in court. That may help protect Hewlett-Packard from legal hassles, but after that memo was distributed, all types of E-mail usage at Hewlett-Packard—gossip as well as company business—dropped by two thirds, sources say.

California employees may be able to claim some privacy rights, but few others around the country can. In most states laws simply don't support the notion that employees should be allowed to tell their bosses to get their noses out of their business. As attorney Shipman admits, if he were trying these cases anywhere but in the Golden State, "I'd have to think of some creative lawyering to make them stick."

But, other attorneys note, worker concern around the nation about E-mail snooping is growing dramatically and isn't likely to die down soon. What's more, activism surrounding this issue could be the cata-lyst for a host of other employee privacy initiatives—protests against videotaping, bugging, databanking, and surveillance. There may not be many immediate victories in store, but, says Eric H. Joss, a Santa Monica corporate lawyer, workplace privacy will likely be the "hottest employment-law topic of the 1990s."

Loyalty Redux

Employers—even those who find it distasteful and a waste of time to keep tabs on everything their employees are doing and to tiptoe through raw information on dozens of computer databanks before hiring somebody—say they've been forced into these activities by the nation's current civil rights, legal, and social climates. "Traditional avenues for checking workers out have been shut down," says employment attorney Lee Paterson. So companies have to use new and more devious means of figuring out who they're hiring and who's working for them.

They've got a point. There's a long list of personal information employers are no longer allowed to ask prospective and current employees about: questions about age and citizenship, race and religion, lifestyle and children, marital status, and arrests that did not lead to conviction are all off limits. Face-to-face talks are nothing but legal minefields. And that's just the beginning. References are also of little value. Previous supervisors are afraid to supply negative reports on former workers because a few have been successfully sued for defamation of character when they've done so. And polygraphs were outlawed a couple of years ago.

Although these regulations have helped to crack down on discrimination, to a large extent the rules have backfired against those they were set up to protect. Because of these regulations, employers looking for clues to the personality behind the person are not allowed to plumb far below the surface anymore. This sends employers retreating to databases and private investigators to find some hint about whom they're hiring or paying a weekly check to, and turns them into voyeurs with pinhole cameras, computerized monitors of minute-by-minute work habits, and E-mail readers.

And it doesn't end there. Now there's a new legal notion emerging from dozens of court cases that runs wildly counter to these civil rights rules, the so-called negligent hiring theory. This holds a boss liable for a worker's crimes or negligence on the job if the employer fails to screen for personality quirks or past misdeeds—in short, if he doesn't pry deeply enough into the heart and soul and hidden corners of his employees' lives, those very nooks and crannies that civil rights decisions forbid employers to look into. "If Encyclopaedia Britannica sends a convicted rapist door-to-door the company will pay mightily in court if something goes wrong," says Lawrence Z. Lorber, attorney for the American Society for Personnel Administration.

It's an employer's dilemma: ask-no-questions antidiscrimination requirements and ask-all-questions negligent hiring rules would appear to be incompatible, yet employers have to answer to both. And both wreak havoc on the idea of privacy. Only databankers and private investigators get rich and fat from them.

The loser in all of this is company loyalty. Recently Safeway Stores, Incorporated, in Oakland, California, installed dashboard computers on its 782 trucks. Their purpose: to record driving speed, oil pressure, engine RPMs, idling time, and how long a truck is stopped. If anything is abnormal—if the computer report shows that the truck's engine idled for twenty-five minutes on a trip for which average idling time is only ten minutes—the driver is questioned. And he may be suspended or discharged.

"When the computer says the trucker stopped two minutes longer during a break than what Safeway feels is appropriate, he can be brought up on charges," says George Sveum, secretary of Teamsters Local 350 in Martinez, California.

Safeway argues that its onboard computers hold down maintenance and fuel costs and keep drivers on their toes, because they know the data can be used to build a disciplinary case against them. But, as it turns out, Safeway's system has done damage particularly to driver morale, and it's driven a wedge between the truckers and the company.

That's what a Safeway driver—a forty-year veteran of supermarket deliveries—says. He recalls how he used to love his job because "you were on your own—no one was looking over your shoulder. You felt like a human being, and one of the team." Now, he says, going to work is pure drudgery. "I feel pushed around, spied on. There's no trust, no respect, anymore. It's them against us."

Sentiments like these leave an unspoken change in worker attitudes: the company, which used to be for this Safeway driver as central to his life as his family, has turned its back on him. It's become an enemy. And that hurts a lot. So much, in fact, that, says Sveum, for every man-minute of productivity Safeway has gained from its computers it's lost an equal amount in loyalty from its truckers.

This is not happening only at Safeway. More and more veteran employees view their companies with distrust these days, especially as other longtimers are summarily laid off, increases in high-tech monitoring distance supervisors from staffs, and machines replace colleagues. And recent hirees seeing this are just as cynical.

Corporate life for most workers "is adversarial," says Gary T. Marx, a technology and personnel consultant. "Workers feel violated and powerless in the face of new monitoring technologies and new management techniques that only put space between supervisors and those under them. That breeds low morale and even destructive countermeasures. When workers feel challenged to beat the system—as opposed to being part of the system—they react out of anger and estrangement."

Perhaps what's most important about this fundamental change in corporate America is that it has significant ramifications far from the workplace itself. Like many technological and lifestyle shifts in modern society, the right to privacy, it turns out, is affected by it. Data mania has increased worker cynicism about the corporation, and now that very cynicism is, in turn, facilitating more data mania. With corporate pride and the work ethic fading anachronisms, it's not hard to find employees who will sell private, internally held information, either about a company or a company's customers, to the highest bidder. It's easy to do, it offers the excitement of anonymously hanging out on the wrong side of the street, and it's a way to show that the corporation has no lock on loyalty. What's more, some people are even padding their pockets by doing it.

And with databanks that contain our most personal information—from bank records to telephone calls, from credit reports to tax files—sitting in computers on the desks of clerks, salespeople, telemarketers, bill collectors, bookkeepers, receptionists, and just about everyone else, information that some people would pay a premium to know is readily available in hard copy or digitally to hundreds of thousands of workers with just the press of a button. And there's virtually no audit trail when they access it.

It's no wonder, then, that a key conduit through which personal information flows from supposedly secured databanks in the private sector and the government to those outside who aren't authorized to see it is faceless, sullen, bored workers.

It's a conundrum that reverberates with an unkind echo. Workers scream mightily when snooping employers rob them of their so-called reasonable expectations of privacy—and their chance to get a job. But the knowledge that this occurs more and more often has only made workers less timid—indeed, mischievously aggressive—about opening the faucets on the computers sitting on their desks and leaking to anyone the secrets that the rest of us have in the course of our daily lives made available to these machines.

8

Body of Information

Whatsoever things I see or hear concerning
the life of men, in my attendance on the sick
or even apart therefrom, which ought not to
be noised abroad, I will keep silence thereon,
counting such things
to be as sacred secrets.

Hippocrates, ca.
fifth century B.C.

Tommy Robinson's career seemed poised to skyrocket in 1990 when, after six years in the U.S. House of Representatives, the Arkansas Republican ran for his party's gubernatorial nomination. Not that it wasn't a risky step. Even if Robinson won the party primary, he—or, for that matter, any GOP candidate—would have a tough time defeating Bill Clinton, the popular four-term incumbent, in the general election.

But that didn't concern Tommy Robinson. Winning and losing—even in the primary—wasn't really the issue. Either way, as Robinson saw it, he'd come out ahead. Not widely known in Arkansas, Robinson figured that by participating in a statewide campaign he would at least become a household name. And this could serve as a springboard—the beginnings of a political base—for good things in the future. Robinson didn't expect, though, that before the election was over what people would be saying about him when they mentioned his name would make him long for obscurity again.

Robinson's plans soured when his boyhood friend Jerry Jones, owner of the Dallas Cowboys, clipped him but good. In March, according to Robinson, Jones obtained a copy of Robinson's medical record from a local insurance agent and leaked it to Robinson's opponent, Sheffield Nelson. Nelson then allegedly passed it along to the *Arkansas Democrat,* the biggest newspaper in the state.

The medical file wasn't a pretty sight. It said that Tommy Robinson drank a pint of bourbon a day. The following Sunday, that's also what the *Democrat*'s banner headline read.

"I was smeared," protests Robinson. "None of what was said is true. Sure I drink, but only moderately—more like a pint of liquor a week, not a day." True or false, the damage was done. Robinson's reputation was damaged irreparably and Nelson roundly defeated him in the primary. Clinton, as expected, thrashed Nelson in the general election.

Today the fifty-year-old Robinson farms seven thousand acres and "has no interest in politics anymore." A bitter man who feels betrayed by his political party and one of his oldest friends, he says, "I will take care of Jerry Jones in due point in time." Jones says the incident is in the past, and he doesn't want to talk about it with anyone.

But how did Jones obtain the damaging medical record? The tangled intrigue and interplay of key characters that led to its release play out like the plot of a Southern Gothic novel.

As Robinson tells it, Jones and he had a farming partnership, and Jones wanted Robinson to take out a life insurance policy to cover the losses the business would incur if Robinson died. So Robinson was contacted by an insurance agent—"a friend of Jones," says Robinson—who told him that, although a physical was required before the policy could be underwritten, there was no need to waste any time with that. Instead, Robinson was asked just to provide a copy of the results of any recent physical for the insurer's files.

"Now this is where it gets weird," says Robinson. "I had taken a physical a year or so earlier. During the exam, the doctor asked me if I drank. I told him, 'Sure, about a pint of bourbon a week.' That damn doctor wrote down a pint a day. And I turned that over to the insurance agent, without even reading the file."

But the insurance agent clearly read it. And when he saw Robinson's "drinking problem," he decided that this was something Jerry Jones would find very interesting. So he shared it with Jones.

Says Robinson, "Nelson's gas company had just cut a sweetheart deal with Jerry, buying his gas reserves at a price much higher than they were really worth. And this gave Jones the cash he needed to buy the Dallas Cowboys. My medical report was Jones's way of saying thank you to Sheffield Nelson."

For Robinson, the pain of this episode lingers. "Everybody thinks I'm a damn drunk," says Robinson. "Denying it does no good. The damage was done big time in that one headline. I wouldn't want anybody to go through what I went through where something so personal—and so wrong—is spread around like idle chatter."

Robinson isn't suing Jones. Despite the apparent defamation of character, it would be a tough case to win for one simple reason: medical records are not private. There are no federal laws mandating exactly under which circumstances and to whom a medical record may be revealed, and when it must be kept under wraps.

Some state statutes exist that allow for the release of medical records only with a patient's approval. But such authorization is frequently automatic. Consent is obtained through small print on an application for insurance, a loan, revolving credit, employment, or virtually anything else for which a complete background check, including examining medical records, may be conducted.

"It's a search warrant without due process," says University of Illinois professor David Linowes. That's especially so because many consent forms have no expiration date, meaning that they can be used as the justification for unrestricted access to a consumer's personal records at any time without further notification.

Generally, then, discretion and old-fashioned ethics are the sole confidentiality safeguards in medicine. But these are gentlemanly boundaries. And like many uncodified privacy protections, they're locked in a losing battle with technology. Most medical records are now stored on computers at a variety of sites, among them doctors' offices, hospitals, and insurance companies. Gaining access to the records, with authorization or without, as is the case with all data in this information-rich world, poses no difficulty for the curious.

"We used to have a medical system that was confidential," says retired Harvard School of Medicine neurosurgeon Vernon Mark. Mark recalls that when he was practicing, and, indeed, when his father, grandfather, and great-grandfather hung their shingles out, a patient's file "stayed with the doctor. My father used to treat a lot of people who had sexually transmitted diseases. For him to reveal that kind of information would have been unthinkable. Now we need laws to ensure the same kind of protection that we all used to take for granted."

There almost was such a law, but it was derailed by a nasty non sequitur uttered on the floor of the House of Representatives on December 1, 1980. It occurred during debate over H.R. 5935, a bill that would have finally made patient records private and that contained strict procedures to follow before a medical file could be revealed.

To make it palatable to a broad political constituency on Capitol

Hill, the bill was watered down significantly. For one thing, it permitted physicians to dispense patient information freely to the Secret Service and covert intelligence agencies. And it allowed disclosure of medical files without a patient's consent if an M.D. felt circumstances were extraordinary enough to warrant it, for instance, if a patient was a danger to the community because of his mental or physical state.

But to ensure that this "go with your judgment" section of the law wasn't misapplied to the point that the bill lost its bite, the measure warned that flexibility in the legislation should not be used as an excuse to take the release of medical records lightly and allow it without considerable soul-searching. This was particularly pertinent, the bill said, to psychiatric files, which, when released to outsiders, can be extremely embarrassing and damaging to a person's reputation.

Chances for passage were slim. Privacy legislation hasn't been—and still isn't—a priority in Washington. But a healthy debate ensued nevertheless. Many legislators, like most Americans, were unaware that medical records enjoyed no privacy sanctions. And some lawmakers quietly began to question how they could vote against a bill that made such inherent sense.

Negative positions seemed to be shifting slowly, and proponents even began to harbor thoughts that H.R. 5935 might pass. That is, until Representative Edward Boland (D-Mass.) rose to drop his bombshell, to make the offhand, ill-chosen—some even say ignorant—comment that disengaged the pendulum that had begun to swing in favor of this bill.

Boland, then chairman of the House Select Committee on Intelligence and a high-profile lawmaker with clout, announced that he couldn't support the bill. To be sure, he said, the privacy of medical records is an important idea, worthy of careful consideration. But this bill, he screamed loudly, thrusting his fist in the air, waving a sheaf of papers to emphasize the magnitude and weight of what he was about to say, this bill is a threat to national security, plain and simple.

The House chambers were suddenly hushed. Perplexed expressions spread from one Representative to the next. Let me explain why, Boland continued: The bill flatly "encourages psychiatrists to refuse to provide mental health information to government agencies." It even goes so far, he added, as to single shrinks out, warning them to take special care not to broadcast their files. And that's unacceptable,

Boland concluded. If this bill passes, the wrong message will be sent and we'll have a slew of serious security breaches to contend with.

Boland didn't have to be any more specific than that. It wasn't necessary to remind his colleagues in the House of the open wounds left by recent history. In 1971, soon after Daniel Ellsberg released the once top-secret and classified Pentagon Papers, the FBI launched an investigation of him. During the course of it, agents asked his psychiatrist for clinical information about Ellsberg. The psychiatrist demurred, refusing even to acknowledge that Ellsberg had ever been under his care.

Richard Nixon was enraged by the failure of the FBI to dig up any dirt on Ellsberg, whose name appeared near the crest of his enemies list. A couple of years later, he sent first-string "plumbers" Howard Hunt and G. Gordon Liddy to Ellsberg's psychiatrist to see what they could find out.

They, however, didn't visit during office hours, when the door was unlocked. Instead, they tiptoed in during the dark of night and ransacked the psychiatrist's files. Hunt and Liddy came away empty-handed, but they succeeded in accomplishing one thing that they didn't want to accomplish: they got the case against Ellsberg dismissed. When a federal district judge dropped all criminal charges against Ellsberg for revealing government secrets, he cited the burglary of the psychiatrist's office as a key reason for his decision.

The specter raised by Boland—that this medical privacy bill could be taken as tacit approval for the actions of Ellsberg's psychiatrist and would make it difficult to get other psychiatrists to cooperate in investigations to prosecute infidels like Daniel Ellsberg—touched an exposed nerve.

It didn't matter that the wording of the legislation probably would have actually accomplished the opposite. Its evenhanded language would likely have made it easier to force reticent psychiatrists to be more forthcoming if the situation demanded it—or to get a court to authorize the release of therapy records. And it didn't matter that the bill actually bent over backward, perhaps to a fault, not to be overly restrictive. Boland's statement was an emotional one. Coddling enemies of the CIA and the intelligence community was not politically smart in these decidedly more conservative times. It really had nothing to do with the facts, just with making sure that some unruly ghosts left behind by Nixon's White House didn't come back to haunt.

Seven weeks later Ronald Reagan was inaugurated. Privacy was not a Reagan pet project. It was a right that, in his view, required far too much government intervention to ensure, so it took a backseat to corporate laissez-faire and business deregulation, both of which gave information companies a relatively free hand to harness technology and private information for substantial profit. Nobody in Congress since has been able to muster enough support even to hold a hearing on legislation to codify the confidentiality of medical records.

Mud Baths

Unfortunately, the need for medical privacy laws hasn't diminished since 1981. Quite the opposite: it's become more acute. Each new wrinkle in the nation's rapidly changing health care system—whether it be computer-based technologies for diagnoses and record keeping, the expansion of third-party payment plans, or the snowballing of the amount of intimate information maintained in patients' files—increases the need to protect medical records.

In fact, the medical records environment is so open-ended now that the American Medical Association has identified twelve categories of information seekers outside of the health care establishment who regularly peek at patient files for their own purposes, among them employers, government agencies, credit bureaus, insurers, educational institutions, and the media. Tack onto this list unauthorized data gatherers such as private investigators and people with a vested interest in uncovering all they can about someone they want to turn a dirty deal on, and it's clear the amount of medical information making the rounds these days is monumental.

In a typical hospital, "charts travel all over," says Dr. Molly Cooke, an internist at San Francisco General Hospital and a medical ethicist. "Thirty to forty people may look at one during treatment: X-ray technicians, dietitians, occupational and physical therapists, social workers, medical students, and pharmacists. If the patient has an unusual illness, the number of people looking at the record could double. And the fact is that total strangers could also look at the charts, the way most hospitals leave them lying around."

Not to mention that hospitals and physicians are notorious for attaching access codes for computerized medical records to computer terminals, something that private investigators and other clandestine information seekers are well aware of.

Physicians also often tell more about patients than they have to. As San Francisco personal injury lawyer Bennett Cohen explains it, "If an insurance company wants records to see if someone has an asthma condition, and that patient also saw the same doctor for VD infection five years ago, the insurer gets that information too. No one in the doctor's office is going to go through fifteen visits and segregate out the [relevant] records."

And this "has an enormous impact on people's lives," says Alan Westin, a Columbia University professor and a privacy expert. The information in a medical record "affects decisions on whether they are hired or fired, whether they can secure business licenses and life insurance, whether they are permitted to drive cars, whether they are placed under police surveillance or labeled a security risk, or even whether they get nominated for and elected to political office."

Psychiatrists claim they're hit the hardest. Paul Fink, chairman of the Department of Psychiatry at Albert Einstein Medical Center in Philadelphia and medical director at the Philadelphia Psychiatric Center, says that he gets "requests to review my files constantly. But my files are extraordinarily sparse. I keep most of what I know about my patients in my head. We're not enlightened enough as a society to allow people to be open about their treatment."

Unfortunately, not all doctors are as conscientious about protecting patient privacy as Fink. And when physicians release medical records these days they're sharing, as the American Medical Records Association puts it, "more intimate details about an individual than can be found in any single document."

To comprehend how accurate this statement is, just consider the incredibly detailed and wide-ranging information that a typical medical record contains: patient's name, address, age, and next of kin; names of parents; date and place of birth; marital status; religion; history of military service; Social Security number; name of insurer. And that's before getting to the patient's history, which details chief complaints and diagnosis; past medical, social, and family history; previous and current treatments; an inventory of the condition of each body system; medications taken now and in the past; use of alcohol and tobacco; diagnostic tests administered; findings; reactions; and incidents. Only fifty years ago what a physician maintained about a patient was on an index card in a file cabinet, and it listed only the dates of the treatment, the medications prescribed, and how much the visits cost.

With so much information about people available from one source now, it's no surprise—considering the data-gobbling tenor of the times—that a cottage industry has sprung up around the medical record. Surreptitious trafficking in medical information is "common and nationwide," according to a Senate subcommittee that during the 1980s investigated data selling in the United States.

Dale Tooley, a former district attorney in Denver, Colorado, learned this firsthand. He led an investigation of a twenty-five-year-old company whose sole business was obtaining medical information and selling it for a hefty profit. Unfortunately, with medical privacy laws nonexistent, Tooley couldn't convince a grand jury to indict the outfit for any wrongdoing. But here's how the company operated, according to Tooley's testimony before the Senate subcommittee:

> There was an instruction book the company had whereby it trained its investigators to pose as doctors on the telephone. File cards were maintained on hospitals in virtually every state in the country, on military hospitals and doctors' offices. I can recall one note in a card file on a Chicago hospital which said: call after midnight, talk with a black accent, and you can get whatever records you need. It was that precise in detail.
>
> Sometimes sources were paid [for patient records]: interns, nurses. . . . Occasionally mail was used under false pretenses. But the telephone was the main method. . . . The firm was ninety-nine percent successful in being able to pierce the medical records protection system of health care providers.
>
> We located literally hundreds of copies of broad-based solicitations sent out to insurance companies which said, "We can secure medical records without authorization from the patient."

But to what end?

"A mud bath" on the Senate floor in 1989, as some observers called it, offers a hint. During hearings on the nomination of John Tower to be Secretary of Defense, an information melee broke out that left a lot of destroyed reputations in its wake. It started when retired Air Force sergeant Bob Jackson told the FBI and leaked to the press that he had seen Tower quite drunk on a couple of occasions at an Air Force base in Texas.

Angered by what Jackson had done, a Tower supporter, Senator John McCain (R-Ariz.), a Vietnam War hero, used his military ties to obtain a copy of Jackson's medical record surreptitiously from the Air

Force. Then he read excerpts of it into the Senate record—especially the parts that said, "Sergeant Jackson exhibited symptoms of a mixed personality disorder with anti-social themes and hysterical features."

Shocked by McCain's exposure of Jackson's private records, one Republican Senator called it "raw sewage." And Washington right-to-privacy attorney Ronald Plesser said it "was a clear violation of the spirit of the Privacy Act."

But it wasn't unlawful. The heavily watered-down Privacy Act does not cover Congressional activities and there are no legal protections for medical records.

Jackson says that the parts of the report McCain failed to read vindicate him. But the damage was already done. Tower may have been seriously besmirched by the nomination hearings, but his accuser, Jackson—after having the tables turned on him—fared no better.

Disclosing medical records is a natural weapon in politics. For better or worse, the American system is an unforgiving one: a single flaw, a sole dismaying wart, as Tommy Robinson discovered, is enough to destroy suddenly a high-flying or budding career in government. And what better and more direct way to find an imperfection than to examine the overwhelming minutiae of one's personal life deposited in a medical record?

But for every leak of a medical record for top-drawer political intrigue there are literally dozens of cases involving people who are not prominent. "The real problem with medical confidentiality is that most breaches don't result in a big scandal," says Mary Joan Wogan, a director at the American Medical Record Association. "There are usually no headlines and hardly ever monetary awards. Just personal distress."

Take David Castle, a free-lance artist in Southern California. Castle tried to buy disability coverage from three different insurance companies and was turned down by all of them. This frustrated him, but he didn't think that anything was awry. He figured the insurance companies were simply being prudent, at least by their criteria. "Friends told me that because accidents occur more often at home, insurance companies are not very comfortable giving disability insurance to people that work out of their homes," he says.

That may be true, but it wasn't the reason Castle couldn't get insurance. There was a more frightening explanation: information about

Castle that was in the files of the Medical Information Bureau (MIB), the largest repository of medical records in the United States. MIB is virtually unknown to most people, yet its databanks contain summaries of health conditions on more than twelve million Americans and Canadians. Insurance companies feed MIB's cavernous mainframes whatever they learn about individuals from insurance applications, physicians' files, and hospital records. Then when someone applies for a policy, underwriters scan MIB's computers to see if there's an existing data file about the applicant that can help the insurer decide how much to charge for the policy, or if the policy should be issued at all.

MIB, it turns out, was incorrectly saying that Castle has AIDS—damaging information indeed, because AIDS sufferers are not welcome at many insurance companies. Castle grasps at straws when searching for a reason to explain how such inaccurate data got into his MIB file: "I guess the fact that I'm thirty-five and unmarried makes me suspect."

That would be too easy. It would be almost comforting to say that it was simple ignorance tinged with prejudice that had tainted Castle's MIB record. But Castle is caught up in something far more complex: a confusing double-tiered web of misinformation, in which nobody responsible for the bad data is able to explain why they put it there. And incredibly, no one can pull Castle out of its sticky grip.

The first tier was laid bare when Castle applied to a fourth insurance company for disability coverage. At that time he told the agent how difficult it has been to get a policy in the past, and a lengthy investigation of his case was conducted. What was discovered was mind-boggling. Castle's doctor, completely erroneously, had written on his file that "I'm gay," says Castle "and that I'm HIV positive." And this information was passed along to MIB, along with all of his records, by one of the insurers he applied to.

Castle's doctor says he doesn't know why he described his patient as a homosexual, but he can explain why he wrote in his files that Castle has AIDS. It was the result of a second deeply damaging mistake that Castle innocently fell victim to. Earlier in the year, Castle had a sinus CT scan. Inexplicably, the radiologist, in his report to Castle's doctor on this test, said—without any evidence—that Castle was "an HIV positive man."

Now Castle's doctor, embarrassed by his patient's straits, is trying to correct the mess and straighten out Castle's MIB file. "He sent my file again to MIB, but this time he circled the HIV-positive notation, and added a note saying, 'This is incorrect,' " says Castle.

That doesn't seem to have helped. Since then, the free-lance artist has been turned down by seven other insurance companies for disability insurance, even though he finally took an AIDS test, which came out negative. "That's what is really horrifying about this: when misinformation appears in a computerized file, it has a life of its own and remains there virtually forever," says Castle.

In one way or another. MIB will not delete the AIDS and gay notations in Castle's file, even though his doctor has amended the information and said that it is patently incorrect. Instead, MIB will merely add the new data—the notation that there is an error in the record—to the existing file. Leaving the misinformation, Castle says, "sort of negates the retraction."

Castle's case is not unusual. There are many others caught in the same battle of wills with MIB's emotionless databanks. Like Charles H. Zimmerman of West Roxbury, Massachusetts. Zimmerman never imagined he'd have any trouble getting disability insurance at a fair price. After all, he was the picture of health, and didn't drink or smoke. So he was shocked when an underwriter at Guardian Life Insurance Company in Boston told him he would have to pay about 25 percent more than the standard rate for coverage. Zimmerman demanded to know why. Guardian was surprised he asked. After all, the underwriter told him, all alcoholics pay a higher rate.

Zimmerman was flabbergasted. Alcoholic? He hadn't had a drink in more than seven years. But that's not what his medical record said. "I'm a public employee used to dealing with bureaucracies, but for the life of me I couldn't figure out what was going on here," says Zimmerman.

He soon found out. Zimmerman's supposed bout with alcoholism slipped into MIB's databanks when he first applied for disability insurance in 1987, two years before he contacted Guardian about a policy. At that time he mentioned on the application that he had attended Alcoholics Anonymous (AA) many years earlier. But this was not for a drinking problem per se. Zimmerman, a fan of holistic and alternative approaches to health care and well-being, says he felt that AA "could overall improve my life by helping me understand any addictive behaviors I had. And it worked: AA helped me quit smoking."

This subtlety eluded MIB's databank, which in its files simply indicates with one of more than two hundred codes if a medical condition exists, or if a person participates in an activity or maintains a lifestyle that could affect longevity. MIB codes are so wide-ranging that numbers are even assigned to such nonmedical attributes as skydiving, poor driving, sexual deviation, and unhealthy appearance. In Zimmerman's case, attending AA meetings put the code for alcoholism in his MIB record. This raised a red flag when Guardian checked on him.

Zimmerman finally got the disability policy from Guardian without the surcharge, but it took a year of letter writing to MIB, Guardian, and the original company he had given the information to before he could set the record straight.

MIB staunchly defends its part in the insurance underwriting process. After all, says MIB president Neal Day, it's essential that a databank exists to record people's medical histories and catch those attempting to lie to insurers. Otherwise, premiums would rise inexorably. Insurers wouldn't be able to balance the number of risky policies they're signing up against the less risky ones, and accurately figure the prices for premiums they have to charge to each group. "MIB helps the insurer make better decisions, and the average consumer wins because prices of all premiums don't go sky high," says Day. "Those at higher risk pay more and other consumers don't subsidize them." What's more, adds Day, "for every mistake that MIB makes, there are a thousand cases of fraud that MIB catches, and that's not a bad ratio."

Perhaps. But those mistakes hurt. John Friedkin, a free-lance writer in a tiny upstate New York hamlet, learned how much when he applied for a life insurance policy recently with New England Life. "I got a call the next day from my insurance agent, who was livid," says Friedkin. "He asked me, 'Why the hell didn't you tell me that you were being treated for extreme psychosis?' "

Friedkin told him because he's not: "The only time I was under psychiatric care was for mild anxiety—and that was years ago and only for a few sessions."

An investigation ensued. What turned up was the fact that MIB had got it wrong; it was an error of input. Whoever had typed Friedkin's record into MIB's database had tried to enter the code for mild anxiety. Instead, the clerk mistyped just one number. As a result of that simple slip of a finger, the code for psychosis had landed in Friedkin's file.

What's most disturbing about MIB, consumer advocates say, is that the databank is virtually unregulated. Try to get a copy of your medical report from MIB. The huge databanker used to refuse to supply reports at all. Now, under pressure to be more accommodating to the public, it will send a report, but only to the patient's physician. Considering how difficult it is to communicate with physicians and break into their busy schedules, that's a procedure that in many cases completely discourages access to MIB files; it's far too complicated and usually unworkable.

And, says privacy advocate Robert Ellis Smith, it may not work. Smith claims that when he requested his report, it took him three years to get it.

The inability to control the personal medical information that MIB and insurers are sharing is alarming, precisely because they know so much about us. Two out of three Americans have life insurance, 82 percent are covered by health insurance, and nearly everyone who owns a home or car has insurance for these possessions. To these insurers MIB distributes nearly thirty million reports a year.

That's a lot of private information sprinkled among companies made up mostly of nonmedical employees such as clerks, salesmen, and investigators. Loose lips here can sink lives. *New York Times* reporter Bruce Lambert says he came across a case in which an insurance company denied a policy to a prominent small-town businessman when his AIDS test came back positive.

A few days later, according to the businessman, a consultant to the insurer gossiped about the test results at a public dinner held in the applicant's hometown. Grappling with the terminal disease was bewildering and, at this early stage, almost more than the businessman could take. But hearing the whispers and suffering the fire-and-brimstone stares of neighbors he passed in the village heightened beyond anything he could have ever imagined the loneliness of his sudden rush toward death.

Eugenics

MIB, like most databanks, is insatiable. Each new bit of relevant information builds a more complex profile of a person's medical background. And medicine, which refreshes its diagnostic techniques with each new wave of technology, is compliant. Clinical researchers constantly add to the extant information available about each of us, deducing not only the present, but what's yet to come. Genetic screening is a good example of medicine's taste for the total picture—and MIB's thirst for ever more savory data.

The fifteen-year, $3 billion federal Human Genome Project is aimed at identifying all hundred-thousand-plus human genes. The goal is to make it possible to predict with some degree of certainty who carries genes for such genetic diseases as Down's syndrome, hemophilia, Alzheimer's disease, and cystic fibrosis. Additionally, genes will probably be uncovered that contribute to key killers such as cardiac disease and cancer.

A well-intentioned program, built on the best of purposes. But although genetic testing is just in its infancy, this new technology is already further muddying the boundaries of medical privacy. It's early yet: fewer than five thousand genetic disorders have been identified through DNA analyses so far and there are fairly reliable tests for only four or five dozen of them. Still, numerous anecdotes are circulating about people whose personal lives have been sullied by what outsiders do after peeking at the results of their genetic tests. Says Dr. Paul Billings, a genetic specialist at Pacific Presbyterian Medical Center in San Francisco, people found to have a "particular genetic trait are stigmatized and their privacy [is] victimized, in the way that many of the seriously sick are."

Those choosing DNA screening to dispel fears of predisposition to a genetic illness, such as Huntington's disease, or to ensure that a child is not born with a life-threatening condition, are taking positive, desirable steps to rid themselves of worries about impending disease and to protect the gene pools of their families. At the same time, though, if something even the slightest bit out of the ordinary is found, the repercussions may overshadow and completely erase the value of what they've learned. The aftermath could make people wish they had never taken the genetic test in the first place.

That's because those found to be gene deficient, to have abnormal genes, whether recessive or dominant, are shunted into a new category of individual, according to Billings: "the asymptomatic ill—treated as if they are already disabled or chronically ill by important segments of society. And access to jobs, insurance, or social entitlements may be limited."

One reason is that the Medical Information Bureau is keenly interested in what genetic tests say, and regularly broadcasts the results to its subscribers. And that data interchange—that new bit of gossip—can compel insurance companies to intrude on extremely sensitive and private decisions, even to force their will on a couple trying to decide whether a baby should be born or aborted, or to dictate with economic sanctions whether a couple should conceive or not.

In 1985, Robert and Amy Freeze of Paris, Illinois, were expecting their first child. During a routine checkup in February, Amy's sixth month of pregnancy, the gynecologist told her that the baby wasn't as big as it should be at its gestation age. A month later the baby still was far too small, so the doctor decided to do an ultrasound test to see what the problem was.

The Freezes were shattered by what the test uncovered. The unborn baby, the test showed, was suffering from Meckel-Gruber syndrome, a terminal disease characterized by enlarged, cyst-riddled kidneys and severe lung deficiency. It isn't likely, the doctor told the Freezes, that the baby will survive for much more than a few hours out of the womb.

"We were advised to have labor induced immediately," says Amy. "We were already suffering extreme emotional distress over the impending loss of our baby. So the feeling was why put off the inevitable—and go through months of torturous pain—when we could begin to put it behind us that much sooner."

On March 6, Angela Freeze was born and then died immediately.

Soon after, the Freezes underwent a series of genetic tests. It was discovered that both had a recessive gene for Meckel-Gruber, meaning that they were carriers of the deadly condition. They would never get it, but there was a 25 percent chance that any child of theirs would.

The next year, under the care of genetic counselors, the Freezes decided to try to have a healthy baby again. Amy was soon pregnant and this time genetic tests on the fetus showed that the baby was completely normal. Amy gave birth to Sarah Freeze on November 20, 1986. The tab for prenatal, delivery, and postnatal expenses was picked up by Amy's health insurance—a policy she got through her job as a teacher in nearby Terre Haute, Indiana.

Amy decided to quit teaching and stay home with Sarah full-time. And that was the start of a virtual war between the Freezes and the insurance companies. Sarah and Amy needed health insurance. Robert, a farmer, had a policy, but it was expensive and adding his wife and daughter to it was prohibitive. So the Freezes began searching for another carrier. That's when they learned that their genetic history—and MIB—had stacked the deck against them.

No insurer will issue a policy to the Freezes now, because of their genetic flaw. After looking at their medical records, Amy says, an insurance agent told the Freezes recently that "the cost of keeping a baby with Meckel-Gruber alive for seven months, which is about all it will live even with heroic medical intervention, is astronomical. And the company doesn't want to pay for that."

The irony is that the Freezes aren't even sure that they want to have another baby, but, says Amy, "we sure don't want any insurer to tell us whether we can or not." But without medical insurance, they could never afford to cover the thousands of dollars it would take to give birth.

Still, Robert and Amy have promised—in fact, agreed to put in writing—that they would abort any baby who in prenatal genetic tests was shown to have the disease. Even that doesn't satisfy the insurers. "They simply are saying, 'We make the decisions, you don't,' " says Amy. " 'And our decision is that you can't have health insurance because you're genetically deficient. And you can't have another baby—healthy or not. You can't be a parent again.' "

Robert and Amy's anguish is just a hint of what could come when genetic testing becomes a more common practice. "The insurance issues raised by genetic screening are about to grow phenomenally," says Harry Ostrer, a geneticist at the University of Florida.

Suppose, posits Heidi Beaver, a DNA counselor at Washington University in St. Louis, a fetus is found to have cerebral palsy, but the parents don't want to abort. Instead, they choose to raise the child, who, after all, except for his severely limited physical state is normal in all other ways and could conceivably live to an old age. "Unless they're rich, these parents will soon change their minds," says Beaver. "It's unlikely that a medical insurer will allow them to make that decision, and cover them."

"That smacks of a revival of eugenic social policies," adds Dr. Paul Billings of Pacific Presbyterian Medical Center.

The counterargument, of course, is that with the nation's health care costs ballooning, insurers have a right—indeed, a fiscal responsibility to shareholders and policy owners—to minimize financial risks posed by chronic, costly diseases. It's standard procedure for insurers to want to know everything they can about an applicant before making a decision.

"But that penalizes people for taking advantage of the best medical technology at their disposal," says Heidi Beaver. "Faced with insurers using genetic tests as a hammerlock, some might find it more prudent not to test the condition of the fetus and to, in ignorance, deliver untold numbers of extremely damaged Meckel-Gruber babies along with those that you would want to see live who have, say, cerebral palsy. At least the parents will be insured and avoid the traumatic decision of having to abort a fetus that deserves to live. If insurers, who are woefully undereducated about genetic diseases, continue to use DNA testing to punish, more people are going to decide not to test and take their chances—until that choice is taken away from them, too."

The problem is not even that simple. It's compounded immeasurably by the fact that the activities of insurers are spilling over to the workplace, where employers have taken on many of the same concerns as underwriters. Eighty percent of the nation's fifteen hundred largest companies manage or finance health insurance programs of their own. Like insurers, these companies are also squeezed by the price of health care benefits, and they want to cut costs desperately. To help them do this, one approach they've adopted from the insurance industry is tapping prospective employee medical records for, among other things, the results of genetic tests, and then making hiring decisions based on what they find.

In a recent survey of people who underwent genetic testing, Paul Billings uncovered the case of a young woman who took a DNA scan and learned she had Charcot-Marie-Tooth disease (CMT), a nonfatal neuromuscular condition that is often unnoticeable and not debilitating. Despite the diagnosis, she had practically no CMT symptoms and hardly ever felt fatigued as a result of the disease.

Soon after, she applied for a job. The employer obtained her consent to examine pertinent confidential records, both financial and medical; the company's recruiter told her that this was just a formality. On the face of it, the recruiter said, everything looked good. The job was for all intents and purposes hers.

But there was a sudden change of heart. A couple of days later, she received a call saying that someone else had been hired for the position. Why, she asked? Because her medical record showed she had tested positive for CMT, the company responded. After reading up on CMT's pathology in a medical reference book, the company decided that the job she had applied for, though not very taxing physically, wasn't appropriate for someone with a muscular disease.

Employers doubling as insurers check on much more than genetic tests. Many also monitor the kinds of drugs employees are taking and how much they spend on them. Typically, this analysis is performed by an outside firm such as HealthCare Data Corporation of Rhode Island or Health Information Designs in the Washington, D.C., area.

Employers supply these databankers with the details of employee visits to the drugstore, generated by insurance reimbursement records, and ask for identification of employees whose drug use raises eyebrows: some may be abusing drugs, others may be mixing prescriptions inappropriately. Ostensibly, employers want these names so they can take steps to hold down corporate prescription expenditures.

Carl Fink, chief operating officer at Health Information Designs, says there's nothing venal about this arrangement. "In this age of specialization, physician B, unaware of what medicine a person is taking, might prescribe a drug for gastrointestinal problems that's toxic when taken with drugs for high blood pressure prescribed by physician A," says Fink. "That's something we would flag. Of course, we also find cases of people refilling their Valium script twice a month, instead of once every two months, or buying too many sleeping pills or painkillers."

Fink, whose company serves such corporate clients as General Motors, Ford, Chrysler, and Goodyear Tire & Rubber, emphasizes that HealthCare Data shares none of this information with the employer. "It's all sent to the patient's doctor so that he can take appropriate actions," Fink explains. "At this point we're not trying to give employers data that they could use to slap somebody's wrist."

But that's missing the point, medical confidentiality advocates say. As they see it, what these companies are doing is tantamount to surveillance on people when they're away from their jobs, supposedly on their own time. They're unraveling more details of employees' private lives—each Saturday afternoon drive to the pharmacy becomes yet another entry in a databank—and distributing this information on tattle sheets to a system that's dying to know whose names are on them.

That they send data only to physicians is little protection, adds Jerome Beigler, a Chicago-based psychiatrist and former chairman of the American Psychiatric Association's Committee on Confidentiality. He argues that with so many doctors now working directly for employer-financed health maintenance organizations or similar programs, "it happens more and more frequently that companies analyzing their health care expenditures ask employees' physicians overly inquisitive questions about their patients."

Beigler declines to be more specific, but he claims that just such employer-physician interactions are behind "the number of cases I found recently where schoolteachers are let go or demoted after undergoing psychiatric treatment paid for by their school system's health plan."

And there are indications that soon asking a doctor verbally for sensitive information about a patient may not be necessary. It might be possible, instead, to get physicians' records directly via computer. A company called Physicians Computer Network (PCN) in Laurence Harbor, New Jersey, provides a blueprint for how this may occur.

PCN's is a novel approach to medical data gathering. It seeds doctors with free computers to manage their practices. In return for the gratis PCs, PCN requires that the computers it supplies always be connected to the PCN electronic network, via continuously live telephone lines. Then from time to time PCN, which is field-testing its service now, will scour the patient records of the M.D.s, look for interesting tidbits, and pull data from them for marketing lists.

These lists, PCN says, will not contain patient names but only aggregate statistics, such items as the fact that, say, 50 percent of hypertensive patients in the Northeast with a systolic reading of 140 are prescribed a beta blocker and 25 percent are told to take nothing—information that's worth its weight in gold to drug manufacturers.

But PCN is causing concern because it's proposing to do away with human-to-human communications that, at least, have served as a barrier for those who would breach the confidentiality of medical records. It's building one of the first silent and invisible links directly into the nation's doctors' offices, with no mechanism for detecting when a pair of eyes, authorized or unauthorized, is prowling through the database on some distant computer, and what information is being unloaded. It's an unregulated electronic pathway to personal information—even if no names are yet attached to the data—that most patients visiting a PCN doctor are completely unaware of and that would probably cause them to flinch if they knew about it.

So far, in early testing PCN has signed up more than two thousand physicians, mostly on the East Coast. During the next few years, with a full-scale marketing campaign planned, that number could grow to well over one hundred thousand nationwide. "For every M.D. that says they won't participate because they don't want to compromise the privacy of their patient's records, there are twenty that have no such problems with the system, and even find it very useful," says a PCN official.

That kind of attitude among physicians and marketers only validates the fears of privacy advocates that the day of the confidential medical file is virtually over. "Every time you build a new computer network and attach yet another group of sites—in this case doctors' offices—to the big electronic highways we're so enamored of constructing now, the network grows bigger and more opportunistic," says Vincent Brannigan, a computer systems specialist at Georgetown University. "It never becomes more restricted and ethical."

A small news item that has gone mostly unnoticed is testimony to just how far the opportunistic impulses to acquire information can go. It's striking because it shows that in the face of high-tech advances, even the privacy of the most honored dead can be suddenly wrenched from them.

The story concerns Abraham Lincoln. The National Museum of Health and Medicine has in its collection samples of Lincoln's hair, bone chips, and bloodstains. Now, 127 years after his death, the museum has asked for the go-ahead to do a genetic test on these samples to see if Lincoln suffered from Marfan's syndrome.

Marfan's is characterized in part by a tall, gangling appearance. It weakens bones, joints, blood vessels, and the heart. Some historians feel that Lincoln was possibly dying from Marfan's and would have passed away prematurely, perhaps before finishing his second term in office, even if he had not been assassinated by John Wilkes Booth at age fifty-six.

A group made up mostly of leading geneticists said that the Lincoln DNA test is a good idea. The study "should be encouraged," affirms Dr. Victor McKusick, who headed up the panel and is a professor of medical genetics at Johns Hopkins University.

But critics ask why. The DNA test, they point out, will add nothing to the medical knowledge about Marfan's. The only thing it will accomplish, these critics claim, is to satisfy the gossipmongers who for some perverse reason want to use their latest piece of medical information technology to prove that Abraham Lincoln was disease-ridden, at the expense of his privacy. "They're using the corpse of a revered President of the United States for a public relations stunt," says Jeremy Rifkin, the head of the Washington-based Foundation on Economic Trends and a longtime opponent of genetic testing.

It's hard not to agree and wonder, considering more recent history, about the political hay Major General George McClellan, Lincoln's opponent in the hotly contested 1864 election, would have made if he had gotten his hands on the President's medical record and found a hitherto unrevealed reference to Marfan's. The hubbub that would have resulted is certainly something Tommy Robinson of Arkansas could appreciate.

9

Shadow of Technology

Be careful, his bowtie is really a camera.

Paul Simon

We were sitting in a cramped anteroom on the second floor of a turn-of-the-century Victorian home in rural Clinton, New Jersey. Clinton is one of those reconstructed towns that could die of quaint. The waterfall in the center of the business district, the old mill converted into a shopping center, the Colonial brick storefronts with eighteenth-century-style signs lining squeaky-clean sidewalks—it all seems a bit too studied, too perfectly planned. Unfortunately, subtlety and spontaneous charm are about the only things Clinton failed to overdo on.

But in the house we were in, haphazard mystery is everywhere, from the wisteria creeping in and out of the hidden corners of the front porch to the chipped, dark-oak banisters and deep-lacquered walnut trim that snakes upward to the second floor from the stained-glass doorway. At the stairwell, the foyer is draped in sinewy shadows that crisscross the flight of steps and ceiling like bars on an empty prison cell in a ghost town. And the walls, even in the room we were in, are colored in somber pastels: grays, blues, and ochres.

It's an appropriate house for Murray Associates. Kevin Murray is a counteroperative, hired to ferret out skulkers in dark corners. I had spent hundreds of hours with dozens of information junkies and data abusers in pinstripes and jeans during the preceding few years; it seemed fitting at the end of my research to call on Kevin Murray, because Murray is refreshingly unlike them. Destroying confidences and sharing secrets is not his stock-in-trade. He deals in the opposite;

rooting out surveillance equipment, sweeping for hidden microphones and telephone bugs, and catching information thieves. In short, he says, "I protect people's privacy."

The forty-one-year-old Murray has worked for some well-known corporate clients, 30 percent of the Fortune 1000—companies that suspect somebody is listening in on conversations in the boardroom or CEO's office, hacking on their computers, or walking out the door with pieces of their databanks.

Usually Murray outfoxes his prey, but he concedes that the technology he comes up against is getting more ingenious. Take one of Murray's latest adversaries: the Keep Alive. It's a device that's deposited deep in a telephone and, thus, is virtually impossible to find. When the Keep Alive is in place, all an eavesdropper has to do is dial the compromised phone and hang up. That activates the Keep Alive and transforms it into a hidden microphone that transmits to the unauthorized caller every noise and conversation taking place at that location.

The Keep Alive has spawned its share of imitators and offspring, such as the Infinity Transmitter. This device isn't hidden in a telephone. Instead, it's attached to an incoming line. When the snoop dials in, a phone doesn't even ring at the victim's site, but the bug is turned on anyway.

"Too many people give away their privacy these days without even realizing it," says Murray quietly, with a rueful sigh. "Why do they allow people to get inside to plant this eavesdropping equipment in the first place? And why are their computers so vulnerable that downloading their databanks is so simple? New technology is overwhelming to most people. They don't know where to begin to protect themselves anymore."

Murray's a Rod Steiger look-alike—he has the same curly gray hair, fleshy body, and soft, smooth voice. And he exudes confidence. His even Irish tenor drips self-assurance—the perfect counterpoint to the fidgety clients who call him quaking in fear, asking him to comb their homes and offices, sure that somebody is secretly listening in or silently stealing data from their computers and hoping to peddle the information on the street like watches in a trench coat.

One of Murray's favorite cases—because it's emblematic of the deep double crosses that characterize so many relationships between people these days, which make figuring out who's spying on whom, who's the snoop and who's the victim, impossible—involves the disgraced televangelist Jim Bakker. Bakker's office at the PTL Club in Fort Mill, South Carolina, was on the upper floor of a four-story building that like a pyramid was widest at its base and narrow at the top. In March 1987, "a day after Bakker was expelled from the PTL Club," recalls Murray, "I was called in by the people that took over, who said Bakker had been spying on them for years. They wanted me to find and remove the bugs he had supposedly planted."

Murray scoured the building for hours, pulling apart telephones and light fixtures, analyzing the spaghetti wires that supported the telecommunications and computer networks. But he found nothing.

"My clients weren't satisfied," says Murray. "They told me to check his public address system. It seems he had a microphone in his office that was hooked up to numerous speakers throughout the building. And the wiring was zoned so Bakker could select different floors or offices to address. They were certain this setup allowed him to also activate different locations to listen in on.

"It didn't help that Bakker kept the microphone in his office hidden behind a plant. All that hokey 'talk into the plant' stuff you see in bad movies had my clients spooked."

But Bakker's secretary laughed when Murray told her about the suspicions on the PTL office grapevine.

"The microphone is behind the plant because it broke down about a year ago," she told Murray, looking at him as if his sanity must have deserted him if he'd taken the paranoid ravings of the shell-shocked, leftover PTL staff seriously. "And in the disarray that this place is in, nobody bothered fixing it. Bakker just wanted it out of the way."

Murray examined the offending communications device anyway. Within moments, he knew the secretary was right. This old-fashioned microphone, connected to big vintage-1950 elementary-school-issue speakers hung throughout the building, couldn't bug anybody. But to satisfy his clients' concerns, Murray conducted a thorough investigation of the outmoded system.

"I followed the wires and found out why the system had broken down," says Murray, his eyes squinting as a broad smile came across his face, telegraphing the punch line. "They wended down to a first-floor janitor's closet where I made the most amazing discovery: Somebody had actually taken the wires from Bakker's public address system and attached them to an old car-radio speaker. Then they retrofitted the electrical connections throughout the building. I attached my equipment to this microphone line in the janitor's closet and guess what? I could hear everything going on in Bakker's office.

"Somebody had spun the tables on Bakker and was listening in on him without him knowing, somebody who was still working there—one of my clients, who was probably shaking in his boots when I was brought in to comb the offices for bugs."

Murray gave PTL Chief Operating Officer Harry Hargrove his unexpected findings, figuring that the COO would act on it quickly and discipline the staffers who took part in this attack on Bakker's privacy. But Hargrove told a different story to the media. He announced that an extensive investigation uncovered that the disgraced PTL chief had installed "an elaborate bugging system . . . capable of transforming the building public address system into a Big Brother–style listening post. Activated by telephone, you could listen to anything in the building . . . from anywhere in the world. . . . Everybody was shocked."

At least by what Hargrove was saying. According to Murray, there wasn't a shred of truth in it. Still, based on Hargrove's statements, the FBI began an investigation to find out whether Bakker had broken the nation's wiretap laws. Murray provided the FBI with his report. After reading Murray's report and conducting an independent countersurveillance sweep of its own, the FBI dropped the case. But unfortunately for Bakker, Murray's side of the story never came out.

It's Alright, Ma, I'm Only Listening

Murray got up from the overstuffed armchair he was sitting in. "Want to see something really weird?" he asked. "Follow me."

I did so, perhaps too automatically, trailing behind Murray mechanically. I had already been entangled in the privacy story for about two and a half years: I had examined dozens of databanks; interviewed more than a hundred privacy advocates, legislators, consumer activists, information compilers and resellers, data buyers, and underground electronic-gossip purveyors; and patiently listened to the stories of numerous victims of crimes against their privacy. And I felt numb.

Nothing anyone could show or tell me was surprising anymore. What more was there to see? I had easily uncorked carefully sequestered details of the private lives of the Vice President and the nation's most famous anchorman. And I had viewed data of every stripe and confidence funneled into shared networks with security so lax that even the most inept interloper could find a node willing to spill all to him. More importantly, I had seen people tormented at the hands of information renegades, and met corporate and government higher-ups too dependent on the fast profile that data provides. Indeed, the question I sought to answer when I started my investigation—"Is nothing private?"—had long been answered with a thunderous "No, nothing is."

So by the time Murray offered to demonstrate yet another piece of technology gone awry, another untraceable way to sneakily insinuate oneself into someone else's private affairs, I understood better than I ever had before the tortured ambivalence, equal parts curiosity and fatigue, that Bob Dylan expressed in his lyric "Okay, I've had enough. What else can you show me?"

Murray took me into his laboratory, a small, cluttered, slapdash room with a long workbench against one wall. On the other walls were shelves containing mostly books strewn aimlessly, left however they fell when he pulled one out or put one back. Scattered on the work-bench were half a dozen skeletal, partially dissected electronic boxes with tubes, microchips, and wires fully exposed. Surrounding these remains pell-mell were semispliced components of all sizes—wires, circuit boards, condensers, you name it.

Murray walked over to a four-foot-high lazy-Susan-style storage unit next to the workbench that contained dozens of tiny plastic drawers. Searching from one drawer to the next, he finally found what he was looking for: some alligator clips, wires, and chips. He lifted up one of the metal boxes on the workbench, pulled out a few parts, plugged in some others, and turned the machine on. It hissed loudly, static swooping in and out like a swinging wrecking ball—the beginnings of communications from outer space in one of the older "Doctor Who" segments. Then it focused in. Suddenly voices could be clearly heard on the machine.

"How are you?" a woman was saying. "Somebody told me you were sick."

"I'm feeling better," answered another woman. "The flu. Or maybe allergies. Who knows? Are my tickets set?"

"All set. You and your husband are leaving Thursday, May first, on the two o'clock flight from Newark. That's United Airlines 368, nonstop to Los Angeles, arriving at five o'clock. Your return flight is on May twenty-second, United 456 at five o'clock in the evening. The cost for both round-trip tickets is $692. I need your credit card number to put through the order."

"Okay. It's United Jersey Bank Visa 4101-XXX-XXX-022."

"Expiration date?"

"December 1992."

"What name is on the card?"

"My husband, John DaSilva."

"And his Social Security number?"

"133-45-XXXX."

Murray turned the volume down a bit. "That's a conversation occurring right now on a cordless phone between a travel agent here in town and a customer," Murray explains.

I thought I had come in contact with everything that's possible in the antiprivacy lunatic fringe, but this was remarkable. This conversation—broadcast over, according to Murray, a $250 radio frequency scanner from Radio Shack—was as vivid as if we were in the same room. Better than that, really, because we were able to hear what was being said on both sides of the call.

"That's a lot of private information we picked up in about fifteen seconds," says Murray. "If we were burglars it wouldn't hurt to know that the DaSilvas are going to be away in California for three weeks. If we were thieves that liked to work electronic databases, we know DaSilva's credit card number and his Social Security number. And it's legal to snoop like this."

That's because the call was on a cordless phone. It wouldn't be legal, however, if we were listening in on a conversation between people talking on cellular phones, the mobile kind that you find in automobiles or that you see people talking on in the streets of, for instance, New York and Los Angeles. The privacy of cellular phones, unlike that of cordless phones. is protected by law. But although the cellular phone industry succeeded in getting Congress to make unauthorized eavesdropping on cellular calls as illegal as unwarranted wiretapping, that hasn't stopped many people from doing so.

"It's not something we want to go out and publicize," says Gary Brunt of the Cellular Telecommunications Industry Association, "but we don't deny that it's still going on—in a big way."

One reason is, if you convince a jury that you were just listening for fun and not for personal gain, and that you had no malice in your heart, the penalty for a first offense is only a $500 fine. The other reason, says Murray, "is who's going to catch you if you do?"

Particularly when federal government and law enforcement authorities are some of the worst offenders. Although the Internal Revenue Service won't discuss the policy, in 1990 it formulated new regulations for its criminal investigators authorizing them to eavesdrop without a warrant on suspected tax dodgers while they chat on their cordless or cellular phones.

And the nation's case logs are rife with examples of people who were encouraged by the police and district attorneys to tap into juicy cellular conversations and then report back what they found out.

In one such incident, Richard and Sandra Berodt were playing around with their radio scanner and overheard a telephone call on which their neighbor Scott Tyler was discussing what sounded like the beginnings of a drug deal. The Berodts told a county sheriff's investigator what they picked up. He urged them, without court authorization, to continue monitoring. The Berodts did and even taped subsequent conversations.

Tyler was eventually indicted, and convicted—although on an unrelated offense, because the taped conversations were not admissible as evidence. However, despite that, Tyler's civil suit against the Berodts for eavesdropping on him was dismissed. The courts couldn't find anything sufficiently wrong with what the Berodts did to justify continuation of the case.

Roy E. Barker, a retired Indianapolis car salesman, is a veteran of cellular eavesdropping on his twenty-five-year-old scanner. Barker's favorite coup: in 1986 he heard a state official and a local CEO making arrangements for a clandestine meeting before the state took up the company's request for leniency on waste-dumping charges.

"When you make a call on a cellular phone you might as well be calling a newspaper," says Thomas Bernie, president of the Cellular Security Group, a consulting firm based in Gloucester, Massachusetts.

Cellular calls are so easy to intercept because they're carried on ordinary radio waves within a band of 800–900 megahertz. Typically a car phone sends a signal between 820 and 840 megahertz to a cell site, from which it's transferred to a regular telephone line. The return signal is then transmitted at a frequency exactly 45 megahertz higher than the caller's signal. So to listen in on both sides of the conversation, all one has to do is tune the scanner's frequency to a frequency 45 megahertz above that of the first leg of the call.

Cordless phone calls pose even less difficulty. The radio bands they travel over are closer to the middle of the dial, next to many popular stations. "Any housewife can pick up a neighbor's cordless call completely innocently when she's just trying to tune in her favorite talk radio show," explains Murray.

There are devices that encrypt conversations on cellular and cordless phones, but they're out of reach of most people, costing about $3,000 to purchase and $50 per month in service charges.

"It's gotten so bad that companies are actually hiring people, usually shut-ins, to spend all day listening to scanners for any conversations that might tell them something, anything, about the competition," says Murray.

He spun the scanner's dial again. Nothing but static until we finally heard two distant voices, lost in the sound of paper rubbing against gravel. He fine-tuned the machine slowly. The voices came in clearly.

"I prefer to close Thursday morning," a man was saying, "because if it's done slipshod, it will give me enough time to get Jennifer to do something about it."

"The question I have is does he have enough money in his account to cover the deal? I mean, $100,000 up front and $5 million over five years seems out of his league."

"I agree, however . . ."

He paused for a long time. Nothing but dead air for seconds. "However what?" Murray asks impatiently, leaning closer to the radio scanner, as if that might make the man on the car phone finish his thought more quickly. "Now he has me interested."

I understood what Murray meant. We were both transfixed by the conversation we were overhearing. Murray makes a living as a self-described privacy gatekeeper, yet here he was listening to people on a cellular phone conversation, hopelessly smitten by the allure of eavesdropping on the sweet sound of gossip.

"However," the man finally continued, "he's been beaten down before and always emerged at the top."

"This time I'm not sure he can do it. Give me his bank account number. I have a source that can tell me how much money he has."

"Okay, it's under Wellington Industries. Account number 2200XXXX-9."

"I'll tell you right now there's no fucking way the deal will go through. The only way to make it work, he'll have to run this loan through some kind of individual trust line he has somewhere. And if he has such a line, I'll find it and get back to you."

Murray turned the scanner off and pulled his hand away from the machine quickly. He continued to stare at it for a moment, though, like a recovering alcoholic putting down a drink he had just sipped and was tempted to try again. He glanced at me sheepishly. "I just wanted to show you what could be done, how hard it is to protect your privacy anymore," he said, looking embarrassed, and as if he owed me an explanation.

Privacy Is Like Clean Air

Murray's demonstration drew an important conclusion for me, an unavoidable one that I had already suspected: technology has become uncontrollable, a rampaging flood, carving its own course. Breakthroughs in computers, communications, electronic networks, and databanks relentlessly sweep away previous discoveries. Meanwhile, there's inexcusably little serious thought given to the implications of these advances for individuals or society.

Indeed, the record shows that we brake the impulse to let technology advance without scrutiny only when something unmentionably horrible happens. As should be clear from this book, there are numerous examples of new technologically based invasions of privacy occurring virtually every day. Some are small and barely noticed, but are jarring nevertheless.

For instance, in one of the latest and most preposterous examples of a company failing to create even minimal safeguards for its customers' private data, the Boston-based mutual fund firm Fidelity Investments lets investors get account information via telephone by simply keying in their Social Security numbers. Fidelity claims it, of course, views account information as confidential, but, says a spokesman, "so are Social Security numbers. So what are we doing wrong?"

Plenty, says Eric Kobren, president of the Mutual Fund Investors Association, which tracks Fidelity and other funds. "I don't know about you, but a lot of people have access to my Social Security number," argues Kobren. "The number is on my driver's license, on the back of checks, on credit reports, and on file with the SEC [Securities and Exchange Commission]. Am I being a bit paranoid?"

Probably not, if Fidelity's recent run-ins with electronic pranksters are any indication. When Fidelity's new teleservice system came to light, dozens of practical jokers looked up the Social Security numbers of Fidelity executives on Securities and Exchange Commission documents. Then they called the Fidelity 800 number and typed in these numbers to find out the sizes of the accounts the mutual fund's senior officials kept with their own company. "We wanted to see if they were really investing where they were telling everybody else to invest," says one telehacker. They were, he adds.

But Fidelity wasn't amused. Learning of this rash of incidents, it blocked the public's access to Fidelity executives' accounts. Unfortunately, Fidelity's less notable investors don't get the same consideration.

Other examples of new privacy intrusions are much larger and more dangerous, such as the unceasing development of new, "collect everything" government databanks that lack significant oversight or adequate notification of the public.

All of these electronically driven information-gathering breakthroughs are allowed to proceed with hardly a whimper by people inured and desensitized to the steady dissolution of individual rights in this country. They're accepted as logical extensions of technology's long-running assault on privacy.

In time, high-tech snooping and databanking could make earlier-generation activities seem naively old-fashioned, as innocent as child's play. When that occurs, our failure to legislate controls over databanking, computer systems, communications devices, and surveillance equipment as they evolved—already a problem today—could overwhelm us, as could our failure to prescribe adequate civil and criminal penalties for abuses of individual privacy committed by government agencies and U.S. corporations.

If you ponder how easily we've adapted to VCRs, personal computers, auto-dial telephones, answering machines, and automated teller machines just in the past decade, it becomes apparent how readily we shape ourselves around technology—and change to conform to it.

This didn't begin with the computer age. Culture in America has always followed technology and reordered itself around it, whether the technology is the skyscraper, the machines of the Industrial Revolution, the telephone, the credit networks, the automobile, or the assembly line.

In each case there has been a trade-off. Improvements in lifestyle, a higher standard of living, a sense of financial well-being, a chance to provide a better future for one's children, and more day-to-day conveniences have accrued in exchange for the steady erosion of long-cherished social virtues. Each steady advancement in technology has eroded the personal relationships that once were a source of support and strength. The family is not as close as it once was because television, the telephone, and the computer, to name just a few technologies, have reset our priorities away from relationships, trust, and intimacy. In the same way, certain essential rights, such as privacy and freedom from unwarranted invasions of one's personal life, have been incalculably diminished since the computer was plugged in some forty years ago.

That's the price Americans are paying for being enamored of new technology and for choosing as heroes such technocapitalists as Thomas Edison, William Paley, Alexander Graham Bell, Henry Ford, and more recently Steve Jobs, William Gates, George Lucas, and Steven Spielberg. Each invention or media experience supplied by these people re-created or modified culture in its image; each was a mindscape with a good and a bad hemisphere. As Neil Postman, a professor of communications arts and sciences at New York University, puts it, "To a man with a pencil, everything looks like a sentence; to a man with a television camera, everything looks like a picture; and to a man with a computer, the whole world looks like data."

To illustrate how naturally culture recasts itself in the wake of technology, Postman likes to use the plot of *The Gods Must Be Crazy,* a movie about a tribe in southern Africa that is "invaded" by an empty Coca-Cola bottle tossed from the window of a small plane passing overhead. Having never seen a bottle or even glass before, the people think it's a gift from the gods. At first, the bottle enchants the natives, as they find all sorts of novel things to do with it, such as blowing through it to make music.

Soon though, the bottle becomes an all-consuming obsession. Examining it and trying out new uses for it replace normal day-to-day activities. And because the bottle is a one-of-a-kind item, fights, jealousy, and greed break out as the haves try to fend off the have-nots. The tight-knit thousand-year-old culture is almost rent apart. The people are saved only when the tribal chief, certain that the gods must be crazy, throws the bottle off the top of a mountain.

Says Postman, "That movie raises two questions of extreme importance to our situation: how does a culture change when new technologies are introduced to it, and is it always desirable for a culture to accommodate itself to the demands of new technologies? The leader of the Kalahari tribe is forced to confront these questions in a way that Americans have refused to do. And because his vision is not obstructed by a belief in what Americans call 'technological progress,' he is able with minimal discomfort" to shuck the technology in order to preserve the structure of his tribe's society.

No one says that we have to go to the lengths of the tribal leader. There's no need to dump our computers, telephones, fax machines, bugs, and Bionic Ears into the sea in some wild-eyed ritual of purgation and salvation in order to reclaim our lost privacy and personal autonomy. Indeed, there are things we can do as individuals and as a society to slow down the steady fury of technology, to make it accommodate itself to us.

But for this to happen, people have to stop hiding under rocks and quaking in the shadow of computers, snoopers, and databankers. Among the things that you as an individual can do are:

- Get a copy of your credit report often, checking for inaccuracies and evidence that unauthorized snoopers have accessed it. Notify the credit bureaus of any errors and question the snoopers about what they were doing.
- Don't share personal information with anybody unless you're absolutely sure that whoever has requested it has the right to it. That means, for starters, don't write your Social Security number, credit card numbers, address, and telephone number on checks or documents if you don't feel it's appropriate to do so. And don't provide this information over the telephone to unknown callers who tell you you've just won a new TV set, a trip to Hawaii, or any other prize you'll probably never receive.
- If you don't want to receive junk mail—most of it now the result of personal information taken from credit reports, bank records, your latest shopping spree, and census data—notify the credit bureaus, credit grantors and the Direct Marketing Association in New York City that you'd like to be removed from their mailing lists.
- Strike back when somebody has invaded your privacy. If you find out or suspect that a bank, doctor, hospital, employer, telephone company, or any other person, organization, or corporation has

without your consent shared personal information about you with others, notify the offending party that you're appalled by its actions and won't do business with it anymore. And then tell the sordid tale to anybody with the power or media access to make sure it doesn't happen again, such as Congressmen, the American Bankers Association, the American Medical Association, the Federal Communications Commission, the Federal Trade Commission, the American Hospital Association, the Better Business Bureau, and magazine, newspaper, and TV journalists.

- If you learn that a private investigator has inappropriately accessed information about you, notify local licensing authorities.

Clearly, it's up to the individual to safeguard his own secrets. But that's not always easy to do. Sometimes, in fact, the only way to find privacy is to buy it.

Take the Caller ID ruckus. To many, Caller ID systems, which automatically display on the called party's phone the telephone number of the person placing the call, are odious. With these systems, anytime you call a carpet store, auto dealer, clothes outlet, or any other retailer to inquire anonymously about a price or an item, your phone number can be collected by the retailer. And he can use that piece of information to find out your name and address. This data can then be the basis for mailing and telemarketing lists, which the retailer may use himself or sell to others.

That's not the worst of it. Caller ID also threatens to destroy the anonymity people used to have when contacting crisis hot lines, which counsel on alcoholism, AIDS, spouse beating, suicide, and numerous other medical and social ills. Frightened, paranoid, desperate individuals are less likely to seek help from these ostensibly discreet 800 numbers when the possibility exists that the person on the other end of the line knows who they are—and may reveal the details of their supposedly private conversation.

Still, for those who crave telephone privacy, there is a solution—but it will cost you. Call 1-900-STOPPER and you'll hear a dial tone. Then just punch in the area code and the phone number you want to call. Since you're going through the 900 number's telephone lines, even if the party you're calling has a Caller ID system, he'll never be able to identify your phone number. But this little piece of privacy doesn't come cheap: it's $2 a minute.

Unfortunately, no matter how prudent people are about protecting their own privacy, their efforts will probably amount to little unless they're accompanied by an equally serious commitment from Congress and the courts to scrutinize technology's impact on privacy and on the right of individuals to live their lives without being at the mercy of those who would pry into their private affairs, on a whim or for malice. Key privacy issues that have been ignored for decades are now on the national agenda. Answers must be found to such questions as:

- Who should be allowed to get personal information such as credit reports? Currently this list includes—besides legitimate credit grantors—private investigators, attorneys, employers, landlords, auto dealerships, and anybody else who claims to be doing business with somebody he wants to look up.
- Are laws needed to safeguard the confidentiality of unprotected data such as medical, bank, and telephone records?
- Do we need a European-style Data Protection Board to be an ombudsman for any citizen who feels that an individual or company has abused his right of information privacy, and to pass judgment on corporate and government use of private information and databanks?
- Should there be civil remedies for breaches of privacy, with monetary redress even if the victims cannot prove tangible damages? The cost of the loss of privacy is often difficult to assess because it produces personal suffering that may not have a clear-cut monetary value.
- How can surveillance and telecommunications equipment manufacturers and sellers be better controlled?
- Are there some innovative approaches to the commercial use by third parties of personal information that should be examined? One idea being floated is to pay individuals a royalty each time a credit bureau, bank, marketer, medical records provider—in short, any databanker—resells information from their digital dossiers.
- Should consumers automatically be provided free credit reports each year?

The questions are complex, but bug buster Kevin Murray doesn't believe that the problem is insurmountable. Optimistically he asserts that each onslaught of culture-altering technology—such as the automobile or the mechanized factory—at first opens up the floodgates to new real and potential abuses of individual rights, and gives the criminal or more sinister element original ideas about ways to use it against others. Then the regulators tone down this impulse with legislation and licensing rules that make the new technology coexist better with society's goals and precepts.

The same could be done for computers, databanks, surveillance equipment, and communications networks. "As has been shown by all obtrusive dictatorships, people don't flourish in a world without privacy," Murray says. "They feel caged and their incentive to produce is destroyed. The desire to make the most of their lives—the chances for individual achievements, which are what made America stand out in the world—is diminished immeasurably."

But, Murray adds, something has to be done soon, or we may miss the chance and change the quality and tenor of our lives forever:

"Privacy is like clean air. At one time there was plenty of it. Now it's just about gone."

Notes

Chapter 1   Glass Houses

Page

13. *It was a story out of a Hitchcock film*
    Details of Rebecca Schaeffer's murder were obtained from interviews with Los Angeles prosecutor Marsha Clark, private investigator Anthony Zinkus, and sources in the Los Angeles Police Department who requested anonymity, as well as evidence and testimony in the trial of her murderer, Robert Bardo.

17. *". . . let alone seek redress for, misuse of their records."*
    From *Electronic Records Systems and Individual Privacy* (Office of Technology Assessment, June 1986).

23. *Florida resident Mallory Hughes learned recently how far marketers will go*
    Anecdote supplied by Denny Hatch in his newsletter, *Who's Mailing What!*

25. *regularly ask their computers to comb the databanks and create "propensity profiles" on American citizens*
    From *Computers and Privacy: How the Government Obtains, Verifies, Uses and Protects Personal Data* (General Accounting Office, August 1990) and *Privacy Act: Federal Agencies' Implementation Can Be Improved* (General Accounting Office, August 1986).

25. *Valerie Hubbard, a Social Security worker in Newark, New Jersey*
    Details of this incident were obtained from law enforcement sources, indictment papers, and courtroom transcripts.

Chapter 2   The Secret Sharers

Page

32. *and most of the information they maintain is extremely confidential*
    Information about the credit industry in this chapter was obtained from interviews with nearly one hundred sources from the credit bureaus, credit grantors, Congress, consumer and privacy movements, and information underground. Key material was supplied by John Baker, Jack Rogers, and Jim Perkins of Equifax; Richard Whilden, Edward Barbieri, Edward F. Freeman, Michael Van Buskirk, Dennis Benner, D. Van Skilling, and William Tener of TRW; Allen Flitcraft, Oscar Marquis, and W. R. Rodgers of Trans Union; Louis Giglio of Bear, Stearns; Jean Noonan, formerly of the Federal Trade Commission; Robert Ellis Smith of the *Privacy Journal;* Evan Hendricks of the *Privacy Times;* Mary Culnan of Georgetown University; Barry Connelly of the Associated Credit Bureaus; Representative Richard Lehman (D-Calif.); Representative Charles Schumer (D-N.Y.); former Senate aide Ken McLean; and

former senator William Proxmire (D-Wisc.). Other sources requested anonymity.

39. *but you have to bump into someone like James Duke*
James Duke is a pseudonym. Because of the sensitive nature of his activities, he requested anonymity.

43. *The credit M.D.s in the Southwest have made a living from*
Details about the Texas credit doctors and, in specific, Walter "Waldo" Hilton, James Lawson, and Christian Financial Services, Inc., (CFS) were obtained from courtroom testimony and depositions involving these individuals and organizations, as well as interviews with Houston and federal law enforcement authorities working on credit industry cases and senior executives in the credit industry. Key sources include credit-card fraud expert Joseph LaBranche; Houston police detective David Hefner; and Stephen Mansfield, an assistant United States Attorney in Los Angeles. Other sources requested anonymity. Additional material was obtained from published reports in local Texas newspapers and the article, "Identity Crisis: To Repair Bad Credit, Advisers Give Clients Someone Else's Data," in *The Wall Street Journal,* 8/14/90, page A1.

49. *Chandler Corcoran was seventy-two years old when I met her*
Chandler Corcoran is a pseudonym. She requested anonymity to protect her privacy.

50. *somebody named Denise Davis*
Denise Davis is a pseudonym.

52. *is rapidly becoming an epidemic of mayhem spread mostly by mobs of young foreign nationals*
From interviews with nearly a dozen sources in the Secret Service, the Federal Bureau of Investigation, Congress, and law enforcement agencies, as well as private investigators. Key information was supplied by David Leroy of the Drug Enforcement Administration, Martin Biegelman of the U.S. Postal Service, and Dale Boll of the Secret Service. Other sources requested anonymity.

54. *Typical is the prosecution of thirty-four-year-old Nigerian Bola Allen*
From interviews with Texas prosecutor Wallace Zeringue, published reports, and sources close to the case who requested anonymity.

Chapter 3   The Man Who Knows Too Much
Page
63. *I had just gotten to sleep when John Branch called me*
John Branch is a composite character. Everything that John Branch does and says is based on firsthand experiences or stories I was told by or about the people I met in the information underground. But to protect the identity of

numerous information undergrounders, I created the vehicle of John Branch to describe the sensitive nature of their activities.

63. *freely traffic in sensitive data, no matter how personal or private, or how illegally obtained*
Details about the information underground in this chapter were obtained from nearly fifty interviews with well-placed figures in the underground. They are a highly secretive and surreptitious group, and only those few quoted by name in this chapter were willing to speak on the record. Others requested anonymity, preferring to conceal their somewhat ticklish activities.

69. *I learned later from sources who know Dan Rather*
These sources include two co-workers and two friends.

79. *Joseph Van Winkle, a security VP, had taken me on an eye-opening journey*
Joseph Van Winkle is a psudonym. Fearing repercussions from his employer if his discussions with me were made public, he requested anonymity.

86. *a veteran high-level secret-information seller based in Seattle*
Details of this incident were obtained from Justice Department and prosecution sources close to the case, from sealed documents describing the settlement, and from colleagues of the information seller.

Chapter 4   Bull's Eye

Page

90. *direct marketing has become an aggressive, extremely competitive business*
Information about the direct-marketing business and the sale of lists by credit bureaus was obtained from interviews with nearly one hundred sources from direct-marketing firms, the credit bureaus, Congress, federal agencies, and the consumer and privacy movements. Key material was supplied by John Baker and Tom Chapman of Equifax; Richard Whilden, Dennis Benner, and Cynthia Copus of TRW; Robert Ellis Smith of the *Privacy Journal;* Evan Hendricks of the *Privacy Times;* Mary Culnan of Georgetown University; Jonathan Linen of American Express; attorney Anita Boomstein of Gaston & Snow; Rose Harper Kleid of the Rose Harper Kleid Company; Ken Phillips of the Committee of Corporate Telecommunications Users; Marc Rotenberg of the Computer Professionals for Social Responsibility; Ken McEldowney of Consumer Action; attorney Ronald Plesser; Denny Hatch of *Who's Mailing What!;* Robert Stanley of Dateq; Ed Burnett of Ed Burnett Consultants; Jean Noonan, formerly of the Federal Trade Commission; Alicia Mundy, formerly a reporter for *U.S. News & World Report;* and the staff of the Direct Marketing Association. Other sources requested anonymity.

102. *free of direct-marketing appeals*
Information about this incident supplied by Wayne Wallhausen of Arby's, sources at the demographic databankers National Decision Systems and

Claritas who requested anonymity, and a marketing vice president at the local newspaper in the center of the dispute, who also asked that his name not be used.

102. *the people living in lower East Point*
The names "lower East Point" and "upper Point" are neighborhood designations used by demographic data companies and are not formal names for these sections of East Point, Georgia.

Chapter 5   A Trace Left Behind
Page

106. *Christina Danvers had a warm, full-throated, gentle voice*
Christina Danvers is a pseudonym. She requested anonymity to protect her privacy.

107. *the producers at WABC got a willing couple to serve as guinea pigs*
Ted and Alice Darling are pseudonyms. They requested anonymity to protect their privacy.

113. *the one involving Mark Koenig*
Details about this case were obtained from interviews with Secret Service and Federal Bureau of Investigation sources who worked on the Koenig investigation. They requested that their names not be used. Additional material was taken from evidence and testimony in the Koenig trial and newspaper reports.

Chapter 6   Hollow Acts
Page

124. *analyze their ability to satisfy their tax liabilities*
This Internal Revenue Service activity was uncovered by Evan Hendricks of the *Privacy Times*. During interviews he provided information about it to me and he supplied internal IRS documents detailing the activity's scope and dangers.

125. *than it was before the Privacy Act was on the books*
From *Computers and Privacy: How the Government Obtains, Verifies, Uses and Protects Personal Data* (General Accounting Office, August 1990) and *Privacy Act: Federal Agencies' Implementation Can Be Improved* (General Accounting Office, August 1986).

127. *creating the Law Enforcement Assistance Administration (LEAA)*
Details about LEAA, the death of Karen Silkwood, and the Regional Information Sharing System were obtained during interviews with approximately two dozen federal investigative agency staffers, Central Intelligence Agency and FBI operatives, Congressional aides, private investigators, and privacy watchdogs. Key sources include journalist and colleague Robert Ratner;

Glen Roberts of *Full Disclosure,* a newspaper; attorney Danny Sheehan; and private investigator Bob Lesnick. Other sources, many of whom provided essential material, requested anonymity because of the extremely sensitive nature of the subjects and the roles they played.

129. *the Federal Bureau of Investigation's National Crime Information Center (NCIC)*
Details about NCIC and the FBI's new DNA databank were obtained from interviews with a dozen Justice Department and Congressional sources, as well as from testimony provided during Congressional hearings. Key information was supplied by Representative Don Edwards (D-Calif.) and his staff, Professor Philip Bereano of the University of Washington in Seattle, attorney Janlori Goldman of the ACLU, Marc Rotenberg of the Computer Professionals for Social Responsibility, and William Bayse of the FBI. Other sources requested anonymity. Additional material was taken from *Criminal Justice: New Technologies and the Constitution* (Office of Technology Assessment, May 1988).

136. *databanks sprouting throughout post-Watergate Washington*
Details about the Financial Crimes Enforcement Network and the Treasury Enforcement Communications Systems were obtained from interviews with a dozen sources at federal investigative agencies, Congress, and private investigation firms. Key information was supplied by Representative Don Edwards (D-Calif.) and his staff and by Glen Roberts of *Full Disclosure.* Other sources requested anonymity. Additional material was taken from *Money Laundering: Treasury's Financial Crimes Enforcement Network* (General Accounting Office, March 1991), *Money Laundering: The Use of Cash Transaction Reports by Federal Law Enforcement Agencies* (General Accounting Office, September 1991), and *Money Laundering: The U.S. Government Is Responding to the Problem* (General Accounting Office, May 1991).

138. *conducted a secret survey of TECS II in 1990*
A copy of this General Accounting Office report was obtained from a Congressional source. The report was never released to the public.

140. *a little-known activity called computer matching*
Details about computer matching and memos pertaining to Joseph Califano's development of Project Match were obtained during interviews with two dozen sources, including privacy advocates and sources at the Office of Management and Budget and Congress, as well as from published newspaper reports and testimony during Congressional hearings. Key information was supplied by Joseph Califano, former Secretary of Health, Education, and Welfare; Robert Veeder of the Office of Management and Budget; attorney Robert Belair; Hale Champion, a former Califano colleague; former OMB director James McIntyre; Jean Noonan, formerly of the Federal Trade Commission; and Evan Hendricks of the *Privacy Times.* Other sources requested anonymity.

141. *127 computerized matches conducted by the federal government*
From *Electronic Records Systems and Individual Privacy* (Office of Technology Assessment, June 1986).

144. *According to the Congressional General Accounting Office*
From *Privacy Act: Federal Agencies' Implementation Can Be Improved* (General Accounting Office, August 1986).

Chapter 7   Hard Work
Page
154. *In its vast mainframes, EIS maintains upwards of a million files*
Details about EIS were obtained from interviews with David Czernik of the Louisiana Consumers League; attorney Kenneth Pitre; EIS counsel Rutledge Clement; nearly a dozen unemployed workers, including Ernest Trent and Rod Stevens, whose names are in EIS's databank; and half a dozen EIS subscribers, chiefly King Fisher of King Fisher Marine Service.

157. *employers are combing databases of all kinds*
Details in this chapter about the use of databanks and surveillance devices by employers were obtained during interviews with two dozen information resellers, employers, labor leaders, Congressional staffers, federal agency officials, and employee relations attorneys, as well as from published newspaper and magazine reports. Key sources include attorney August Becquai; private investigator Bill Callahan; Becky Van Winkle of the Human Resource Information Network; Thomas Lawson of Apscreen; J. Ray Reid of the Industrial Foundation of America; Steve Mednick of CDB/Infotek; attorney Lee Paterson of Sonnenschein Carlin Nath & Rosenthal; Sharon Guenther of Information Resource Service Company; William Sharp of Fidelifacts Metropolitan New York; attorney Noel Shipman; David Karas of Equifax; José Millan, deputy labor commissioner of California; David Foerster of the Resource Center; George Sveum of Teamsters Local 350; and Jean Noonan, formerly of the Federal Trade Commission. Other sources requested anonymity. Additional information was taken from *Employee Privacy* (Conference Board Research Report No. 945 [1990]), *The Electronic Supervisor* (Office of Technology Assessment, September 1987), and *Electronic Monitoring in the Workplace: Supervision or Surveillance* (Massachuesetts Coalition on New Office Technology, February 1989).

Chapter 8   Body of Information
Page
177. *There almost was such a law*
Details about the attempt to generate Congressional support for a medical privacy bill were provided by two Congressional sources who spearheaded the effort. They requested anonymity.

180. *the need for medical privacy laws hasn't diminished*
Details about the lack of privacy for medical records were obtained during

interviews with two dozen medical ethicists, physicians, privacy advocates, and medical information resellers, as well as from published newspaper and magazine reports. Key information was supplied by Carl Fink of Health Information Designs, Caroline Smith DeWaal of Public Citizen, Mary Joan Wogan of the American Medical Record Association, Molly Cooke of San Francisco General Hospital, psychiatrist Jerome Beigler, psychiatrist Paul Fink of the Albert Einstein Medical Center, Neal Day of the Medical Information Bureau, psychiatrist Ellen Fischbein, and attorney Paul Tobias.

183. *Take David Castle, a free-lance artist*
David Castle is a pseudonym. He requested anonymity to protect his privacy.

184. *the Medical Information Bureau (MIB), the largest repository of medical records in the United States*
Some material about MIB was taken from *For Their Eyes Only: The Insurance Industry and Consumer Privacy* (Massachusetts Public Interest Research Group, April 1990).

186. *John Friedkin, a free-lance writer*
John Friedkin is a pseudonym. He requested anonymity to protect his privacy.

188. *Genetic screening is a good example*
Details about the use of genetic data in information banks were obtained from interviews with about a dozen genetic experts, medical information resellers, privacy advocates, medical ethicists, and health care professionals. Key sources include Deborah Stone of Brandeis University, Mark Rothstein of the University of Houston, Dorothy Nelkin of New York University, Paul Billings of Pacific Presbyterian Medical Center, Amy Freeze, and Heidi Beaver of Washington University.

191. *survey of people who underwent genetic testing*
From Paul Billings et al., "Discrimination as a Consequence of Genetic Screening" (unpublished).

Index